"What if someone were to do something unimaginably horrific to you or your family? *The Devil in Pew Number Seven* is a riveting true story of one woman's journey of forgiveness, the depths of which most of us will never experience. Ultimately, Becky's harrowing account serves as an inspiration to us all, especially to those who are struggling with forgiveness in their own lives."

**DR. TIM LAHAYE**
*President, Tim LaHaye Ministries; coauthor, Left Behind series*

"As little girls, we're all scared of something. For five-year-old Becky, it was a bomb-setting madman in her daddy's church—with her family as the target. Against the odds she survived and has had to learn that 'forgiveness is the language of heaven.' This is must reading for anyone struggling to forgive."

**SHELLEY BREEN**
*Point of Grace*

"As Christians we often pray, 'Forgive us our sins, for we also forgive everyone who sins against us.' It's a lot easier to ask God for forgiveness for our own failings than it is to extend forgiveness to those who have wronged us. Becky's story shows us that, with the Lord's grace, forgiveness and healing are possible, even in the most horrific of situations."

**JAMES D. DALY**
*President and CEO, Focus on the Family*

"Becky has reached a level of forgiveness where few will ever have to go. In going there herself, she leads us on a path of freedom that is both riveting and revolutionary. We loved every page."

**RON AND LYNETTE LEWIS**
*King's Park International Church, Durham, North Carolina*
*Morning Star New York, New York City*

"Without a doubt, this is one of the best books I have ever read. I believe Becky's story will be greatly used of our Lord to change the lives of countless numbers of people."

**SHERRILL BABB, PH.D.**
*Chancellor, Philadelphia Biblical University*

"Becky relives the 'shop of horrors' in which she grew up, as her pastor dad and family were the target of vicious attacks. You will be dumbfounded and heartbroken over the extent to which evil can be perpetrated by bitter hearts. You will be vexed by the apparent triumph of injustice and perplexed by the seeming inactivity of God at times. And you will marvel at the grace of God to enable His children to forgive their enemies, overcome evil with good, and hold fast to hope that a day is coming when He will right all wrongs and vindicate His own."

**NANCY LEIGH DEMOSS**
*Author,* Revive Our Hearts *radio host*

"Forgiveness seems so unnatural. For the offended to be able to remove the debt of the offender can only be a 'God thing.' *The Devil in Pew Number Seven* proves that point very well."

**H. B. LONDON, JR.**
*Vice President, Church and Clergy, Focus on the Family*

"At the heart of solving most of our relational conflicts is one all-important word—*forgiveness*. Becky's remarkable story will unlock multitudes from their past and propel them into a life of freedom, success, and peace. I highly recommend this book."

**LARRY TOMCZAK**
*Author and Speaker*

"Get ready to be captivated and inspired by Becky's testimony. We simply could not put the book down."

**SAM AND KATHI KATINA**
*The Katinas*

"Bless those
who persecute you;
bless and do not
curse."

# The Devil in Pew Number Seven

A TRUE STORY

Rebecca Nichols Alonzo

with Bob DeMoss

*Tyndale House Publishers, Inc.*
*Carol Stream, Illinois*

Visit Tyndale's exciting Web site at www.tyndale.com.

*TYNDALE* and Tyndale's quill logo are registered trademarks of Tyndale House Publishers, Inc.

*The Devil in Pew Number Seven*



Designed by Ron Kaufmann

Published in association with the literary agency of WordServe Literary Agency, 10152 Knoll Circle, Highlands Ranch, CO 80130.



---

**Library of Congress Cataloging-in-Publication Data**

Alonzo, Rebecca Nichols
The devil in pew number seven / Rebecca Nichols Alonzo with DeMoss, Bob.
p. cm.
Includes bibliographical references (p. ).
ISBN 978-1-4143-2659-7 (sc)
1. Alonzo, Rebecca Nichols 2. Nichols, Robert (Robert F.) 3. Nichols, Ramona. 4. Free Welcome Holiness Church (Sellerstown, N.C.)—Biography. 5. Victims of violent crimes—North Carolina—Sellerstown—Biography. I. DeMoss, Robert G. II. Title.
BX7990.H62A46 2010
277.3'082092—dc22
[B] 2010007670

---

Printed in the United States of America

16 15 14 13 12 11 10
7 6 5 4 3 2 1

*To Mom and Dad for being servant-leaders, for showing God's endless love to the unlovable. Thank you for writing your memoirs so this book could be written. Our journey together continues through the years.*

*To my brother, Daniel; you were not only an answer to Mom and Dad's prayers but mine as well. Without you, I would have been a lonely only child.*

*To Aunt Dot, my constant guide and number one fan. I'm grateful for your love and wisdom. Your devotion to our family knows no bounds.*

*To Kenny, my husband and best friend. Thank you for all of the years of love and devotion, for being a man of integrity, and for holding my hand through the smiles and tears. You continue to amaze me.*

*For Kolby, my valiant warrior; your mighty heart toward the Lord and love for justice bless my life.*

*For Katelin, my delicate rose; the love of God is a sweet-smelling fragrance from your tender heart and is precious to me.*

# CONTENTS

# AUTHOR'S NOTE

Let me be clear about one thing.

The story you're about to read actually happened, every last detail of it. As the plot unfolds, my hunch is that you'll need to remind yourself of this reality more than once. If you've ever required evidence to prove the adage "Truth is stranger than fiction," look no further. To be redundant, this *is* a true story.

In a way, I wish it were not. And at times I'm glad it's true.

Some of what transpired occurred before I was born, which, for obvious reasons, means I have no firsthand knowledge of those events. Likewise, there was a time when I was too young to comprehend the events swirling around me. However, my parents wisely kept thorough personal journals, thick family photo albums, stacks of newspaper clippings, an 8 mm film reel, and a priceless cassette tape narrated by my father. (Some of those photos appear on the opening pages of the chapters in this book. A list of captions is included on page 272.)

As if these items were not proof enough that this story actually occurred, as I wrote, I had at my disposal my memories, a federal court transcript, and crime scene reports and photographs. I also conducted numerous interviews with those witnesses who are still alive today. These invaluable resources provided a trustworthy road map through the minefield that was—and is—my life.

I don't share the following pages because I am looking for sympathy. Far from it. Rather, I invite you to travel with me to the very end where we discover perhaps the most disturbing part of the story: you and I have no choice but to forgive others . . . even if they are the monsters next door.

After all, forgiveness is the language of heaven.

CHAPTER 1

# Walking, Crawling, Dead or Alive

I ran.

My bare feet pounding the pavement were burning from the sun-baked asphalt. Each contact between flesh and blacktop provoked bursts of pain as if I were stepping on broken glass. The deserted country road, stretching into the horizon, felt as if it were conspiring against me. No matter how hard I pushed myself, the safe place I was desperate to reach eluded me.

Still, I ran.

Had a thousand angry hornets been in pursuit, I couldn't have run any faster. Daddy's instructions had been simple: I had to be a big girl, run down the street as fast as my legs could carry me, and get help. There was nothing complicated about his request. Except for the fact that I'd have to abandon my hiding place under the kitchen table and risk being seen by the armed madman who had barricaded himself with two hostages in my bedroom down the hall. I knew, however, that ignoring Daddy's plea was out of the question.

And so I ran.

Even though Daddy struggled to appear brave, the anguish in his eyes spoke volumes. Splotches of blood stained his shirt just below his right shoulder. The inky redness was as real as the fear gnawing at the edges of my heart. I wanted to be a big girl for the sake of my daddy. I really did. But the fear and chaos now clouding the air squeezed my lungs until my breathing burned within my chest.

My best intentions to get help were neutralized, at least at first. I remained hunkered down, unable to move, surrounded by the wooden legs of six kitchen chairs. I had no illusions that a flimsy 6 x 4 foot table would keep me safe, yet I was reluctant to leave what little protection it afforded me.

In that space of indecision, I wondered how I might open the storm door without drawing attention to myself. One squeak from those crusty hinges was sure to announce my departure plans. Closing the door without a bang against the frame was equally important. The stealth of a burglar was needed, only I wasn't the bad guy.

Making no more sound than a leaf falling from a tree, I inched my way out from under the table. I stood and then scanned the room, left to right. I felt watched, although I had no way of knowing for sure whether or not hostile eyes were studying my movements. I inhaled the distinct yet unfamiliar smell of sulfur lingering in the air, a calling card left behind from the repeated blasts of a gun.

I willed myself to move.

My bare feet padded across the linoleum floor.

I was our family's lifeline, our only connection to the outside world. While I hadn't asked to be put in that position, I knew Daddy was depending on me. More than that, Daddy *needed* me to be strong.

To act. To do what he was powerless to do. I could see that my daddy, a strong ex–Navy man, was incapable of the simplest movement. The man whom I loved more than life itself, whose massive arms daily swept me off my feet while swallowing me with an unmatched tenderness, couldn't raise an arm to shoo a fly.

To see him so helpless frightened me.

Yes, Daddy was depending on *me*.

Conflicted at the sight of such vulnerability, I didn't want to look at my daddy. Yet my love for him galvanized my resolve. I reached for the storm-door handle. Slow and steady, as if disarming a bomb, and allowing myself quick glances backward to monitor the threat level of a sudden ambush, I opened the storm door and stepped outside. With equal care, I nestled the metal door against its frame.

I had to run.

I shot out from under the carport, down the driveway, and turned right where concrete and asphalt met. The unthinkable events of the last five minutes replayed themselves like an endless-loop video in my mind. My eyes stung, painted with hot tears at the memory. Regardless of their age, no one should have to witness what I had just experienced in that house—let alone a seven-year-old girl. The fresh images of what had transpired moments ago mocked me with the fact that my worst fears had just come true.

I had to keep running.

Although I couldn't see any activity through the curtains framing my bedroom window, that didn't mean the gunman wasn't keeping a sharp eye on the street. I hesitated, but only for a moment more. What *might* happen gave way to what *had* happened. I had to get help. Now, almost frantic to reach my destination, I redoubled my efforts.

I ran on.

To get help for Momma and Daddy. To escape the gunman. To

get away from all the threatening letters, the sniper gunshots, the menacing midnight phone calls, the home invasions—and the devil who seemed to be behind so many of them.

But I'm getting ahead of the story.

CHAPTER 2

# Once upon a Dream

The snow drifted.

Thick plumes of whiteness blanketed the frozen streets of Bogalusa. Layer upon layer of soft-packed snowflakes settled in near silence, forming a quilt of feathery ice crystals. This quaint Louisiana town, nestled against the border of Mississippi, a scant forty miles north of the Gulf of Mexico, resembled a winter wonderland worthy of Santa himself.

Traditional red and green Christmas garlands hung from front doors. For some, windows and rooflines sported strings of flickering lights. Families huddled together with cups of hot chocolate while children eyed brightly colored packages beneath tree limbs adorned with ornaments and candy canes. Each in his or her own way was celebrating the birth of Christ.

I did not witness these happenings.

However, at age twenty-seven, my mother, Ramona Welch, did. Although Christmas was usually a time of joy for her, this particular year, 1963, was especially hard on her soul. She was as miserable as if she were living during the Great Depression. Chief among reasons for her heavy heart was the unmistakable fact that most of her friends were married and she, for reasons known only to God, remained unwed. A lonely old maid, as she wrote in her journal.

In every other aspect of her life, things were going great. Her career as a bookkeeper paid well. Her boss loved Momma's work ethic and sometimes flew her to New York to handle one of the company's accounts. She had a closet full of clothes, a new car, and until this year, lots of friends. Momma was not melancholy by nature. On the contrary, she was as effervescent as a freshwater stream.

But while her peers lived in apartments or houses of their own, she was still living with her parents—as well as with her recently divorced younger sister and her sister's four-year-old son. She longed for companionship, for independence, for someone to share the dreams of her life. For years she had prayed that she'd marry a preacher. That was the unmet desire of her heart.

Not that Momma wasn't close to her family. She was. Every workday she traveled home during her lunch break to watch *As the World Turns* with her mother, a routine as regular as the rising of the sun. They had each other, but she didn't have someone to call her own. Momma managed to mope through Christmas. Even with the new year fast approaching, bearing promises of new beginnings, Momma's otherwise upbeat, unquenchable spirit remained frozen in the grip of the winter doldrums.

On New Year's Eve, the snow fell again. For three solid days, a heavy snowstorm dumped a pale shroud of white flakes until the roads became impassable. Momma had been trapped at home, unable to celebrate New Year's with old friends or coworkers. No shared fireworks. No colorful hats. No noisemakers. Midnight hugs and laughter were in short supply. She had to settle for watching Guy Lombardo and his band playing on television as the ball dropped in New York City.

As if to add insult, the blizzard crippled their phone service. A simple phone call to share the moment was out of the question. Momma never felt more isolated in her life. Needing to do something, anything, to take her mind off her loneliness, Momma, bundled up in mittens, boots, and a scarf, headed to the backyard to make her own company. Maybe she figured that, if God wouldn't bring her a man, she'd just have to make one for herself.

Hours later, she had hand-fashioned a life-size snowman tall enough to match her five-foot-seven frame. Even as pictures were taken of Momma standing with her arms draped around her make-believe man, an avalanche of frosty emotions swept over her. This snow creation, no matter how perfectly crafted, could never melt the chill within.

She was a single adult in a world made for couples.

Two days later, on January 3, 1964, her snowman vanished, vanquished by unseasonably warm, coastal winds. In the wake of his abrupt departure, her longing for a man, one who wouldn't melt with the snow, wash away with the rain, or disappear into the night, intensified.

The cold returned.

The first weekend of the New Year brought with it an intense gloom, thick as fog. Once again, Momma had nothing to do and no friends with whom to brighten her Saturday night. Living across the street from the Warren Street Church of God, an intimate community church where she had worshiped since childhood, she decided to practice several songs on the organ. To Momma, music was like a treasured gem, one she polished to a shine as often as possible.

Musically gifted and able to play a number of instruments by ear, Momma could make a piano, accordion, guitar, and saxophone sing. Those around her would often dance as she serenaded them with song. Whether playing a hymn, a folk ditty, or the boogie-woogie, she was the life of the party. Recognizing her talent, the pastor had asked her to serve as their organist.

Momma headed out the door with her energetic four-year-old nephew, Stevie, in tow. Much to Momma's dismay, her mother had asked—as a favor to her sister—for this spirited child to accompany her. Rather than sing the blues in protest, Momma figured she'd just have to drown out Stevie's cacophony of sound with the organ. That's all there was to it.

With no plans of meeting anyone, she wore a run-of-the-mill blouse, an ordinary skirt, loafers, and a scarf. Her long locks of chestnut brown hair were rolled tight in the clutches of twelve pink curlers. She made her way across the street, slipped into the vacant building, and cranked up the organ. With the exception of Stevie running between the pews, she was alone in her private sanctuary of song.

That's when the side door opened.

That's when he walked in.

A stranger.

The most handsome man she had ever laid eyes on.

The unknown guest paused just inside the sanctuary door, Bible in hand, standing tall. His shoulders, broad and sturdy, appeared as if they could carry the weight of the world without breaking a sweat. His brown eyes sparkled like perfectly matched quartz gemstones. He glanced around the room and then settled on the source of the music.

Struck by his unexpected appearance, Momma lifted her fingers from the keyboard as if the keys had suddenly become hot to the touch. The music stopped and was instantly replaced by a chorus of questions. Who could this man be? Where was he from? What was he doing here, of all unlikely places? Had he been listening to her playing through the door? If so, for how long?

More to point, was he married? If he didn't have a wife, what kind of first impression was she making with her hair wrapped up in neat rows of pink rollers? Her face, with its otherwise fair complexion, flushed beet red at the thought and then reddened even more as a new reality dawned on her: What if this visitor, this perfect specimen of a man who'd just walked into her world, was single and assumed little Stevie was her child? Would he dismiss her out of hand as being married? Would he, like her snowman, vanish in the night just as quickly as he had materialized?

With long, smooth strides he spanned the distance between them. Momma rose from the organ, flattening out her skirt as she stood. Nothing could be done to conceal the rollers sitting atop her head, drawing attention like a lighthouse beacon. He offered his hand in greeting. She took it. Rather, his mitt-size hand engulfed her petite fingers, yet with care, as if handling a rare, delicate flower.

The newcomer introduced himself as evangelist Robert Nichols, from Mobile, Alabama. His smile, as wide as the Mississippi River, seemed to brighten the room as if a drape had been pulled back, admitting the morning sun. The fact that it was night only served to heighten the winsome beam he projected as he spoke. Robert explained that he would be holding revival services at the church starting the next day and continuing for a month of Sundays.

This was news.

This was exciting news, though she wondered why she hadn't heard he was coming. After all, she was the church organist, and her father was the choir director. Surely news of a revival would have found its way to her. Nevertheless, she was delighted, especially when she noticed Robert wasn't wearing a wedding ring. At the thought, her heart fluttered inside her chest like a butterfly trying to escape. Dare she believe he might be the one she'd been praying for?

They chatted for several delightful minutes. The private exchange would have been perfect had it not been for Stevie's high-energy distraction. It was to be Robert's second revival series after leaving the Navy—those years in the military explained the confidence and strength he displayed. The first two weeks, Robert explained, were designed for the church members and would be followed by two weeks of messages for those outside the church family whom he hoped the regulars would invite in.

Before he excused himself, Momma offhandedly let him know that the impetuous child running circles around them was her nephew, Stevie, not her child. She, of course, wasn't married—for the record. After saying good-bye and giving her another firm handshake, Robert turned and left her standing there with her heart beating faster than she thought possible. He would be coming back. Tomorrow. For a revival.

She'd see him for four weeks—without rollers.

For the first time in ages, she floated home.

In spite of her best efforts to remain calm, Momma couldn't hide her excitement as she told her parents about the unexpected visitor. Her mother was quick to encourage Momma's hope that Robert might just be the guy for her, the answer to a decade of prayers. Like two schoolgirls comparing notes on the playground, they talked at length about Robert. Her dad, however, frowned during the whole discussion. Rather than launch into a lengthy discourse, his opinion was reduced to three words.

"Ramona, forget it."

During the first two weeks of the revival, it seemed her dad had been the more realistic of her parents. Robert was there to preach, not to date. His heart was burdened for the impact of the gospel message on those filling the pews. Although he was polite, Momma felt largely ignored. Night after night, Robert preached until his pressed white shirt was soaked around the collar. Riveted to her seat, she hung on to every word as if each syllable were a treasure. If, by chance, Robert made eye contact, her face glowed pinkish red as if a sunlamp had been turned on.

After services, her smile still beaming as if she were privy to a secret joy, Momma lingered with the crowd, hoping for a turn to express how much she got out of the message. Robert maintained a polite, professional distance. If Robert had feelings for Ramona, he managed to keep them close to his vest, causing Momma to wonder whether her feelings for him were a one-way street.

Maybe he was seeing a girl back home. If not, why didn't he warm to her? He was single. She was single. Both were of marrying age. Was there something undesirable about her? Maybe he would notice her if she were to dress more like her sister, Sue—the flashy dresser in the family. After years of practice, Sue knew how to use makeup to her advantage. But slathering on mascara and wearing hoop earrings that jingled when she walked wasn't Ramona's style.

Rather, her beauty treatment amounted to the discreet application of pancake makeup. She preferred dresses with gathered skirts, most of which she and her mother handmade themselves, and the practicality of loafers. She had no use for gold necklaces or shiny rings. Applying clear nail polish was about as glitzy as she cared to venture into the world of cosmetics.

For two weeks she talked late into the night with her mother about the mystery of attracting a man, this man in particular. Would it be such a bad thing to spice up her image? Should she ask her sister if she could borrow one of her store-bought dresses? What about fixing her hair differently? How about a splash of perfume?

Although sympathetic to the war of emotions raging within Ramona, her mother had little use for such window dressing. In her heart of hearts, Momma knew that her mother, her best friend and coconspirator in love, was right. To put on a show would be to become someone she was not. No, there was nothing wrong with her appearance. Robert would have to be drawn to her vibrant spirit and inner, godly glow. That's all there was to it.

Which is not to say Momma was unattractive. She wasn't. Like a rose, hers was a classic beauty. Resolved to be the person God created her to be, refusing to apply so much as a layer of lipstick, she continued to trust and pray that the man who captivated her heart would one day accept her for who she was. Would that day ever come?

Maybe. Maybe not.

That decision was beyond her control.

The veil of uncertainty cloaking Robert's feelings parted fifteen days after their initial meeting. As was his practice, Robert concluded the evening service with an altar call. After talking and praying with those who had come forward, he lingered as the attendees retraced their steps to the parking lot. Much to Momma's surprise, Robert took her aside and, lowering his voice as if the room had been bugged, asked if she would like to go somewhere and get a cup of coffee.

These were the words she had yearned to hear. Her ears burned around the edges as he spoke. Did he have feelings for her after all? Could this be the beginning of something special? Of course she'd enjoy the pleasure of his company and said so—although she fought the temptation to appear too anxious. Desperation wasn't attractive, no matter how nicely she was dressed. Escorting her outside, this young evangelist—her tall, handsome knight—held the car door as she gathered her dress and slipped inside the chariot.

He circled around the front of the hood and appeared at his door. This was no dream, no wishful thinking. At the sound of the engine roaring to life, she remembered to breathe. They navigated all too quickly the short distance to the Acme Café, a local hot spot in the heart of Bogalusa. If she could, she would have gladly arm wrestled with Father Time to slow down the clock for the night.

They were seated across from each other in an oversize, avocado green and orange booth. The butterflies in her heart fluttered with a renewed burst of energy when her feet accidentally brushed against his under the table. She hoped he didn't think she was being forward. Given that each booth was outfitted with a personal coin-operated jukebox, and grateful for a chance to pull the focus from the unintentional physical contact, Momma fished a dime from her purse and selected a favorite tune, "Danny Boy."

Waitresses buzzed from table to table, like bees scuttling between buds on a honeysuckle shrub, taking orders and refilling drinks. Considering Momma had been to the café many times before with friends, the harried pace and general pulse of the scene felt familiar but different. This time, rather than scan the faces in the room, Momma, feeling as charmed as Cinderella, gave her full attention to soaking in the view across the table.

Robert sipped coffee while Ramona drank in the moment.

For two weeks she had been early to every one of his revival services. Day by day she grew deeper in love with his heart, his boldness, and his voice of conviction. He was the real deal. A man of God. Sitting with her. Not only was he great looking up close, she found his gaze as warm and inviting as a spring day. She felt as if she could tell him anything—and yet she didn't want to say too much.

It was just coffee, right? Or was it?

She could have listened for hours. And she did.

When the evening was over, she sailed home, buoyed by his

request to meet again the next night after services. Sleep, of course, was out of the question. She'd keep the moon company while she replayed their conversation in her mind over and over until, at long last, her eyelids conceded. She drifted off to sleep with a smile still embossed on her face.

During their second coffee, she discovered they had more in common than she'd ever imagined. Both had been previously married—Ramona, at age twenty, to a hot-tempered, controlling man devoid of love and, on occasion, verbally abusive. When he hit her the first time, that was the last straw. The short-lived marriage was annulled.

Robert, too, had married young while serving in the Navy. He had fallen in love with his commanding officer's daughter. Enthralled with this woman, Robert was quick to tattoo her name on his left arm. Not long into the marriage, he left for a tour of duty with his ship. Upon his return, the young serviceman learned she had abandoned him. A Dear John letter on the kitchen table announced that she was leaving town with her father, who had received orders transferring him to another naval station. She made it clear Robert was not to follow—and for the record, her father was having their marriage annulled.

Which is why Robert had appeared to ignore Ramona for the first two weeks. Love had wounded him before. The last thing he wanted to do was make the same mistake twice. He had to see what kind of person Ramona was before daring to get close to a woman again. Yes, he had been watching her, studying her character at arm's length. He warmed to her humor, her giftedness, her simplicity, the way she interacted with others, and above all, her heart for God. What he saw led him to believe she'd be the perfect helpmate for him.

For the next fourteen days of the revival, she drank more coffee—with Robert—than she'd had in her entire life. The couple concealed their growing love from the parishioners, who, in turn, were floored at the announcement of their wedding on Tuesday, February 11, 1964. Six weeks after her unexpected encounter with Robert in the chapel, Momma and Daddy pledged each other their lives—for better or worse, in sickness and in health, until they drew their last breath.

Standing that day, arms entwined under a white, arch-shaped trellis, surrounded by family and friends, there was no way they could foresee the trials that lay ahead like a snake in the shadow of their garden of paradise. Trials that would test their faith, threats that would shake their emotions, and bullets that would target their commitment to God and to each other. All they knew or cared about in that joyous moment was the unmistakable fact that God had brought them together.

Their first house was a small trailer in which Momma gladly set up housekeeping as if it were a palace. The humble abode didn't bother her in the least. A big house held nothing that she didn't already possess. She had a great man who loved and cherished her, a man with an unmatched passion for the Lord. That was better than the finest mansion money could buy.

For the better part of six years, Daddy, Bible in hand, and Momma, toting her accordion, planted churches and held revivals wherever God's calling took them. Throughout Alabama, Arkansas, and Texas, they lived in motels while Daddy preached the Good News to whoever would listen. They spent several of those years serving as missionaries to the Native Americans in Oklahoma.

In spite of their best efforts, times were hard, and finances were lean. On one occasion, with just three potatoes and some cooking oil in the pantry, my optimistic momma suggested they head to the creek and catch some fish for supper. Daddy dug for worms and grabbed two poles, and away they went. Evidently the fish weren't as hungry as they were. After three hours, and with no nibbles to show for their efforts, Daddy announced, "Let's go!"

Momma wasn't about to let the fish win. Time they had. Money they didn't. Besides, once she got something in her head, she wasn't easily dissuaded. Momma said, "Wait a few more minutes. I know we're going to catch *something.*" I'm sure in that moment Daddy gained a new insight into his new bride: He had married one tenacious woman.

She was also creative at meal planning whenever they traveled to conduct revival services in other cities. When packing the car, she made sure she had an electric coffeepot and a frying pan to cook dinner in their motel room. Skipping restaurants was a sure way to keep costs down. Momma's resourcefulness knew no bounds, except in one area.

Having children.

Try as they did, Momma couldn't get pregnant.

Robert was as disappointed as she that kids weren't a part of their story. He loved children. Always quick to pass out candy to the youngsters or to tell tall tales to entertain their young ears, he couldn't imagine going through life without raising at least one child of their own making.

During the early years of their marriage, Momma saw three doctors in search of a solution. After running a number of tests, the first physician broke the bad news: Momma had endometriosis. Nine out of ten women with her condition could not have children. She heard him speak the words, but the reality was slow to register. When it did, the news almost crushed her. Momma hoped and prayed she would be one of the few who defied the odds.

She also sought a second opinion.

Sitting across the desk from her new doctor, Momma explained her deep desire to have children. After examining her, the doctor threw up both of his hands as if being held at gunpoint and said, "I'm sorry, Ramona, I can't paint you a pretty picture—the capacity to have children just isn't there." The third doctor echoed what she had already been told and then suggested she consider adoption.

Momma's heart was shattered. The thought that she'd never embrace a baby who was her own flesh and bones was too much to bear. She desperately wanted to give her husband a child. But the verdict was in. There was nothing more that could be done—at least not humanly speaking.

She had reached the end of the road, and she knew it.

There would be no baby blue or pink pajamas, no high chairs, no little feet following her around, no birthday candles to blow out atop a brightly decorated cake. She'd never experience the joy of hearing a little voice laughing while swinging in the backyard or opening presents on Christmas morning. Her ears wouldn't be graced with the precious words, "I love you, Momma."

Her empty arms ached at the thought that they might never be filled. At the same time, Momma clung to the conviction that coming to the end of ourselves always brings us to a place where we find Jesus. If she were ever going to enter into the marvel of creating life, a supernatural intervention to correct whatever was wrong within her womb would have to occur. She never doubted that it could.

And when it did, she had no idea what was wrong.

One morning, Momma became too queasy to stand. Drained as if she had expended every last ounce of energy running a triathlon, she lingered in bed, head glued to the pillow. The knotted-pine walls of their rented bungalow seemed to grow as dark as the Black Forest with depression. She kept her eyes closed as if that might prevent the waves of nausea from washing over her.

With no explanation for this sudden shift in her demeanor, Daddy took her to see a doctor who, though not wanting to raise their hopes, ran a fresh battery of tests. The doctor returned to his desk, wearing a smile so wide his face almost couldn't contain it. With the enthusiasm expected from a proud grandfather to be, he announced there was no mistake: Momma was pregnant!

It was Daddy and Momma's turn to rejoice at the unbelievable news. Their countless prayers had been answered. Soon there would be a third plate at the table.

They'd be a family.

Now what?

The doctor provided a book detailing the important vitamins Momma should take, a prescription for even more potent vitamins, and a list of foods she should be sure to eat. Like a student studying to pass an exam, Momma pored over the material to ensure she did everything in her power to fuel proper fetal development. This was going to be the healthiest baby in the world. It was also destined to be the most spoiled—that is, if the grandparents had anything to say about that.

Momma's pregnancy—and Daddy's decision not to serve as a traveling evangelist for a season—gave birth to a whole new routine. Having settled down in Baton Rouge, Daddy worked as a self-employed painter and, on occasion, was a guest preacher on an "as needed" basis. His schedule was as unpredictable as the stock market. Momma's days looked different, too. In the past, she had spent her time cleaning, sewing, and preparing dinner in anticipation of Daddy's arrival. Now, she passed the time dreaming about setting up a nursery. Whenever she could get to a phone—their rented house didn't have one—she'd call her mom and talk about baby clothes, her sudden cravings, and her latest favorite baby names.

What's more, she didn't feel so alone during the day. True, Momma's little miracle couldn't communicate with her yet. But she delighted in serenading the growing baby anyway, humming a tune as she busied herself in the small home. Like any expectant mother, she glowed as if the sun's rays illuminated her face everywhere she walked. Life was good, and it was about to get better.

Three months into her pregnancy, when stepping out the back door of their home, the unthinkable happened. Momma's ankle buckled as she walked down the steps. She fell sideways, hitting the stonelike earth. Hard. Too hard. As she struggled to pull herself upright, the weight of fear pressed down on her like a vise, crushing her with the thought that she might lose her precious baby.

The baby they had prayed God would provide.

The child she envisioned cradling in her arms.

A grandbaby for her parents.

Without close neighbors and with no phone to call for help, she battled her fears like a mother bear about to be robbed of her cubs. Nursing a twisted ankle and a bruised side, she hobbled to bed and slipped under the covers cocoonlike. The comforter did little to muffle the voices of shame swirling like a storm inside of her head: . . . if only she had been more careful . . . if only she had placed her hand on the handrail to steady herself down the two short steps . . . if only . . .

Thoughts of shame gave way to anxiety.

Had anything happened to her baby?

If so, how could she face her husband? What would she say? How might he handle the news? He wasn't a man easily given to anger, but this was a big deal. Bigger than if she had lost their life's savings. Money could be replaced. Life has no price tag.

Alone with nothing but a cold silence to answer her endless questions, she cried out to God. Tears soaked her pillow as she begged Him to be merciful. She had faithfully endured the dry, desertlike years consulting doctors only to have received bad news at every turn. How could God allow her to savor those glorious feelings soaring within upon learning she had defied the odds? She couldn't lose this child. Not now.

Not after all she had been through.

+ + +

It was hours before Daddy returned home to learn the awful news. True to form, he was kind, understanding, patient, and above all, prayerful. The matter was in God's hands as is all of life. Turning out the lights, they tried to get some rest. An unbearable pain, the struggle within her womb, prevented sleep.

The bleeding started at midnight.

Daddy rushed Momma to the hospital. She begged the nurses for something to ease her pain. In spite of their efforts to make her comfortable, she felt as if she would explode. Blood rushed to her head as her blood pressure spiked. Four nurses hovered over her, calling her sweet names while placing cool washcloths on her forehead, but they couldn't prevent the trauma at work inside.

Two hours before dawn, Momma lost the baby.

She was undone, limp from exhaustion.

+ + +

After surgery to remove that part of her she had hoped to treasure for a lifetime, Momma was wheeled back to her room to recover, although there was no way she could really recover what she had lost. Her priceless miracle baby was gone, gone forever, never to be replaced. With a vital part of her now missing, she felt like an empty shell. Sure, time has a way of healing things. Yet Momma instinctively knew this kind of emptiness wouldn't be easily filled.

To put some distance between themselves and their loss, my parents relocated to Mobile, Daddy's hometown. When they consulted the want ads in the paper, one particular listing caught their eyes. A large homestead, nestled in a heavily wooded area fifteen miles out in the country and several miles down a beaten path from the highway, was available for rent by a doctor.

After driving out to the property, they walked around in the shade offered by a canopy of tall trees. The house was picture perfect; the moment Momma laid eyes on the place, she fell in love. Even without entering the home to see the inside condition, Momma blurted out, "Let's take it!" Much to their surprise, the doctor's wife had recently remodeled the house and left the home completely furnished, including an old wood-burning stove.

While others might have been troubled by the fact that the nearest dwelling was two miles away, my parents were not. If anything, the privacy would allow them to try to start over. The peace and tranquility would give them a much-needed respite. Hunting, fishing, and long, unhurried walks in the dry autumn leaves with my daddy would provide time for Momma's heart to mend from the loss of the child they didn't get to meet.

God had supernaturally intervened once, hadn't He?

Would it be too much to believe He'd do it again?

CHAPTER 3

# Shotgun Justice in Sellerstown

The leaves fell.

Maple and oak trees shed their summer gowns without embarrassment. A potpourri of discarded foliage covered the path, ankle deep. Each new leaf, drifting peacefully from its roost overhead, took its turn to paint the ground in a palette of brown, yellow, and orange shades. A restless few engaged in cartwheels before lying still.

Brisk country air, scented with the fragrance of fallen leaves, filled their lungs as Daddy and Momma walked hand in hand. They traveled in the wake of a beagle blazing a trail twenty paces ahead of them. Tail wagging, nose sniffing the earth, their newly acquired pet remained on high alert for small game. Catching a faint whiff of a hare, possum, or coon, tail now upright reaching for the sky, he'd pause before continuing his search for the elusive prey.

Deeper in the woods they roamed.

Finding a clearing, a break in the dense timberland, they sat down under a towering red maple whose bare branches seemed to tickle the clouds. The relative silence was broken only by the beagle's four paws, shuffling through leaves, pursuing the hunt solo. Leaning against the tree trunk, Daddy and Momma listened and waited for the sound of a deer or turkey—or, more consequentially, the voice of God to answer their unspoken questions.

For six months Momma had been struggling to heal from the loss of her baby. My daddy knew that slowing the pace of life was what his bride needed most, so he left his itinerant preaching with its heavy travel demands and instead put his skill as an electrician to work at a local plant. Most afternoons, he'd arrive home by 4:15, where an early dinner awaited. After he and Momma had eaten, they'd slip into jackets and boots and head down the winding path leading to this oasis of reflection.

During these late-afternoon hikes, she wondered whether or not she should trust God for another child. Dare she hope for a second miracle? Would such hope be presumptuous on her part? What if He didn't grant her request? Would her view of God change? Would He be any less loving if He chose to deny her this one wish?

After Momma lost the baby, Daddy had his share of healing to address as well. That night, pacing the halls in the hospital, he had cried out to God to save their unborn child. He clung to the thread of hope that all would be well. In the dead of night, when the doctor broke the news that their baby was gone, the news took Daddy to the edge of himself.

He was mad at God.

He was mad at his wife.

He was mad at himself.

Daddy had enough sense, though, to keep a muzzle on his mouth. An outburst from an irate husband was the last thing Momma needed.

True, he had managed to rein in his anger when he first learned of her slip and fall. Now that hope was lost, it took everything in his power to summon a reluctant dose of verbal restraint.

The blame game was a game with no winners.

And yet the loss of their child had shattered a part of his heart he hadn't known could break. Was there something he could have done differently to prevent their loss? What kind of man would leave his pregnant wife in a home without a telephone in case of trouble? At the very least, Daddy knew if he had been there, he could have ventured outdoors instead of his wife, and she, in turn, wouldn't have miscarried.

Regrets for what he might have done differently gave way to nagging questions about God's hand in the matter. Even after Ramona's fall, God could have prevented her miscarriage, right? Why, then, did this God of love allow such pain to scar their dreams? Was there a lesson God wanted him to learn the hard way? Wasn't there an easier way for God to make His point?

Was he being punished for something?

Or were they being prepared for something?

A series of clipped barks pulled him back from his musing. Their beagle, ever vigilant, dashed off in hot pursuit of an unseen quarry. Neither Robert nor Ramona saw fit to join the chase, although Robert had his rifle within reach should a wild turkey emerge from the brush.

Watching the dog disappear in the dense undergrowth, he returned to his thoughts. For whatever reason God saw fit to take their child, he knew his wife's miscarriage was not some sort of punishment or payment for past misdeeds. God had already bought his life with a heavy price. His sins had been covered, his debt had been paid. No further payment was required. God had already sacrificed His only child on Daddy's behalf.

In spite of his intense grief, Daddy yearned to tell others about the God who had a yet-to-be-revealed purpose for their present grief. God was still good, even when life sometimes didn't make sense. After all, this was the same God who had rescued him from a life of unrestrained vice. He was living proof that God changes lives.

Before making his peace with God, Daddy could raise Cain with the best of them. As a young man in his midtwenties, fresh out of the Navy, Daddy had spent his free time going to bars and brawling just for the thrill of it. Giving no thought to anyone or anything else other than the pursuit of beer and women, Daddy took frequent jaunts on the wild side.

Recognizing the self-destructive path Daddy had been traveling, my grandpa urged Daddy to attend a revival service at their small country church. For five weeks Daddy rebuffed the offer. A revival service? Right. There were bars to visit. Drinks to be shared. Friends to laugh with and women to chase. Going to hear some preacher rattle on about sin wasn't just low on Daddy's list; it didn't even make his list.

Grandpa persisted, prayed, and asked again.

During the sixth week of the revival, Daddy agreed, albeit reluctantly, to attend. Anything to humor his father and get him off his back. At first, he only half listened, checking his watch in the hope that he could catch up with his friends at the bar while there was still beer left on tap. Everything about the revival made him feel as awkward as a pig at a barbecue, even though, with the skill of a mason, he had constructed a wall around his emotions. The wall was a tribute to his first wife, who had taught him a hard lesson: the more you love someone, the more you have to lose when that someone decides you're no one. And yet there was something about the preacher's message of faith that chipped away at his heart of stone.

One by one the bricks were knocked out of place.

He stopped checking his watch.

By the end of the service, he was convicted by the simple truth of God's love for him. With knees on the ground, Daddy prayed for Jesus to come into his heart. His life would never be the same. For starters, Daddy lost his taste for beer and gained an insatiable thirst for the Scriptures. At night he'd read the Bible until the sun crested the horizon. He loved talking with other godly men from church for hours on end.

More than that, he learned to love God so much that if he wasn't holding a Bible, he made certain he had one tucked into his pocket. He'd steal unused minutes from the day to absorb every ounce of truth on the printed page. Daddy's transformation was every bit as spectacular as when a caterpillar morphs into a butterfly.

How could he not tell others?

Not surprisingly, Daddy's old drinking buddies weren't thrilled at this changed, Bible-toting man. Much to their surprise, when they'd invite Daddy out for a night on the town, Daddy would tell them he didn't live that way any longer and then turn the tables by inviting them to church with him. They liked the old Bob Nichols, the ex-Navy womanizer who chased the skirts and drank long past midnight.

So radical was the change in Daddy's life, and his zeal for God so infectious, his pastor asked Daddy to preach his maiden sermon just two months after his conversion. Within half a year of falling in love with the Lord, Daddy felt the hand of God, like a powerful magnet, drawing him into full-time ministry. He gladly quit his factory job at the Scott Paper Company to hit the road as an evangelist.

On January 5, 1964, Daddy walked into the Church of God on Warren Street in Bogalusa for what would be his second revival. There was no way at the time he could have known that God had someone special waiting for him at the organ. Someone who would be a perfect helpmate for him.

Someone with neon pink rollers in her hair.

Momma.

Now almost four years later, Momma was waiting for him again. This particular autumn afternoon, with their dog prancing through the underbrush and chasing small game, she wanted to know what was weighing so heavily upon his heart. She knew Daddy struggled with his desire to be a father. And yet, she sensed there had to be some deeper longing, some unmet desire, tossing and turning within him like a storm at sea. Content to wait until he felt safe enough for the words to be expressed, she didn't pry.

As if reading her thoughts, Daddy turned to Momma and said, "You know what, Mona? I was called to preach the gospel, but here I sit at ease in Zion. I will rest just as Jesus took time to rest," he said. Then he added, "But when He opens a door, I won't hesitate to return to my calling."

Momma wasn't entirely surprised to learn what had been stirring within her husband. She knew once people have a call on their lives to share Christ, they're not happy doing any other type of work. In a way, she resonated with this longing. She missed the joy of sharing Jesus with others. The thought that maybe it was time for them to reenter the ministry had been growing in her, too. They were, after all, a team.

Month by month her body was growing stronger. Even her wounded heart was beginning to mend. She knew there was nothing that could change the past, and with courage, they would once again face the future. While it was still light enough to see the trail, they started back home with an unspoken yet renewed sense of purpose.

In July 1969, the call came. Sensing an inner prompting from God to reenter the "harvest fields," as he was fond of calling them, Daddy wasted no time resigning from his job and made plans to reenter the ministry. Part of his transition back into the pulpit required Daddy to attend a series of meetings in Montgomery, Alabama. Without hesitation, thrilled at the chance to help the lost dedicate their lives to the Lord, Momma packed their bags, frying pan, and coffeepot for the trip.

That's when the unexpected happened.

Momma became ill. Not just sick as if she had a head cold. Day after day, she struggled to get out of bed as if shackled to the mattress. Morning would give way to noon, and she'd still be trying to pull herself out from under the covers. When she did manage to emerge, she stumbled through the motions of getting ready to face the day.

She wasn't depressed. Far from it.

Her husband had a new fire in his eyes as he reported the details of his various meetings. As far as they could tell, they were in the center of God's will doing exactly what they should be doing. Depression had nothing to do with the queasy, nauseated feeling rocking her emotional boat. The evidence seemed to point in one direction.

With a mixture of faith and apprehension, Momma asked Daddy to take her to see a physician as soon as he could clear his schedule. When the doctor returned with her results, he was all smiles. God had given her another chance to be a mother.

She would finally fill that empty place in her soul.

With me.

During the early weeks of her pregnancy, after the nausea had passed, Momma felt impressed upon her spirit to visit friends in North Carolina while she could still travel. An extended road trip might seem crazy—if not borderline irresponsible—since she had just lost a baby. But she was neither insane nor reckless. I can only imagine that Momma must have had a powerful indication from the Holy Spirit to undertake such a journey while pregnant.

Although Daddy didn't feel the same tug in his heart, he listened to his bride, trusting that she would have prayed about such an important decision. They traveled to the charming town of Lumberton, North Carolina. A popular rest area for tourists, Lumberton is situated halfway between Florida and New York. The Lumber River, a scenic blackwater river, cuts a whimsical path through the town, adding to its laid-back appeal.

However, Daddy and Momma were not tourists seeking a haven of rest. To be sure, they would have appreciated the local beauty. And, given Daddy's love of fishing, it's easy to imagine they made some time to cast their lines in the Lumber River. But they had had their season of rest and now were anxious to be fishers of men.

While in Lumberton, Daddy was invited to bring the morning sermon at a local church. His topic was "Seek Those Things Above." Upon hearing the passion with which Daddy preached his message, the ministers suggested he sow some seeds of faith in the outlying communities of North Carolina. To my daddy's way of seeing things, I'm sure the idea of planting the seeds of truth among the area's farmers had a certain ring about it. Eager to serve, he agreed to their proposal, and three revivals were scheduled.

Their first assignment was to conduct a series of revival services at the Free Welcome Holiness Church, a small independent church eight miles south of Whiteville, North Carolina. Armed only with their Bibles and the conviction that God had opened this door, Daddy and Momma pointed their car south toward Whiteville, a thirty-minute ride.

With fewer than four thousand residents, Whiteville wasn't exactly a large town. It really wasn't much larger than a whistle-stop. But at least it was a town, complete with a city hall, bank, grocery store, doctor's office, gas station, hardware store, motel, and restaurant. As Daddy and Momma continued south, the signs of city life quickly fell away as the two-lane stretch of blacktop took them deeper into the sparsely populated outlying area, closer toward whatever awaited them in Sellerstown.

As Daddy and Momma were quick to discover, while there *was* a street called Sellerstown Road, technically speaking there wasn't a *city* of Sellerstown—at least not in any official sense of the word. Unlike Whiteville, Sellerstown was little more than a tract of farmland and residential dwellings. No banks, no businesses, no city hall. Just acres of farmland. In spite of the fact that Sellerstown is unincorporated and not noted as a town on any map, the locals had been calling their community by that name for four generations.

They still do.

More than a hundred years ago, four Sellers brothers moved to this beautiful stretch of wide-open country. With an eye on farming, three of the brothers purchased all the land on either side of the two-mile road that would ultimately be named after them. A thousand acres or so became home to their extended family tree, where the Sellers clan promptly put down deep roots in the rich, virgin soil.

There, they built their homes and raised corn, tobacco, and soybeans. For better or worse, they lived, worked, played, and fought together. With a few rare exceptions, everyone in Sellerstown was related to one another in some way. Which is why at times, shotguns in hand, they watched out for one another. The Sellers kin are true salt-of-the-earth people . . . although some were saltier than others.

Willie Sellers* comes to mind.

+ + +

For ten years, Willie Sellers ran a service station. His was an explosive personality, dynamite looking for a reason to detonate. He possessed

* Willie Sellers is a pseudonym.

both a volatile temper and a short fuse. Willie was the kind of hothead you didn't want to cross. His legendary anger would flare up at the slightest provocation.

What's more, Willie was obsessed with the thought that someone might swipe a pack of cigarettes or a stick of gum without paying. He patrolled his turf with an eagle's eye. No one would take advantage of him, not if he could help it. If a stranger walked in seeking directions, Willie got straight to the point, having no use for small talk. Chitchatting was for women. Assisting the customer took a backseat to running a tight ship.

If there was one thing that made Willie madder than a hornet's nest when poked by a stick, it was hired help that didn't show up to work. Such was the case one Saturday morning in the mid-1960s. Left alone to pump gas, fill kerosene cans, and run the register, Willie ran back and forth, in and out of the store, like a headless chicken. Midmorning, with more business than he could juggle, Willie called his cousin E. J. Sellers and asked if he could lend a hand. E. J. would pump the gas while Willie watched the store.

Glad to help, E. J. arrived and got busy, although Willie remained in a sour mood, his forehead perpetually snarled in a knot. As E. J. tells it, three youth in their midtwenties rolled to a stop at the pumps. Who they were or where they were going was no business of his. Minding his own affairs, E. J. gassed the car and washed the windshield, applying enough elbow grease to adequately scrub away all visible bug remains. With that done, the driver stepped out of the car, entered the building, and paid his bill.

On the way out, however, he took a quart of oil from the display case between the pumps without paying for it. At the time, a quart of oil cost all of twenty-five cents. Still, money was money, and E. J. wasn't about to let the guy off the hook. When he asked for payment for the oil, the driver denied taking it. Words were exchanged, but neither the oil nor the payment was handed over.

E. J. went inside and told Willie what had transpired. The news was more than Willie could handle, the final straw in an otherwise horrendous day, at least from Willie's heated point of view. He raced to the back room of the store, grabbed a pistol from the shelf as if arming for battle, then sprinted outside to confront the driver as he opened his car door.

Willie barked so loud, anyone within a block would have heard him: "Hey, you! Did you take that quart of oil? You owe me!"

The driver turned and stood his ground. "I didn't take no oil, and I ain't paying for oil I didn't take."

"I'm warning you," Willie yelled. "Pay me for that or else—"

The driver told Willie to back off—only in making his point he used a string of profanity as colorful as the shades of red on Willie's face, which was about as smart as pouring gasoline on a bonfire. The young man hopped in his car and started the engine to leave. E. J. watched in stunned silence as Willie raised his gun and shot the driver—and, in the heat of the moment, one of the other passengers as well, for reasons E. J. still doesn't understand.

Never in a thousand years did E. J. think his cousin would actually pull the trigger. He knew Willie could lose his cool, especially if he had been drinking. But Willie hadn't touched a drink all day. He was just at the boiling point when the heat was turned up. If E. J. had had any inkling that his cousin was capable of taking a man's life, he would have kept the incident to himself and gladly paid for the oil out of his own earnings.

The passenger who had been shot lived.

The driver, however, died.

The law was called, and Willie Sellers was arrested. His family was quick to raise the $100,000 bail money, and Willie was released.

When the tragic incident went to trial, E. J. was called to testify. If E. J. was shocked by the senseless murder, he was dumbfounded when the jury returned a "not guilty" verdict.

Less than thirty minutes after leaving Whiteville, Daddy and Momma spotted Sellerstown Road, a side street branching off to the right. Tucked in the shadow of the Route 701 Service Center—a one-story, two-pump gas, snack, and repair station—it would have been easy for them to miss the turnoff. Considering the events soon to take place on Sellerstown Road, it might have been better if they had.

They slowed, then turned right.

Watts Farm Supply, immediately on the left-hand side of the street, greeted them. As the only game in town, the store provided the necessary nuts and bolts to keep the farming community running smoothly. Parked behind this white, cinder block building, a modest collection of trucks, tractors, and trailers in various stages of disrepair sprouted from the field like turnips. The neglected and forgotten assortment of clutter stood in stark contrast to the otherwise serene country setting they had enjoyed since leaving Whiteville.

Aside from this disheveled patch of land, to the naked eye there was nothing ominous about the Sellerstown community. No dark, sinister clouds lying low like a shroud in the sky. No sudden heaviness in the air. No uneasy feeling, premonition of impending doom, or even a lone black vulture circling overhead, keeping watch in anticipation of death.

My parents didn't have the slightest reason to turn back. They didn't know about Willie Sellers, who settled disputes with a gun. Besides, they had a host of reasons for pressing on. They had been called, they had their marching orders, and now they were headed to

Sellerstown to do the Lord's work. It would be up to God to reap a harvest of souls.

As they had done before the start of every revival, once they arrived in Sellerstown, my parents planned to meet their local contact, survey the hall where the revival services would be held, and then find a place to stay for the duration of the meetings. They knew a member of the congregation might provide accommodations in his home. Plan B usually meant setting up housekeeping in a nearby, inexpensive motel—though they soon discovered Sellerstown had none.

Although I can't say for sure, they probably drove toward their destination with the windows rolled down. It was, after all, a typical sunbaked day in Sellerstown. The mid-eighty-degree temperatures were the by-product of an August sun standing high and proud in the sky as if it were about to receive an award. Without air conditioning in their 1964 Plymouth, a brown sedan which had seen better days, it's safe to say they would have invited the token breeze to bring some relief.

Within a minute of turning onto Sellerstown Road, they passed Mount Pilgrim Missionary Baptist Church, a humble white, cinder block structure, no larger than a four-car garage, planted like a cemetery headstone in a small plot. A clutch of tall trees surrounded the property like sentries, with just enough of a clearing to permit parking on the grassy side yard.

This, they would learn, was where the black folk attended, with room for no more than forty or fifty worshipers. Most of the members worked as hired help on the local farms in this agricultural community.

As the church took its place in their rearview mirror, they smelled, then saw, a tobacco barn fifty paces from the road. A gentle wind filled the air with the sweet, almost fruity scent of drying tobacco and a hint of freshly turned earth. As picturesque as a page torn out of *Southern Living*, rows of perfectly planted cornstalks, too numerous to count, awaited their turn for harvest in the unhurried patchwork of farmland beyond the barn.

Behind a trailer at the far end of the field, laundry pinned to clotheslines swayed as the grayish white lengths of rope drooped under their loads. Directly across the street on the right-hand side of Sellerstown Road, a second church appeared: the Free Welcome Holiness Church. The modest one-story, redbrick building, accented with six windows, backed up to cornfields and felt instantly inviting, even though the white front doors remained closed.

Adjacent to the church stood a newly constructed, almost-completed parsonage. Daddy had been informed that the church had been without a pastor for some months and the sheep were scattering without a shepherd. Perhaps the congregation, twelve women and one man, thought building a residence for the minister would attract a new candidate to fill the pulpit. Whatever their motivation, building the homestead certainly was a giant step of faith for such a small church family to undertake.

My hunch is that Daddy, having served in the Navy and out of habit, might have cruised the length of Sellerstown Road, conducting an informal reconnaissance of the area before stopping inside the church. A preliminary survey would give him a better feel for his audience during Sunday's revival. It was just as likely to prompt a few local metaphors with which to illustrate his message.

If so, Daddy and Momma would have counted an assortment of prefabricated single-wide and double-wide mobile homes resting on stacks of cinder blocks; ranch-style homes, some made of brick, others sporting clapboard siding; three barns with sagging rooflines; and a number of weathered feed shelters peppering the landscape.

When they ultimately arrived back at the church, they were greeted by Rev. Lonzie Sellers and his wife, Alma. Although formally retired, Rev. Sellers had offered his preaching services until a proper replacement could be found. True to form, Rev. and Mrs. Sellers gladly opened their home to my parents with all the Southern hospitality you might expect from a couple who freely gave their lives in the service of others.

With open arms and bottomless pitchers of sweet tea, Daddy and Momma were introduced to the quiet Sellerstown community, a place where everyone was made to feel like family—a task made easy because most *were* family. And, while I was present for Daddy's debut, being *in utero* has its limitations. Without the ability to hear or see the worship service, this much I know from those who weren't confined to their mother's womb: Daddy and Momma were a hit.

Actually, that's an understatement.

They were offered the job virtually on the spot.

The prospect was appealing. My parents had mutual feelings for these new friends. Having been captivated by those whom they met, longing to put down roots and establish a routine for their growing family, my parents felt that Rev. Sellers's overture had all the appeal of an ice cream sundae without the calories. As appetizing as the offer was, over the course of several days, my parents made the decision a matter of prayer.

After all, their extended family lived more than seven hundred miles away. They would soon have a child, and they'd want their baby to know his or her grandparents, aunts, and uncles. And yet delighted over the warm reception offered by these dear brothers and sisters, they accepted the job. Happy to pass the duties of pastor to my daddy, Rev. Sellers invited them to stay in his home until the parsonage was ready.

Daddy was quick to utilize his carpentry skills, nailing sheets of walnut paneling to the living room walls and applying the final coats of paint throughout the parsonage. Likewise, Momma, making several polite suggestions, put her final touches on what would soon be her residence. Among other things, she had a baby coming and wanted the nursery to have plenty of shelving in the closet.

On Thanksgiving Day 1969, Robert and Ramona Nichols moved into their new home. The church threw a housewarming party that was open to the entire Sellerstown community. A fresh turkey, shot, plucked, and roasted, took center stage on the kitchen table. Homemade dishes arranged around the turkey filled the house with an inviting aroma as delicious as the fellowship they shared with their new neighbors.

Momma mingled with the women as Daddy studied the faces, memorizing the names as best he could. Moving from guest to guest, he identified those who currently attended, had once attended, or ought to be attending the church. He knew there was a reason why the congregation had dwindled to about a dozen regulars, and he planned to do everything in his power to make everyone feel welcome under his leadership.

Of course, he knew little about the personal histories of the guests from this tightly knit community now making his acquaintance. For that matter, he wasn't a mind reader, nor could he see into the future. There was no way he could tell that one visitor in particular would soon betray him with the zeal of Judas.

CHAPTER 4

# The Devil's in Pew Number Seven

I yelled.

My eyes were pinched shut against a light as harsh as a solar flare. They stung as if sprayed with salt water. From head to toe, my skin tingled as if a blast of arctic air had swept over me. Chilled to the bone, I couldn't explain the traumatic change in temperature. My body shivered, trembling like a leaf in the wind. And, although I was suddenly cold, my lungs burned with each breath.

In vain, I cried out.

My legs, kicking without regard for the hands that attempted to hold me down, were no match for the masked faces surrounding me. I could not make sense of their muffled voices. Out of control, powerless to hold my head up, I was carried away against my will. With fingers curled into a ball of fury, face as red as Mars, I howled so loudly the wail could be heard down the hall.

Like all of humanity before me, I entered the world staging a protest.

On April 26, 1970, precisely at the stroke of midnight, I was born Rebecca Lorraine Nichols at the Southeastern General Hospital in Lumberton. After the nurses cleaned off my body, weighed, measured, and then wrapped me in a pink blanket, I was presented to my mother. I cannot pretend to imagine the feelings soaring through her heart like an eagle caught in an updraft as she cradled all 8 pounds, 9 1/2 ounces of me for the first time.

Drawing me to herself, inhaling the fresh scent of my newborn skin, Momma whispered a prayer of gratitude. Her arms were embracing a living miracle, and she, more than any of the nurses and visitors doting on me in the crowded hospital room, could fully appreciate the depth of that fact.

I was an answer to her countless prayers.

A dream fulfilled.

A hope granted.

Now that I had arrived, Momma would be my provider, my protector, my friend. And she, no doubt, had big plans to teach me how to sing and play an instrument when I was of age. In due time, she'd teach me about purity, modesty, conversational etiquette, boys, and especially the God who loved her baby. Throughout my life, she wouldn't permit a day to go by without saying, "I love you, Becky."

Even before I was born, she took the time to communicate her love for me, crafting a tender note placed inside my baby book. Putting pen to paper, she captured these reflections:

*A Letter to Our Little Darling*
*Your mommy is writing a letter because you haven't arrived yet. Your Daddy and I are looking forward to seeing you for the first time just two weeks from today. Daddy is like a little boy at Christmas waiting for Santa Claus to bring him a big present.*

*Only Santa won't bring you because you are being sent from Heaven. We prayed for you and Jesus heard us and is sending you to add more happiness to our lives.*

*We have wanted you so much for a little over six years now. But, God has a timetable and we had to wait until He was ready to send you. Our Heavenly Father always knows what's best for us. Your Daddy prays that you will be a good-spirited baby, and your mommy prays that you will be healthy.*

*You are coming from Heaven and I pray too that after your life is fulfilled on this earth that you will return from whence you came. Our greatest desire is that your name won't only be written in this book, but that it will be written down in the Lamb's Book of Life, the great record book in Heaven.*

*May God Bless Our Little Angel*

The joy Momma and Daddy experienced over my birth was shared by the entire church family. I was welcomed into the world as if I were one of their own kin. These dear friends showered gifts and homemade meals, like a heavy downpour, upon our home. A steady stream of visitors flowed in and out of the parsonage, seeking a peek at the miracle baby or dropping by to lend a hand as needed.

My parents couldn't have been happier.

Life was good. Very good.

At least for the first eighteen months of my life.

And then the telephone rang.

A jarring *clang* ripped through the night air. An unseen hammer in the belly of the phone beat against a metal bell with repeated blows as if prodded by a hot poker. Unlike modern phones, this one didn't have a selection of personalized ringer tones to customize the sound of an incoming call. No playful rendition of Tchaikovsky's *1812 Overture*, Beethoven's *Fifth Symphony*, or *Für Elise*. Not even a few bars of a favorite pop tune. The black rotary-dial telephone had a single, raspy voice delivered in one of two volumes: dull loud or loud.

A second ring pierced the silence.

This unsophisticated, low-tech communication device, the great-grandfather of the iPhone, didn't offer Internet access, caller ID, or even a mute feature. At the time, phone customers who loathed being awakened in the middle of the night had to invest some degree of effort to preserve the peace. By design, simply unplugging a phone from the wall wasn't an option for the simple fact that most phones were hardwired to a wall jack.

For a quiet night, it was necessary to remove the receiver from the cradle, creating a perpetually busy signal for would-be callers. Then, unscrewing the three-inch-round earpiece was necessary to avoid the shrill warning tone furnished by the phone company within thirty seconds of inactivity.

With rare exceptions, his role as pastor prevented my daddy from ever taking the phone off the hook anyway—even with a baby. Daddy knew his role as a leading figure in the community meant expecting the unexpected. Day or night, a parishioner might call for prayer, comfort, a listening ear, parenting advice, conflict resolution, or a request to visit a patient at the hospital. If so, he had to be ready to meet the need.

Without a full-time church receptionist to contact, some people would even telephone the parsonage seeking details regarding an upcoming churchwide picnic, fish fry, or hunting trip. In some respects, a country pastor was as "on call" around the clock as was the country doctor.

It just went with the territory.

The high-pitch jangle beckoned for a third time.

There was nothing unusual about receiving this particular late-night call, at least not at first. Although readying himself for bed, Daddy was prepared to grab his Bible and head out the door should someone be in need of a visitation. Even at this late hour, sleep could wait if necessary. Daddy lifted the receiver, placed it to his ear, and offered a friendly greeting.

"Hello?"

Without identifying himself, the anonymous man proceeded to deliver a threat to our family.

Daddy waited, eyebrow raised, listening for more. No response. The phone went dead.

Daddy rested the receiver in the cradle. Could the call have been a prank? A couple of kids fooling around, getting their kicks after dark by startling random people? Maybe. However, the voice didn't have the high pitch of youth. If not a young person making mischief with a juvenile stunt, who could it be? What kind of man would place a threatening call under the cover of darkness?

The people he had met during his first year in Sellerstown weren't mean-spirited. Quite the opposite. They'd be quick to give the shirt off their backs, bring a home-cooked meal, or lend a hand if needed. The Sellerstown he had experienced was a place where neighbors helped their neighbors.

If someone had a disagreement with him, why not just face him in the daylight, man-to-man, to air out their differences? That was the way it was usually done in Sellerstown. Receiving a telephone threat suggested he had been contacted by a disturbed individual with deep psychological issues.

Then again, Daddy might not have been quick to dismiss the possibility that the call was just a harmless prank. Daddy was, after all, married to a practical joker who didn't miss an opportunity to play a prank, even on her own husband, like the time months before when Daddy planned an early morning hunting trip with several men from church.

The men had gathered at the parsonage with their gear just as the timid sun was peeking over the horizon. Right before they set out into the woods, Momma offered the men glasses of sweet tea, which they gladly guzzled.

When the men returned, with a twinkle dancing in her eyes as if she were privy to a private joke, Momma inquired about the success of the hunt. As she could plainly see, the hunters had returned, for the most part, empty-handed. Daddy, sensing Ramona was up to one of her old tricks, explained how the men had been unable to do much in the way of hunting for one simple reason: They had been lined up at the latrine most of the morning taking care of business.

Momma could hardly catch her breath from laughing so hard. Regaining her composure, she confessed she was the responsible party. She admitted to spiking their sweet tea, slipping castor oil in when they weren't looking. Momma had this playful philosophy about humor. She was fond of saying, "The Bible says laughter is like medicine. So, maybe if we laugh for a while, we'll all be well!"

As to the wisdom of playing a joke on men armed with rifles, I'm not so sure. Seems to me that pulling a prank on a women's Bible study would be a safer bet. Nevertheless, the men were good sports about it because they knew how Momma was. According to Aunt Pat, who lived next door, Momma kept more people "cleaned out and regular" than anyone she had ever known.

I should mention that Aunt Pat wasn't really our relative, we just called her that because in many ways she was family to us. Perpetually kind and graceful, she gave me the freedom to drop in at the drop of a hat. Her pantry was an extension of our pantry; snacks and drinks were served with a smile and a friendly tousle of my hair while I ate. Aunt Pat was one of Momma's closest friends. So, yes, if Aunt Pat said Momma kept folks "cleaned out" with one of her "special" drinks, she'd know.

But could this phone call have come from one of the disgruntled hunters seeking to get back at them for the castor oil incident? That would be a stretch. Everyone knew Ramona was the guilty party, not Daddy. He had been duped, too, spending time in the latrine with the rest of the men. How, then, had *he* offended anyone enough to provoke a threatening phone call?

For the better part of his first year, the church had been growing by leaps and bounds under his pastoral care. Husbands were now sitting side by side with their wives who, in the past, attended church solo as if widowed. A large number of young married couples were getting saved and filled with the Spirit. Even the numbers participating in Sunday school shot up, from thirty to approximately one hundred.

As well as sparking a sizable ingathering of people from both Sellerstown and nearby communities, Daddy had initiated a host of improvements to the church facility. The sanctuary received a much needed face-lift. Threadbare carpet was tossed and replaced, while a fresh coat of paint offered the walls and ceiling new life. With the installation of fourteen comfortable pews—seven on each side of the aisle—and an improved sound system, there wasn't a bad seat in the house.

He had done nothing wrong, certainly nothing to merit this sinister treatment. Someone, apparently, felt differently. This same someone went to the trouble of attempting to conceal his identity. Again, who and why? Sifting through the prospects, no doubt Daddy stopped to weigh the possibility that the call might have been instigated by someone very close to home.

+ + +

At age sixty-five, Mr. Horry James Watts, who lived across the street from us, was a wealthy, well-connected, and respected businessman—at least as far as the general public was concerned. Typically sporting a pressed white shirt, tie, slacks, and blazer, Mr. Watts was rarely seen in public without his black wool hat. Tufts of gray hair peeked out from around the bottom of the fedora while black, thick-rimmed glasses rested on the bridge of his nose.

Mr. Watts was one of five Columbus County commissioners, and he served as chairman for several years. During his two terms in office, Mr. Watts helped facilitate the construction of the new Columbus County Law Enforcement Center, a police headquarters and jail complex. His name, along with those of the other commissioners, had been embossed on a bronze placard and prominently displayed adjacent to the entrance to the facility.

By all outward appearances, Mr. Watts was an upstanding citizen and a happily married, devout family man with nine children. But many of the locals in Sellerstown and the longtime neighbors who knew him well testified that, in addition to his respectable public facade, he had a sinister side.

Mr. Watts had a reputation as a womanizer, a control freak, and a kingpin of sorts, a narcissist who didn't hesitate to leverage both his influence and affluence to his advantage. Old-timers claimed that, as a youth, he had once disguised himself before robbing his own mother's house. I cannot fathom the sort of person who would pull a stunt like that.

Case in point.

For a number of years, money was tight, and most banks refused to extend credit to the Sellerstown farmers. Without necessary funds for supplies or equipment, their farms would fail. The lending crisis created the perfect storm, and Mr. Watts was quick to swallow the small fish in town. Stepping in and offering loans from his own funds, Mr. Watts offered cash at confiscatory interest rates.

The farmers took the bait.

What choice did they have?

Money was power. He who had money held all the cards. The more money he loaned, the more control Mr. Watts enjoyed. If someone wasn't making his payment, Mr. Watts hired hatchet men to collect on the debt. One of Watts's favorite lackeys to strong-arm delinquent debtors was Roger Williams, a local bruiser with a less-than-stellar reputation. Roger had served time at the Texarkana, Texas, penitentiary over a firearms violation, making him just the kind of guy Mr. Watts loved to employ in his "informal" collection agency. A show of force was a powerful way to extract cash out of slow payers and nonpayers.

That's exactly what happened to Donnie Ward. When Donnie fell behind in his loan payments, Mr. Watts enlisted Roger to intimidate Donnie. "With your reputation, all you got to do is talk to him, probably; me and you are going to get along good." With Mr. Watts behind the wheel, the two men rode together to Donnie's place to collect. Arriving at Donnie's house, they found him working in the front yard.

With a tap of the horn, Mr. Watts signaled Donnie to approach the car. Roger leaned out the window and said, "I believe you're a little late in your payments. It's time to catch them up—and not be late anymore." I don't know whether it was the unexpected personal visit by Mr. Watts, the big brute with a rap sheet doing the talking, or most likely, the combination of the two, but Donnie got the message. He didn't hesitate to pull a check from his pocket and endorse it over to Mr. Watts.

After cashing the check, Mr. Watts slipped Roger fifty dollars. Then, placing a hand on Roger's leg in a friendly show of affirmation, he said, "That's the way to go, buddy. We'll get along good together." If, unlike Donnie, a borrower couldn't pay, Mr. Watts wasn't above compelling them to sign over the deed to their house and property.

In a matter of years, Mr. Watts seemed to own or control everybody and everything within his power—he even managed to control the church affairs at Free Welcome, which he attended religiously. His favorite pew was the back row, pew number seven. From that comfortable perch, he had the perfect vantage point to mind everyone's business.

He could note who was sitting with whom, who wore what—perhaps a sign they had spent money on clothes that should have been money paid to him for a debt—and who didn't show for services—a possible sign they were avoiding contact with him. Even though Mr. Watts was neither a professed believer nor a church member, the church followed his wishes without opposition.That is, until Daddy arrived on the scene.

Daddy was a quick study. Witnessing Mr. Watts's stranglehold on the church, Daddy made changes to end his dominance. Making the case that church business should be conducted by the church brethren as a whole—not by one or two outspoken individuals—the church family voted to turn the business of the church over to members only. From then on, stripped of his power, Mr. Watts had no say in church matters.

This came as a blow to Mr. Watts, who had been serving on the building committee. It was understandable that the church would rely upon Mr. Watts's expertise when it was time to build a fellowship hall and additional Sunday school classrooms. He had, after all, been a key player in the construction of the multi-million-dollar jail facility for the county. His wealth of knowledge and years of experience would be invaluable.

During the design phase of the building, Mr. Watts believed his recommendations should be followed. At issue was whether to build an addition with a flat-topped or a pitched roof. If Mr. Watts had had his way, the church would have constructed a smaller building with a pitched roof. Although more costly, this design would have matched the existing facility.

The majority opinion, shared by Daddy, was to keep costs down by constructing a flat-topped structure. This infuriated Mr. Watts, who was accustomed to giving advice and orders, not taking them. While Mr. Watts went along with the others and voted for the simpler roofline, inside he was steaming as if trapped inside a pressure cooker.

Unconvinced that more space was needed, angered that his counsel had been rejected, he took Daddy aside, lobbying him to change the decision. His plea fell on deaf ears. Daddy was not to be swayed, saying, "Mr. Watts, I get my advice from the Lord." Mr. Watts wasn't accustomed to being rebuffed, nor did the rejection sit well with him. Mr. Watts had said, "If you don't need any advice, maybe you should get in your car and go back to Alabama."

Daddy probably took his comment with a grain of salt.

Everyone was entitled to their opinion, right?

Besides, Daddy and Momma had faced opposition over a building project years before while pastoring a new church. Back when my parents were starting out in the ministry in Alabama, Daddy had been conducting revival services under a tent pitched on a piece of land purchased the hard way: selling chicken and fish dinners. Between the sweltering heat that soaked Daddy from his head down to his socks as if he had been standing in the rain, and the ever-present bugs that seemed to delight in annoying the faithful, his growing congregation knew they had to build.

A handful of neighbors adjacent to the property, however, protested the idea of building a church within a residential community. A public hearing was arranged before the town board to settle the matter. Several councilmen clearly felt pressure to deny the building permit. After reviewing the architect's drawing, a councilman said, "Mr. Nichols, it doesn't look as if you have enough room for a playground."

A playground? Talk about grasping at straws. Daddy was quick to counter, "Sir, we aren't going to church to play but to worship God."

Another councilman, who underestimated how resilient Daddy was under pressure, said, "Well, Mr. Nichols, with the complaints we have, it looks as though you may be in a hornet's nest."

"Sir," Daddy said, most likely with a wide, disarming smile, "I've been in a hornet's nest ever since I got saved and started preaching against Satan and his evil workers." The permit was granted, and the church was built. The fact that Mr. Watts was fuming about the style of roof on the fellowship hall was, by comparison, no big deal. But there were other issues compounding the old man's rage.

Making matters worse, like tossing gas on an open flame, was a decision to remove Mr. Watts's wife, Ora, from two positions in the church. For years, Ora had been an adult Sunday school class teacher and the church clerk. As teacher, Ora held to the tradition of the old Fire Baptized denomination that believed Christians shouldn't cook or buy anything on Sunday. Ora attempted to put the class under the heavy burden of such strict convictions at the same time Daddy was preaching about God's grace. Seeing the conflict of beliefs, members of the church voted her out as teacher.

But it was Daddy who wanted to take away Ora's duties as clerk once he realized how surreptitiously Ora handled the church's funds. Mr. Watts seemed to feel his wife's position gave him control over the church's finances. In fact, when the members voted in a new clerk,

Ora never turned over any records—only a new checkbook and the current balance.

Bit by bit, Mr. Watts and his wife were divested of their dominant roles in the congregation. This enraged Mr. Watts, who, at first, had welcomed the new preacher. During one heated exchange, Mr. Watts stood up in the worship service and told my Daddy, "You had better not tell my wife that she could not vote in the business." Before sitting down, while the stunned crowd looked on, he groused that Daddy had bought too many songbooks.

Could Mr. Watts be so upset that he was the one behind the call? Was he really willing to stoop to such juvenile behavior just because he couldn't have his way? Then again, the voice on the other end of the line wasn't the low-pitched, resonant voice of Mr. Watts. It had a distinctly dark timbre, much like Al Pacino with a sore throat. Besides, the caller sounded younger.

Of course, it might have been a wrong number.

The caller never mentioned Daddy by name.

The late-night menacing phone call Daddy received wasn't the last one he'd get. Far from it. During the days, weeks and months ahead, someone hiding behind the cover of anonymity would call our home, and quickly hang up—or call, wait for a few long moments, and then terminate the call. Some days there would be several dozen hostile calls designed to create fear in the hearts of my parents.

These acts of intimidation didn't end with the phone. An unsigned letter arrived at our house on December 23, 1972, two days before Christmas. This time the anonymous author pointed a finger of guilt at my mother, asserting that Momma had told a lie in a phone conversation. The letter went on to say she lied a second time to cover up her first falsehood. The accusation was ridiculous. Had the writer said Momma ran a moonshine operation under the cover of dark, he would have been just as wrong.

Momma wasn't a liar.

She didn't even like to tell a fib.

If Momma had one driving goal in her life, it was to live in such a way that she would bring glory to the Lord. Lying, stretching the truth, massaging the facts, dabbling in deception—all would have been as foreign to her as speaking an unfamiliar language. What's more, she made a point of raising me to respect the truth, tanning my hide on more than one occasion for daring to tell a white lie.

Filled with fragmented sentences, repetitions, and typos, the letter, which had been typed in all capital characters, went on to ask,

**HOW ARE YOU GOING TO EXPLAIN TO THE CHURCH AND THE PEOPLE IN THE COMMUNITY? WILL YOU TRY TO COVER UP AGAIN? MRS. NICHLOS (SIC), YOU ARE SUPPOSED TO BE A SUPPOSED TO BE HOLLINESS PREACHER'S WIFE. BUT, WHAT DO THE CHURCH AND COMMUNITY HAVE TO LOOK FORWARD TO? SHAMEFULLY, WHAT A PITY.**

The end of the letter defied logic:

**SIGNED BY MORE THAN 25 CHURCH MEMBERS, NEIGHBORS, AND CITIZENS.**

One problem. There were no signatures. Certainly not twenty-five. The note contained this postscript:

## P.S. HAVE YOU WOKE UP YET?

I'm not sure how my parents would have initially viewed such a message. Were they tempted to toss the letter without giving it a second thought? Did they dismiss it as a tasteless joke? Did they wonder whether someone had consumed too much spiked eggnog and, in an unguarded moment, dashed off this error-filled note? I'll never know for certain, although my hunch is that they rolled their eyes at such foolishness.

Daddy had been polishing his Christmas Eve message while Momma had been busy preparing for our family vacation. There were clothes to pack, presents to wrap, and last-minute Christmas cards to mail. If someone was too cowardly to put his or her name on the claims, and if that same someone was so vague that he or she couldn't even spell out what Momma's alleged lies were, then there was no point wasting time or energy over a nonissue.

At the same time, this wasn't an isolated event.

On December 29, 1972, Momma wandered down the driveway and, with a neighborly wave, greeted Aunt Pat, who was likewise retrieving her mail. Momma emptied the mailbox and returned to the kitchen table to leaf through the assortment of correspondence, bills, and supermarket circulars.

One letter stood out. The message was housed in a plain, vanilla white envelope bearing no return address. Daddy's name and address were typed in the center of the mail piece. As was Momma's style, she slit open the end, fished out the note, and began to skim the words.

Similar in tone and style to the other hostile letters my parents had received during their time in Sellerstown, they didn't need an address to know the madman behind the menacing words.

But this letter had been different. For in it, the threat of inflicting bodily harm to our family was taken to a new level. The cryptic message had been typed onto an ordinary white piece of paper to mask the identity of the sender.

The unsigned diatribe stated that the people at church were weary of the way Daddy had been treating them. They were disgusted with his behavior, especially with the way he allegedly used flattery to brainwash the young people. After suggesting Daddy take a leave of absence, the writer promised we'd be leaving Sellerstown one way or the other ". . . crawling or walking, running or riding, dead or alive."

With the threatening phone call still ringing in his memory, Daddy knew the matter warranted some measure of caution. Trained in warfare, having spent years as part of a Navy crew at sea, Daddy knew one strategy employed by the enemy was a shot across the bow. To ignore such overtures would be a mistake.

With the controversial building project nearing its completion and with the festivities of Christmas behind them, Daddy and Momma packed the car and drove home to vacation with family in Alabama and Louisiana. Since I was not yet three years old, I have no memories of the time spent mingling with my aunts, uncles, and cousins. Nor do I recall Daddy and Momma's stories of the amazing growth of the church and their dreams for the future.

Our return to Sellerstown in January of 1973 was marred by an unwelcome revelation: In our absence, while we were away enjoying a belated celebration of the birth of Christ with relatives, the parsonage had been violated. I'm not sure whether Daddy initially saw, or felt, that something was amiss. His first clue that our home had been invaded might have been the telephone. Pulled from the wall, with its cord sliced, the phone had been knocked to the floor.

Then again, his first impression that there was trouble might have been the lack of heat. Though the thermostat had been lowered while we were away to save on the heating bill, when our family entered the house that evening, it was no warmer than the icy-cold January temperatures outside. The thick blanket of snow covering the roof and ground around our house, while picturesque, only added to the chilly reception.

Upon further investigation, Daddy discovered two reasons for the inhospitable temperatures inside our home: Someone had poured about fifty gallons of water in the fuel tank, causing the heater to malfunction. That, and a shattered window through which cold air continued to enter as easily as the housebreaker had made his or her illegal entry. The broken glass littering the floor would be the least of my parents' problems.

As they soon learned, there was more trouble afoot. When Momma attempted to use the faucet, instead of watching a clean flow of water spilling into the sink, she witnessed an oily substance oozing from the tap. The water and fuel tanks didn't share plumbing. No pipes had burst, causing seepage between the tanks. Puzzled by the water-and-oil mixture, Daddy ascertained this had not been an accident. Someone had intentionally spiked our water pump with fuel oil.

No heat, no water, no phone.

But why? Why would anyone attack our home?

A quick survey of our few valuables indicated that nothing had been stolen. This, then, was an act designed to frighten us. Whoever had done this must have known we were scheduled to be out of town.

Did that mean we had been watched? If so, by whom and for how long? Were we being watched now? Should Daddy and Momma call the law from Aunt Pat's house? Or would involving the police bring unwanted attention to the church? Did this break-in have anything to do with the threatening phone call or unsigned letters?

Repairing the damage was the easy part.
Getting answers was a bit trickier.
Anticipating what might be next, impossible.

CHAPTER 5

# Under Siege

The fog lingered.

On the evening of Saturday, August 17, 1974, a light rain shower swept across the southern region of North Carolina, moving west to east. The rainfall traveled from Fayetteville through Sellerstown and then continued east to Wilmington before sailing out to an unknown destination over the Atlantic Ocean.

The procession of thunderclaps, noisier than the crashing cymbals of a marching band, announced the parade of inclement weather washing over Sellerstown. The restless and moonless sky soon lost its booming voice. In the storm's wake a pale gray fog, accompanied by a gentle mist, settled in for the night around our one-story, redbrick house.

I was four years old at the time.

It's not that I have an extraordinary memory about weather patterns on any given day during my childhood. Nor was I some sort of child prodigy who thrived on all things meteorological. Even today, while I'll consult the Weather Channel, I'm not an avid viewer. True, I happen to be interested in storm patterns since tornadoes are a reality in Tennessee, where we live.

However, I'm not sure I could tell you what the weather was like last Saturday, let alone a Saturday decades ago. Aside from figuring out how to dress my kids for school, I don't typically study the forecast. There is, however, a very good reason why I can report what the weather was like on that night in August.

I checked.

I researched that date for a compelling reason.

I wanted to learn everything I could about the last night before my innocent world was completely—and forever—turned upside down. Hiding behind the blanket of darkness, lurking in the misty shadows of fog, an evil so black, so devoid of compassion, planned to execute its diabolical attack against our family.

While the weatherman had predicted the weather with surprising accuracy, he would have had no idea about the tornado of hate gathering strength nearby. Nor could he have foreseen the vortex of rage that would soon sweep down upon us, hurling everything we held dear, most of which had nothing to do with earthly possessions, to the wind. We were targeted by a madman who, in mere hours, was ready to pull the trigger.

Literally.

+ + +

At the time, unaware of the hostilities about to befall us, we were happily engaged in the routine business of family life on a Saturday night. With a well-worn Bible opened to his text, Daddy sat at his desk in the corner of our family room. He prayed and pored over his sermon notes like an honors student cramming for a final exam. Three pine shelves fastened to the wall, sagging under the weight of thick biblical reference books, were within arm's reach above his head. While Daddy never went to seminary, he had been changed by Calvary and wanted to be as prepared as was possible to lead others to the Cross.

As busy as he was—given his responsibilities on the Lord's Day—Daddy still made time for a good-night hug and a kiss. I'd climb into the safety of his lap, content to linger in his sturdy arms until his large yet tender hands lowered me to the floor. With the inevitable bidding to brush my teeth and head to bed, I'd reluctantly leave his company.

Upon reaching my bedroom, I'd slip into my pajamas while Momma picked out my clothes for Sunday morning's church service. Even with her best efforts, Momma typically ran late on Sunday mornings. It seemed as if there were always a thousand and one things to do, between her need to fix her hair, get dressed, get me dressed, make breakfast, then make me *eat* my breakfast.

Driving her race against the clock was the need to get to the organ in time to play the music *before* Daddy gave her "the Look." You know, that unhappy glance with an eyebrow raised skyward, wondering why there wasn't music playing as the members filled the sanctuary. Sitting in one of the two high-back, oak chairs behind the pulpit, Daddy would turn his head to the left and give her the Look if Momma wasn't ready and in position as worshipers filed in.

I'm afraid I wasn't much help.

Especially at breakfast.

Momma served scrambled eggs and toast. I was fine with the toast. The eggs—forget it. Scrambled, hard-boiled, poached—any way they were served, I hated eggs, and Momma knew it. Still, she'd sit there with me like a sentry to make sure I ate every last bite. I was a growing girl and needed my protein; at least that was her position.

I don't know whether I got my stubborn streak from Momma or from Daddy. Either way, the standoff was nothing less than a battle of our wills. Some days she won. Other days, with time at a premium, she abandoned her post, leaving me and my headstrong protest in order to get dressed. I confess, the moment she left the kitchen, I raked my eggs into my napkin and then threw them away.

In spite of our breakfast skirmishes, I'd have to say that the first four years of my life had been charmed. I enjoyed the unconditional love of two parents; I was doted on by Aunt Pat and half of the church; and my best friend, Missy Sellers, lived conveniently up the street.

What's more, I had my own bedroom; a collection of dolls, some mass produced, some handmade; an assortment of stuffed animals and toys; and a real live puppy named Tina. No bigger than a loaf of bread, Tina was a white poodle-and-Pekingese mix.

Adding to my princesslike childhood, Momma arranged my bedroom with an elegant touch. I had a full-size, snow white poster bed with matching nightstand, accompanied by an upright, five-drawer chest, a long dresser with a picture-window-size mirror, and a desk. Each piece was trimmed with gold accents. A chorus of kindly stuffed animals took their assigned places on my array of furniture. And the drapes, to my way of thinking as a child, were made of pure gold threads, probably woven out of strands of perfectly milled fibers by fairies in the Enchanted Forest.

Knowing how precious little time there was on Sunday morning to get everything done, Momma arranged my Sunday outfit, ironed, of course, on my dresser the night before. She knew her angel needed a head start when she awoke. And, going way beyond the call of duty, placing her as close to sainthood as was humanly possible, Momma would surprise me by placing a little dress or a candy treat on my pillow at bedtime. Not every night, mind you. She didn't want me to be spoiled rotten. Just often enough for me to feel as if I had checked into a fine hotel.

Speaking of bedtime, as was their habit, Daddy or Momma would get down on their knees with me, bedside, to pray together before tucking me under the covers. Lingering over prayers was an especially comforting touch during a thunderstorm. Thankful that the thunder boomers had passed, having said my prayers, I settled in for the night, pulling my blanket to the base of my neck.

During August 1974, I was too young to recognize anything different about my mother. Unlike Daddy, I wouldn't have noticed the sunlike glow on her face, the added bounce in her step as if walking happily on spring-loaded shoes, or on occasion, the need for a midafternoon nap. Any change in her diet, any odd cravings, would have been missed by me, who, most of the time, was happy with a peanut butter and grape-jelly sandwich. Day or night, this was the preferred food of young princesses.

Had I been aware of the secret she carried within her, I'm not sure what difference that would have made to me. Children at that age are typically absorbed in their own universe. I was not an exception to the rule. You could have offered me a million dollars, and still I couldn't have told you that my momma, at age thirty-nine, was three months pregnant. Nor could I have known that she had, once again, defied the odds for a woman with endometriosis. To be three months pregnant was, in itself, a miracle.

When I say that I had a charmed childhood, I believe that's largely a function of what my parents did and *didn't* do for me. While they immersed me in love, laughter, and yes, discipline as needed, they also kept me in the dark when it came to the heated debate over the building expansion, the mysterious letters, and the late-night phone calls. In true princess fashion, I had been spared such unhappy details. Even the home invasion went over my head. About all that registered was the fact that there was something wrong with the heater and water and phone—the kind of stuff best left for grown-ups to sort out.

And when our home had been burglarized a second time in May of 1973, I knew something was wrong, but was again spared the details. While I was unsettled by this invasion and suspected my parents had been, too, they did a remarkable job not allowing the fear they may have been experiencing to dominate their lives. That time, the intruder had stolen both of my daddy's hunting rifles, most likely to disarm us.

Though it wasn't as frightening as break-ins, my parents also had to deal with the antics of Mr. Watts in pew number seven. Yet even when Mr. Watts did his best to disrupt the worship service, my parents didn't allow him to define their joy or cast a cloud over the mood in the church or our home. For instance, Mr. Watts had a deep bag of dirty tricks designed to fluster Daddy while he preached. Like some sort of clown with a bad sense of timing, Mr. Watts made obnoxious faces in the middle of the service. Bringing hand to mouth, he'd clear his throat with gasps, coughs, and grunts as if he had swallowed dry bread, and for variety, he'd suck his teeth and smack his lips as if savoring the last morsels of a steak dinner.

Toward the end of the sermon, Mr. Watts pointed at his watch, arm raised, signaling that Daddy had preached too long—at least too long in Mr. Watts's view. And if that grand display didn't prompt Daddy to wrap things up, Mr. Watts would rise from his pew and make a sudden, noisy exit, slamming the front doors so hard the frame rattled.

To lighten the atmosphere whenever Mr. Watts pulled one of these door-banging stunts, Momma, with a smile and a wave of her hand, would say, "Well, *Amen*!" or "Praise the Lord." If she and Daddy had been unsettled, which would be understandable, they didn't show it. Daddy would finish his sermon, and Momma would play her heart out at the organ. After the service, standing at the back, shaking hands with the departing worshipers, they had the wisdom to be discreet rather than comment on Mr. Watts's weekly misbehavior.

They did, however, have a plan to minimize the racket over at least one of Mr. Watts's tactics. Daddy had the front doors of the church changed from thick, solid wood doors to glass doors that, being lighter, didn't shake the building when Mr. Watts stormed out. This, of course, only made Mr. Watts all the more irritated.

What my parents couldn't do, however, was prevent me from experiencing the hellish actions of this deeply tormented man that were about to unfold. When the initial round of harassment failed to yield the desired results, Mr. Watts was prepared to unleash his full wrath. For the better part of two years, he had dreamed up, and was about to implement, a campaign of terror designed to fill us with fear, drive us away, or send us to an early grave.

All three if necessary.

With just a sliver of the new moon's gray face illuminated as if too bashful to make a full appearance, and thick fog loitering on the grounds like a phantom reluctant to move on, two men, no doubt thankful for the shroud of darkness, carried out their orders in our yard while we slept.

Wielding a knife with precision, they sliced through the telephone line. With that lifeline now hanging helplessly at the back of the house, all contact with the outside world was rendered impossible. Clinging to the shadows, they moved around the side of our house to the front yard like professional soldiers mounting an ambush against the enemy.

There, they slashed the rear tires of both cars parked in our driveway. In less than three minutes, working with the efficiency and stealth of trained mercenaries, they eliminated our means of communication and any hope of a rapid escape in the event of an emergency. Whether or not Mr. Watts had any previous military experience, he did a masterful job of planning the details of the attack.

That done, for reasons still unclear, our mailbox, which had been staked in the ground at the end of our driveway, was shot up as if it had faced a firing squad for some unknown crime. Yanking its metal carcass out of the ground, the shooters carried the battered mailbox and ditched it in the carport. Perhaps they were using the mailbox to send us a message: if we didn't leave town, we'd end up just like it.

It would be at least ninety minutes before the sun, currently held hostage by the night, would begin to assume its rightful place in the sky. This left the mercury-vapor light behind our home as the only means of illumination against the darkness. Situated on the utility pole thirty feet above the ground, this comforting ally was executed with a gunshot to the dome. Eager to finish the main event, no doubt worried that the shattered glass cascading to the ground might betray their position, the gunmen hurried to the front yard to complete their mission.

Exercising the utmost caution, the men positioned ditching dynamite in the ground not more than twenty-five feet from the bedroom where I was sleeping. With the steady hands of a surgeon, someone attached several feet of safety fuse to the nonelectric blasting cap with care so as to avoid an accidental detonation. And while a surgeon's ultimate objective is to save the patient, these hands were engaged in a procedure designed to harm, not heal.

When Alfred Nobel harnessed the power of nitroglycerin and, in turn, invented dynamite a hundred years prior, he must have envisioned its use as a good thing. Perhaps he recognized dynamite's potential for the mining, farming, and construction industries. He might have anticipated some utility for dynamite in warfare. I highly doubt, however, that it was ever his intention for his invention to be used by a neighbor with an ax to grind.

I cannot say whether the men deployed more than one stick of the lethal material. And while I am not an expert in such things, I've learned that one stick of dynamite produces 2.1 million joules of power and that one joule is the energy required to lift an apple forty inches off the ground. With the strike of a match, they'd unleashed an explosive force so powerful it could have sent two million apples airborne.

At 4:30 a.m., Sunday, August 18, the earth shook.

I jolted awake.

A cold fear crawled over me like a second skin. I cried out in the darkness, "Daddy! *Daddy*!" Frightened with a terror that stressed my nerves to the breaking point, I clung to my blue bear. My heart clamored, like horse hooves against cobblestone. What happened? A bad dream? Something imagined? If so, why did my ears ring as if I had been standing too close to the clang of a hundred fireman bells? No, this wasn't my imagination run wild.

A light snapped on.

Daddy, calling my name, scrambled from his room to see that I was unharmed. We nearly collided in the hall as I, now airborne, blue bear in hand, flew to their bedroom for shelter as fast as my legs could carry me.

I cried in my mother's arms, her voice struggling to assure me that everything would be okay, that Tina, too, would somehow be just fine in her dog pen in the backyard.

Daddy reached for the phone to call the law. When he found that the phone was dead, he knew he had to get next door to Aunt Pat's to call for help. And yet he waited.

Listening.

Praying.

Wondering.

Would there be another explosion?

If so, where would the attackers strike? Would the next blast be detonated in the backyard? With a glance out his bedroom window, Daddy could see the outdoor night-light was not functioning. Had it been intentionally destroyed to hide another bomb? Dare he risk leaving his wife and child, even for a few minutes, to seek help while his house was under siege?

At some point, failing to detect sounds of movement around the house, Daddy must have figured we were relatively secure. Or at least safe enough for him to sneak next door to call the law.

Upon his return from Aunt Pat's house, I'm sure Daddy's God-given instincts, as protector of the home, were to get his precious family out of harm's way. It had to have been creepy for him to venture out into the still-darkened, predawn sky and find that both of his vehicles had been sabotaged. Unable to load the family into the car and drive safely away, praying that no further attack was imminent, he had no choice but to wait for help to arrive.

The dynamite repercussions had been so fierce, the intense thrust had rattled the bones of our house. As we'd later discover, clumps of dirt and rock, like projectiles from a cannon, had pelted the brick exterior of our home. Had the walls been made of anything less sturdy, the damage would have been more severe. Even so, the hardened brick surface was riddled with gashes, a nearby window was splintered, and a six-foot crater left a gaping hole in our front yard.

Columbus County Deputy Sheriff Kenneth "Bill" Smith, one of Whiteville's then-eight-man police force, was the first to arrive on the scene. Upon surveying the extent of the damage with Daddy, recognizing this was neither a false alarm nor a small matter, Deputy Smith radioed headquarters to request backup.

Deputy Sergeant George Dudley, the only detective serving all of Columbus County at the time, lived several miles away and, having thrown on a pair of jeans and a shirt rather than the standard tie and jacket required during normal business hours, arrived within minutes. Armed with years of experience, a .38-caliber snub-nose Smith & Wesson pistol hanging from a shoulder holster, Detective Dudley took charge to secure the crime scene.

Retrieving several lengths of colored police rope, the detective cordoned off the sensitive areas to prevent extra foot traffic from contaminating the evidence. Unlike today, the now-popular yellow and black polyethylene crime tape used in police work to seal off crime scenes wasn't in use. Having preserved the evidence, he took a barrage of photographs and pages of notes that would, hopefully, lead to the conviction of the perpetrators.

And, while Detective Dudley had a hunch who was behind this assault, he needed more proof before an arrest could be made.

Word of the early morning attack spread through Sellerstown like wildfire in a dry wheat field. Daddy didn't want to alarm the church, yet he knew there was no use trying to hide the details from the congregation. Besides, some of the members in the nearby areas had heard the blast for themselves. Awakened by the detonation, with their own frightened children seeking answers, these good people would want Daddy's firsthand insight.

During the Sunday morning service, taking his place behind the pulpit in spite of the predawn ordeal, Daddy explained what had happened to those gathered. As he spoke, there wasn't a question mark in anybody's mind who was behind the harassment.

I do not know whether or not Mr. Watts was present that morning, although I'd be surprised if he were absent. Failure to attend would appear suspicious since Mr. Watts virtually never missed a service. Missing church would also mean he'd have one less opportunity to harass Daddy. Not to mention that he'd forgo the sick pleasure of witnessing firsthand the impact that the explosion had made on the pastor . . . and on my pregnant mother.

Reflecting on the attack, Daddy told the church that while he had been surveying the damage, Proverbs 28:1 had come to mind: "The wicked flee when no man pursueth: but the righteous are bold as a lion." He assured the church that he was determined to stick it out and overcome the persecution, come what may.

After the service, many well-wishers offered words of encouragement and promises to pray for our safety. One of them, a visiting missionary from Mexico, said our persecution sounded like life on the mission field. To be sure, Daddy must have thought he had been given a high calling to a low valley—the valley of the shadow of death.

Later that week, borrowing a tractor to fill the crater in our front yard, Daddy had to wonder whether this was the end of the terror or just the beginning of a more aggressive campaign against his family. In spite of what he had said publicly to the church, I wouldn't be surprised if he privately wondered whether the cost of serving Christ in Sellerstown was a price too high to pay.

He had the welfare of his pregnant wife to consider.

And the well-being of his young daughter.

Soon there'd be a baby.

And yet Daddy was hopelessly in love with the Word of God captured within the pages of his well-worn Bible. As was his habit, he'd recite Isaiah 54:17 out loud: "No weapon that is formed against thee shall prosper; and every tongue that shall rise against thee in judgment thou shalt condemn. This is the heritage of the servants of the Lord, and their righteousness is of me, saith the Lord."

As a child, I vividly remember him walking through the house, repeating those words. He drew strength from the promises of Scripture daily. No doubt as the phone company repaired the telephone lines, with a new window taking the place of the old, and as he maneuvered the tractor to fill the crater, he chased away the fears in his heart with the Sword of Truth.

If Daddy had any temptation to strike back, as he might have done without a second thought before giving his heart to the Lord, he would have heeded the words of another favorite passage, "Thou shalt not avenge, nor bear any grudge against the children of thy people, but thou shalt love thy neighbour as thyself: I am the Lord" (Leviticus 19:18).

It took several months for life to settle down.

Understandably, our nerves were on edge, stretched thin like a balloon and ready to burst. For me, going to sleep proved to be a challenge. Even with my daddy's bedside prayers, it would take weeks for me to feel safe enough to sleep in my bedroom. Alone.

In the dark.

Wondering.

Waiting.

Listening for any stray sounds that might prove to be the preamble of another assault, I would often crawl into my parents' bedroom and wedge myself between them on their queen-size bed. Although Momma looked petite next to Daddy, he was a tall man. Between the two of them there wasn't much room for company. Daddy, being my hero, knowing I couldn't make it through the night alone on those occasions, would scoot out and sleep in my room while I snuggled with Momma.

During that season of distress, Daddy began to pray over me the words of Isaiah 54:13, placing special emphasis on the second half of the verse: "And all thy children shall be taught of the LORD; and great shall be the peace of thy children." Even now, if I close my eyes, I can almost hear his warm, unwavering voice reciting those words of comfort and promise, and personalizing it with a subtle change: "great shall be the peace of *my* children."

Indeed, for the next several months, we experienced a measure of peace. Friends and supporters called the house, offering their votes of confidence and support for Daddy's leadership. Their words breathed life into our hearts. True, there were numerous phone calls—upwards of twenty-five to thirty in one day—where the caller remained silent, breathing and nonresponsive to my parents' attempt to engage him. And once the mailbox was replaced, the threatening letters resumed—although these acts of intimidation were kept from me.

The ironic by-product of this persecution was a soaring church attendance, growing with the speed of kudzu vine. People from both Sellerstown and neighboring communities rallied around Daddy, and as the turnout on Sunday mornings swelled to record levels, the building committee explored ways either to expand the sanctuary or build a larger facility at a different location. Such discussions infuriated Mr. Watts, whose sole aim seemed to be to drive Daddy out of the pulpit and, ideally, out of town—not into a new building.

Instead, his hostility only served to solidify Daddy's standing in the community. Mr. Watts found himself on the wrong side of the general consensus, upstaged by a young preacher. It would be an understatement to say that this reality didn't sit well with a man who was accustomed to having his way, which explains why, when Mr. Watts declared war against our family, he wasn't about to back down.

Even if he had to take matters to the next level.

+ + +

On December 4, 1974, my parents were entertaining guests at the parsonage. Brother Billy Sellers, a member of the elder board; his wife, Edna; and their two children, Renee and Billy Wayne, followed us home after the Wednesday evening service for some extended fellowship. Plates brimming with shortbread and oatmeal cookies and coffee brewing in the pot were waiting to be enjoyed. And the best thing about having company, at least as far as I was concerned, was the suspension of my regular bedtime.

With Christmas around the corner, Momma, who loved to entertain, had dolled up our house as best she could on a meager pastor's salary. A modestly decorated Christmas tree, displayed in front of the picture window in the living room, was visible to all who traveled Sellerstown Road. Matching green and red Christmas dish towels hung from the stove-door handle, while white, solitary electric candles graced the front windowsills.

To complete the arrangements, my parents bought me one of those faux brick fireplaces made from 100 percent cardboard—the kind that featured a plugged-in, glowing fire to maximize the effect. I, of course, had insisted that they buy it. How else could Santa come into our home to deliver our gifts? We didn't have a "real" fireplace with a chimney, so Santa would just have to figure out how to make this one work.

I had full confidence he'd work something out.

I even pinned our stockings to the imitation mantel.

With Bing Crosby crooning "I'm Dreaming of a White Christmas," the adults settled in to sip coffee and talk about grown-up stuff. Momma was seven months pregnant, so she and Edna had plenty of baby-oriented talk to keep them happily preoccupied. Brother Billy and Daddy compared notes about an upcoming missions trip to Colombia in South America, scheduled just days away. The ongoing threats also had to be on their minds, since Brother Billy was one of Daddy's right-hand men at the church.

As the adults visited, I danced circles around the oval braided rug sprawled out on the floor adjacent to my imitation fireplace, entertaining Renee and Billy Wayne. Laughing and playing with friends was strong medicine for my soul. During those carefree moments of play, I could forget about the fear that constantly gnawed at the edges of my still-frayed nerves.

At least for a few wonderful moments.

I had been so emotionally impacted by the bombing nearly four months before that I dreaded the thought of Daddy leaving us for his trip. It scared me to death. I needed him. I relied upon his strength. Although exhausted from the duties of being a pastor, Daddy spent countless nights rocking me in his arms until I finally drifted asleep. His courage in the face of adversity comforted me. He was the glue that held our family together. And now he was planning to travel thousands of miles away.

I remember telling my mother over and over again, "Momma, Daddy's *not* coming back. I just *know* he's never coming back. He shouldn't go on that trip!"

She'd take me by the arms and look me tenderly in the eyes. "Becky, don't say that. Daddy *is* coming back."

"No, Momma, he's not. Something's gonna happen—"

"Honey, don't worry yourself. He's gonna be fine."

Whether or not she shared my fears with him, I cannot say. But to be seven months pregnant, her body already bearing enough strain, listening to me ramble on about Daddy not coming home *ever again*, had to be unsettling. While she had every confidence to believe he'd return unharmed, what if she received prank phone calls in the middle of the night? What if there was another attack on our house in his absence? What if the phone lines were cut again?

If something *did* happen, how could she, pregnant and with a frightened four-year-old in tow, get help? Should she take me somewhere to stay while Daddy was gone? Would that look like running? Or would it be the better part of wisdom? If Momma hadn't been considering these questions, she would soon have plenty of reason to do so. While we were enjoying Christmas music and treats, Mr. Watts and an accomplice, veiled behind the thick cloak of darkness, entered our yard.

CHAPTER 6

# Now I Lay Me Down to Sleep

They came.

Sometime after the sun traded places with the moon on that chilly December evening, two men approached our house, unnoticed and unhindered. There was no five-foot privacy fence to scale or high-tech laser-beam trip-wire system to sidestep. We didn't have a hungry Rottweiler for them to evade. My puppy, Tina, hardly qualified as a serious threat to would-be housebreakers. Our yard was nothing but wide-open space with no security measures whatsoever.

And so they came.

Knife in hand, Mr. Watts and his accomplice entered our property while my family and I were singing Christmas carols and eating dessert with friends. They crept toward the back of our house, slashed our phone line, and then crippled the recently replaced mercury-vapor light. That done, they took up a position twenty-five yards away in a soybean field that paralleled the length of our backyard. The field was owned by Mr. Watts's brother-in-law Bud Sellers who, like Mr. Watts, despised Daddy.

We never heard a sound as Mr. Watts and his sidekick prepared to wage their latest assault on us. In some ways I'm surprised we didn't hear them coming. You see, the country possesses a variety of quietness that's vastly different from what passes for quiet in suburbia. In the suburbs when the sun goes down, quiet has a persistent dronelike quality to it: a cadence of soft sounds driven by traffic on a nearby freeway, as tires hum a dull tune to the pavement; a concert of heat pumps or air conditioners cycling on and off; people coming and going at all hours of the night; and the occasional siren wail of an emergency vehicle reverberating in the distance.

When someone in the suburbs is walking about at night, the chorus of muted tones that passes for quiet provides a degree of covering for their movements. Not so in the country. Country quiet at night is different. In Sellerstown, the quiet was so vacuous, so devoid of sound, you could almost hear the ocean waters lapping against the sandy beaches thirty-five miles away. The stillness in Sellerstown rivaled the soundless moon. About the only noise was the occasional bark of a dog somewhere down the street. There was no highway drone, no sirens screeching, no constant whirling of heat and air units providing comfort to street after street of residences slammed together like sardines in a can.

Adding to the hushed serenity was the fact that most of the people living on Sellerstown Road were farmers who maintained a strict schedule: early to bed, early to rise. When the sun retired, a peaceful, dreamy tranquillity settled in for the night. You'd think that, with this intense quietness, we might have heard the night-light executed once again in the backyard, extinguished once again.

We didn't.

Obviously, our merriment inside the home trumped the sound of mischief out back. Even Tina failed to raise the alarm. In spite of her terminal cuteness, Tina displayed her lack of worthiness as a watchdog. She didn't even raise an ear or offer a series of whimpers signaling that trouble was afoot. At 9:28 p.m., a match was struck, igniting dynamite strategically strapped to a small tree five feet above ground. Seconds later, with the thunder of a bomb and the force of a missile, our house trembled down to the foundation.

The explosion could be heard for miles around.

We screamed. We cried. We covered our ears with the palms of our hands to stop the ringing that hurt as bad as if we had been standing beside a jackhammer without proper ear protection. And the Sellers children, Renee and Billy Wayne, and I rushed to the safety of the outstretched arms of our parents.

In spite of her efforts to calm us, I could sense Momma was distressed that her guests were now drawn into the epicenter of terror that had been, for the most part, our private pain.

Sometime during the chaotic seconds following the detonation, Daddy discovered that the phone was dead. Once again, he knew what had to be done. He had to venture out into the darkness, unsure of whether someone might take a shot at him, and run to Aunt Pat's to call the law. This time, at least, Brother Billy was able to stay with us while Daddy sought help.

Deputy Sheriff Bill Smith and Detective George Dudley, both of whom had investigated the first bombing, raced to the parsonage and determined there was, thankfully, little structural damage to our property. And, while nobody was physically harmed, nothing could be done about the damage to our mental states. I have no idea how any of us could have fallen asleep that night after the police left. I never asked, but I'm sure Renee and Billy Wayne had as much difficulty sleeping after the explosion as I had.

The next morning Detective Dudley returned to finish sealing off the crime scene. Aided by the sunlight, he conducted a more thorough investigation to identify the type and placement of the bomb. As Daddy and the detective surveyed the blast site, Mr. Watts and Bud Sellers, owner of the property, walked up. It was clear they hadn't come to offer words of concern or sympathy.

Quite the opposite.

Mr. Watts, arms folded high across his chest, staring through his thick, black-rimmed glasses, had the nerve to inquire whether it was against the law to shoot off dynamite on your own property—not that he was admitting any involvement, mind you. Detective Dudley responded that it was, in fact, against the law.

Standing within a few feet of Mr. Watts, Daddy somehow managed to retain his composure. To think that this man, our neighbor, a fellow churchgoer, and someone with children of his own, would terrorize a pregnant woman, a four-year-old child, and their guests, I would have been livid—on steroids. Or, at least I would have been less than kind had I been in Daddy's shoes. But Daddy practiced what he preached.

When Daddy preached about loving your enemies, those words didn't roll off his tongue with ease. By God's grace, Daddy was a living example of what Jesus meant. Granted, anybody with a Bible and an audience could preach about loving your adversaries. But as a practical matter, I'd say it's impossible, apart from God at work in your heart, to love your enemy when he's setting dynamite next to your house, putting everyone you love at risk.

I'm amazed that Daddy didn't wrestle Mr. Watts to the ground on the spot—if not out of anger, just to put the fear of God into him. In a man-to-man contest, Mr. Watts was no match for Daddy, who, standing five inches taller, towered over Mr. Watts like an elm tree. Daddy's strapping shoulders, muscular forearms, and powerful hands could have put Mr. Watts in a headlock faster than the drop of a hat.

But Daddy didn't fight back. He believed that a soft answer turned away wrath.

He was a firm believer in the power of forgiveness.

The fact that Daddy responded with love to those who were persecuting us wasn't lost on Larry Cheek, a reporter from the *Fayetteville Times*. While there was scant media coverage after the first bombing—perhaps because the local news organizations figured it was an isolated event—several days after this second blast, the press picked up the story. Mr. Cheek showed up personally to cover the emerging conflict in Sellerstown.

Walking around the parsonage with the reporter in tow, Daddy identified the first blast site. Daddy said, "Last week's dynamite hit out behind the house, in the field. Folks heard the blast more than a couple of miles away. That didn't do any damage, except to our nerves. It scared two children who were visiting us real bad too."

Next, Daddy walked over to the house to show how the bombing had damaged the exterior. With Mr. Cheek taking copious notes, Daddy articulated his greatest fear, namely that Momma and I would be harmed, saying, "Trouble is, we don't know what they're liable to do next, or when. My wife's seven months pregnant and Becky, here, is four. I sure wouldn't want to see anything happen to them."

Daddy wasn't the type of person to embellish things. He was plainspoken, preferring to stick to the facts. He didn't know the first thing about media "spin"—that fine art of twisting the details of an event to cast a more favorable light on your side of the story while positioning the opposing side in a negative light. If anything, he was the master of the understatement.

Daddy could have made a big deal out of how we were having difficulty sleeping at night. He could have told the reporter that we suspected every car that went by the house, especially after sundown; that we never knew whether someone was sneaking into our yard to lay some sort of trap for us; or that the fear we tasted played upon our imaginations around the clock. Yet he chose not to elaborate on the toll that this harassment was taking.

Digging for some explanation as to why anybody would want to persecute a pastor with such a forceful display of firepower, the reporter learned about the church feud. When Mr. Cheek filed his report, he summed up the conflict this way: "One side does its fighting with terrorist tactics—dynamite, letting air out of tires, cutting phone lines and shooting out lights. The other side answers with preaching, prayer, patience and the sheriff."

Daddy gave his answers carefully because he was concerned about the way this conflict might play out in the press. The last thing he wanted was for the church, or for the Sellerstown community, to get a bad rap. He loved the people and was there to serve them, which is why he was quick to point out, "The church members are behind me. It's just a couple of families that want to run me out. They want to get the leadership of the church back. . . . But we're not leaving. We're staying."

Daddy explained why he wouldn't abandon the church. "A good shepherd will lay down his life for his flock," Daddy said. "It is a great pleasure to live for the Lord. And there would be no greater honor than to die for Him. After all, all of the apostles except for one died a violent death."

Mr. Cheek raised his eyebrows in surprise: "Are you really willing to die, if necessary? Why not just do what most people would do and fight back?" he asked.

"Violence typifies the spirit of the opposition," Daddy said, dismissing the notion of fighting fire with fire. "They are not Christian people. I know who they are. I know they are violent, mean-spirited people. I will only leave this church if it is the Lord's will. And if it is the enemy's will for us to leave, then it is God's will for us to stay."

During the interview, Mr. Cheek learned about Daddy's days playing football, his four years in the Navy, and his reputation as a former brawler. I am quite sure Daddy wasn't kidding when he said, "Those boys—I know who they are and they know who I'm talking about—just better pray to the good Lord that I don't backslide. Because I have never met a man I couldn't whip."

Mr. Cheek asked Daddy, "Could it ever come to that, Reverend? Could you become so frustrated, knowing who's bedeviling you and your family but being unable to prove it, that you'd revert and go after them?"

"No," Daddy said flatly.

Mr. Cheek noted Daddy had a "faint, beatific smile on his face" as he answered. Rather than retaliate, Daddy admitted, "I'd leave here first. I would never answer them with the same weapons they use against me."

"If so," Mr. Cheek wondered aloud, "when will it end?"

"Only when you read the devil's obituary, I'm afraid," said Daddy. "And I'm afraid that may take more than a few years to happen."

On December 6, 1974, the Friday after that dreadful Wednesday night blast, the mail arrived, and with it, an unsigned, cryptic letter was included in the usual assortment of bills and advertising circulars. Punctuated with threats, filled with bad grammar and typos to conceal the identity of the sender, the letter promised, "We are going to get the job done." Which could only mean one thing: the recent explosion wasn't the last of the bombings in Sellerstown.

There would be more.

We did not receive this ominous letter.

It had been mailed to the home of Mr. Horry Watts. The handwritten note told Mr. Watts "to keep your mouth out of our business" and added that "the job [of getting Nichols out of the area] will be done without . . . your advice or help." Mr. Watts wasted no time making a big deal about how he, too, was being targeted by the anonymous bully. He promptly contacted the police about the note. Detective George Dudley met Mr. Watts and retrieved the letter as evidence.

For his part, Detective Dudley had to determine what to make of this latest development. Had the menacing letter been mailed by the real culprit behind these bombings? Or did Mr. Watts send it to his home in hopes of taking some of the heat off himself for the recent acts of intimidation against us? From the detective's point of view, Mr. Watts had the motive, he had the influence, and as owner of the local farm store, he had the means to secure the raw materials for the explosions.

But circumstantial evidence wasn't enough.

Detective Dudley needed concrete proof.

There's an old saying in the public-relations business: "All press is good press, even when it's bad press." If my family were seeking media coverage, which we weren't, we'd soon succeed by becoming the epicenter of attention in the local newspapers. "Minister's Family Is Harassed," "Field Near Parsonage Dynamited," and "The Embattled Pastor" were among the headlines in just a four-day period.

The news got people talking.

Not all of the talk was constructive.

After all, during the mid-seventies, the newspaper played a much greater role as a media leader and conversation starter in society than it does today. Back then, homes were not wired with cable service. Households didn't use satellite dishes to pull down news from around the globe. And the five-hundred-channel television universe offering several twenty-four-hour news channels was as unknown as it was unthinkable then.

Instead, the newspaper served as an umbilical cord to the local, national, and world events. Major markets often had two competing newspapers offering an early morning edition or a late-afternoon option. People anticipated the arrival of the newspaper. They'd start their days with a cup of coffee and its familiar pages. Having a paper route was certainly more lucrative then than now. Almost every house on your street subscribed, unlike today where newspapers are folding right and left as more news is delivered electronically.

For a story to make the newspaper, of course, it had to be "newsworthy"—something that would captivate the attention of a wide readership. To make the paper, then, you were big news. You were the talk of the town. And with that talk came the gossip.

The more the press dedicated coverage to the bombings and threats, the more people began paying attention to the unfolding drama on our street. As my parents had feared, there was negative fallout on the good people of Sellerstown due to these reports. Certain mean-spirited stereotypes were pinned on our neighborhood.

Driven by her love of those whom she knew in the community, Momma wanted to set the record straight. She did a remarkable thing—especially for someone living in a virtual war zone: She sharpened her pencil and penned what she hoped would be a Christmas gift of affirmation to the community. With her purse on her arm and me in tow, Momma walked through the offices of the *News Reporter*, based in Whiteville.

We found the office of reporter Wray Thompson. Sitting on a metal chair, feet not quite touching the floor, I drank in the smell of newspaper and ink as Momma, with the attitude of a defense attorney, made her case. The stereotyping of Sellerstown was unfair, she said, and her article would offer an insider's viewpoint. Momma handed Mr. Thompson the article. After scanning it, he agreed to publish it. In "Tribute to Sellerstown," which ran on the front page of the newspaper on December 16, 1974, she wrote,

> Since such widespread news coverage of recent happenings around the Free Welcome parsonage, we have had numerous phone calls from people stating their opinions of the Sellerstown community. Also, there have been discussions relating to the reputation that the community has had over the years.
>
> We have learned much about the people of Sellerstown during the five years and one month we have lived among them. First of all, we know there are good and bad, rich and poor, intelligent and ignorant people in every corner of the earth.
>
> Not since the Garden of Eden has there been a perfect spot in this world to live.
>
> Because of outsiders (and those outside the Christian faith), there have been anxious moments here at the Free Welcome Church. It is impossible to please all the people all the time, and it is our desire to try to please God first of all. Due to non-committal to Christ or the church, our enemies have resorted to violence. There are some people who cannot

bring themselves to go along with the majority. Therefore, they prefer to separate themselves from true believers.

Overall, we have found Route 3, Whiteville, a most wonderful place to live. Most of the people here in Sellerstown are related in one way or another; through blood-kin or marriage, and have a deep love and admiration for each other. We have come to love these people with a fervent love and devotion. Here, we have found neighborly love, whereby neighbors care about each other. Something most communities the world over have forgotten, and in most places people do not even know their neighbors' names.

The older people have been hardworking farmers, who worked hard through the years to provide for their families, and to give their children a good education. They also brought their children up in church and taught them to fear God. Inevitably, there are always some who stray from their upbringing. But, with God in one's heart there is love, for God is love.

We have been treated with much love from most of the people of the community, but, our church does not consist only of people of this community. The year 1974 has brought many wonderful families from surrounding communities, and as far away as Shallotte, and Evergreen. There has to be a deep devotion to a pastor and church for those people to drive from such distant places and so many miles roundtrip.

We are proud of our church and the way it has outgrown itself. Due to overflowing crowds, the need is great to arise and build. Plans are being made now to build a larger church in the very near future. The people have a vision and

> a mind to work. Our aim is to "rescue the perishing and care for the dying."

Adjacent to Momma's tribute, the paper ran an article by Wray Thompson entitled "More Harassment at Sellerstown Parsonage." After a summary of the most recent assault, Momma was quoted as saying, "We used to look for the siege of harassment every three months. But now it's every week. My husband, though, is not afraid for himself. He would die for the Lord."

How was Momma's article received by the man behind the persecution? I imagine somewhere, hunched over the newspaper, Mr. Watts read Momma's words while plotting his next move. The timing of the mischief that night could have been a coincidence. More likely it was a direct response to these two articles, sort of like an unconventional letter to the editor. Either way, Mr. Watts aimed to send us another signal that he meant every word of his promise to drive us away.

That night, with yet another gunshot blast, the mercury-vapor light in our backyard was shattered. Thankfully, Momma and I were not at home. We had taken up shelter elsewhere during Daddy's annual eight-day missions trip to Colombia, South America. There was no way he'd leave his pregnant wife and child alone in the house.

Not with Mr. Watts watching our every move.

With the exception of the frequent, daily phone calls designed to keep us on edge, there were no more shootings, bombings, tire slashings, or other acts of physical intimidation during the rest of December. The relative calm remained throughout January, relative in the sense that we lived each day on the narrow edge of fear that *today* might be the day when something terrible might happen to us.

Maybe the attack would come in the dead of the night.

Perhaps during broad daylight, although less likely.

We lived with the dark reality that something awful could strike us at any moment. After several months of being the target of Mr. Watts's campaign of terror, I know I never felt safe. I doubt my parents did either. For me, this tension was greatest as the sun melted into the horizon. Without its warm glow outside my window, I dreaded going to sleep. My mind was tormented by questions that no child should have to entertain.

Why did Mr. Watts hate us?

Why did we have to always live in fear?

Why did life have to be so hard?

Why didn't God stop these bad things from happening?

Would God really allow one of us to get hurt?

Aware that I, at times, dreaded going to sleep, Momma would kneel down by my bed and recite the classic children's prayer from the eighteenth century with me: "Now I lay me down to sleep. I pray the Lord my soul to keep. If I should die before I wake, I pray the Lord my soul to take." Those were not empty words. I meant every word of that prayer. I'm sure she did too.

Much to my surprise, I remember Momma began praying for Mr. Watts. She prayed long and hard for God to take away his root of bitterness and his deep-seated anger toward our family. And she prayed that Mr. Watts would one day give his heart to Jesus. When I asked her about that, she recited Matthew 5:44, saying, "Becky, Jesus said, 'But I say unto you, Love your enemies, bless them that curse you, do good to them that hate you, and pray for them which despitefully use you, and persecute you.'" Part of loving our enemies, she explained, included forgiving them when they wronged us—even if they hadn't asked for forgiveness.

Even if they weren't sorry.

Momma explained that we had been forgiven by Jesus for all of our sins, which is why He expected us, in turn, to forgive others. Taking the teachable moment one step further, she pointed to Romans 12:14, where Paul, a follower of Jesus, calls us to "bless them which persecute you: bless, and curse not." Looking back on those conversations, I can see that Momma was, as best she knew how, teaching me that forgiveness is close to the heart of God.

That forgiveness is the language of heaven.

That forgiveness should be a way of life.

Even when it was humanly inconceivable to do so.

I would soon need to be reminded of this perspective. And yet, thankfully, the welcomed respite from any serious display of trauma continued into February. This was especially good news for my mother, who spent her wedding anniversary giving her husband the ultimate anniversary present: a son. Which was quite the gift, considering she wasn't supposed to be able to bear any children of her own.

On February 11, 1975, Robert "Daniel" Nichols was born, a healthy, bouncing baby boy, at the Southeastern General Hospital in Lumberton. And just as my parents had given me a biblical name, so they gave one to their son, who was always called Daniel.

With the arrival of my brother, the joy returned to our home. I welcomed seeing Momma and Daddy laughing again, unlike the last six months when they had had worried, drawn looks on their faces most of the time. Now that Daniel was finally in his arms, Daddy couldn't stop smiling. I know he couldn't wait to take Daniel fishing and hunting—and teach him about the game of football.

He'd pick Daniel up with his huge hands that engulfed my brother, study his face with proud eyes, and say, "That's my boy!" Daddy knew Daniel would be the one to carry on the family name to future generations. And maybe, just maybe, Daniel would follow Daddy's footsteps and become a pastor—perhaps he'd even fill the pulpit in Sellerstown once Daddy retired.

In the Bible, Daniel obeyed God completely, which I'm sure Momma and Daddy hoped would be the case with their son, too. You know, a great name to live up to. And, whether or not they consciously intended it, there was a deeper significance behind the choice of my brother's name. In the Bible, Daniel was betrayed by those closest to him and then thrown into a lions' den filled with hungry creatures.

Ironically, my brother Daniel had been born into a lions' den of sorts, betrayed by his closest neighbor before he had even taken his first breath. In fact, his doctors noted that Daniel was born with a nervous condition, which they attributed to the impact of the threats and acts of violence against us during Momma's pregnancy.

Daniel wasn't the only one suffering from frazzled nerves. The year before, at age three and a half, I had experienced a complete meltdown that I can only attribute to the impact that two home invasions and the relentless late-night phone calls had made upon me.

During the summer of 1973, my family took a much-needed vacation and traveled to Cherokee, North Carolina. Nestled in the shadows of the majestic Smoky Mountains, the fresh air of Cherokee seemed to be the perfect remedy to the harassment we had been experiencing. We had met up with our relatives, including Aunt Dot, Grandmother Nichols, Aunt Martha, and her daughter, Linda. Momma's friend, Sue Williams, came along on the trip as well.

While window-shopping one afternoon, a colorful Indian feather headdress caught my eye. I just had to have it. You see, both sides of my family have Cherokee and some Choctaw blood. Daddy was a good sport and coughed up the money. After I donned my new headdress, we stopped to pose for pictures at various spots in the

Oconaluftee Indian Village, an authentic replica of community life for the Cherokee Indians in the eighteenth century.

While my parents gravitated toward a frontier church, I was attracted to a Wild West train ride. Happy to please their Indian princess, they paid the fare, and we boarded the train. I sat securely in my daddy's lap as the steam engine belched gray smoke and we started to inch forward. Since it was an open-air train with no sides to obstruct the view, we moved slowly, which seemed fun for me and I'm sure peaceful to my family.

That is, until the cowboys came.

Materializing almost out of thin air, with bandanas masking their faces, the cowboys swooped down toward the train on horseback. With whoops and yells, they fired their guns into the air. Rather than pick up steam to evade the bandits, the train slowed to a stop. I was beside myself. For the life of me, I couldn't understand why we were no longer moving. Didn't the engineer know we were in trouble? Didn't he care that we were under attack? Why didn't someone tell him to get away from them?

Stunned at the drama unfolding, I watched in disbelief as the cowboys dismounted their horses and hopped aboard the train. Walking up and down the aisle, they started yelling for the passengers to hand over their money. What was this? The cowboy bandits had been shooting guns, and now they were robbing people.

I became hysterical.

Try as they did, my parents were unable to comfort me. Daddy scooped me up in his arms and carried me off the train until the "show" was over. How was I supposed to understand it was all just part of the train ride, part of the "fun"? A ride that had started out as an enjoyable afternoon turned into an absolute nightmare for me. While this staged event might have been fake, by age three I knew there were bad men in the world. Men who thought nothing of terrorizing others.

We had one living across the street from our house.

And now this.

I'm sure I ruined the "fun" experience for some of the other passengers. If they had known what was really going on in my little world, maybe they would have understood why I screamed and cried for five minutes straight while turning different shades of red. With hot tears running down my face, I was convinced we were in mortal danger.

And while my reaction may have "embarrassed the fire out of her," as Momma would sometimes say, my hunch is that she completely understood why this event triggered such a distressed response from me. It was too much for my nervous system to handle. She, too, had felt the consequences of Mr. Watts's relentless intimidation.

All of us had.

+ + +

And now Danny, a newborn, had signs of a nervous disorder.

I can't say for certain, but I imagine one of the hopes Daddy and Momma held was that Mr. Watts would have tired by now of his lunatic tactics to get my family to leave the church and our home.

Was it too much to believe that Mr. Watts would somehow come to his senses and realize that we were happier and more resolved than ever to stay? Was it possible that Mr. Watts, watching our home from behind the curtains of his front window, might experience a change of heart? Would he take into account that there were now two small children in our house and, in turn, resist his monstrous desire to attack a harmless family?

CHAPTER 7

# The Toughest Guy in Town

He paced.

Faint rays of midnight moon, like bloodless fingers reaching down through the blackened sky, illuminated his white T-shirt with a feeble glow. The rim of his mahogany brown fedora blocked the moon's frail hint of light; his face remained in the company of dark shadows. Wearing pajama bottoms and plaid slippers, the man appeared to have just rolled out of bed. Heels occasionally scraping against the asphalt, arms swinging as if beating against the muggy air, he peered at our house through thick lenses encased in onyx black frames as he walked.

Like a restless apparition quarreling with an unseen foe, Mr. Watts mumbled to himself with every step. Face twisted into a perverse knot of frustration, muttering a stream of irritated broodings, he marched up and down Sellerstown Road for several hours. Some nights as he stalked the silent street, he wrapped himself in a bathrobe as if he were a king surveying his domain. In spite of the summer heat, at times he'd rub his hands together as if they needed to be warmed, then clench his fingers into fists of rage.

He continued to pace.

Aunt Pat's older daughter, Terri, had a ringside seat during several of Mr. Watts's nightly excursions. Terri and a friend, then both fourteen, slipped outside from time to time to sneak a smoke. They'd hide in a deep ditch near the road to light up. Ironically, the ditch had been dug out around Aunt Pat's house by Mr. Watts and Bud Sellers for no reason other than to annoy Aunt Pat. Since Bud owned the property bordering Aunt Pat's house on three sides, she could do nothing to stop him.

The moatlike trench just so happened to provide the perfect hiding spot to smoke. Like the two mischievous country girls they were, Terri and her friend talked and giggled while engaging in their forbidden pleasure. That is, until they heard the footsteps and the undertone of unintelligible murmuring. Even at low volumes, Mr. Watts's gruff, raspy voice ignited an ominous feeling; a shiver of fear chilled their hearts as he approached.

As unrehearsed as a hiccup, they instinctively ducked down. They hoped that the distinct tobacco fumes wafting overhead, like smoke billowing from a chimney, didn't betray their location. Maintaining a position just below the crest of the hiding place, they watched in silence as Mr. Watts conducted his disquieting vigil. The last thing they wanted was to give him the impression, however false, that they were there spying on him. Life for them would become unbearable if they were discovered. Our family was living proof of what happened if you ended up on his wrong side.

I can only guess why Mr. Watts chose such a late hour to creep back and forth on our street. There was nothing illegal about going for a walk at that time, mind you. It was just so . . . *odd*. Had he been an exercise buff, which he most certainly was not, physical training just made more sense during the daytime. Besides, plaid slippers do little to support a serious workout regimen.

Why did Mr. Watts wander the streets with nothing more than the blanched moon as company? Was his nocturnal activity designed to remind his neighbors—many of whom were indebted to him—that he was always watching? Why did he occasionally stop and stare at our house before resuming his restless quest? Was he wondering why his attacks against us weren't working? Was he scheming new ways to drive us away? It seems to me that the lack of sleep may have contributed to his troubled state of mind.

I knew a thing or two about the impact of losing sleep. When awake, I lived with the constant fear that we were never truly safe. I'd jump at the sound of a car door slamming or at the screech of tires squealing, even if the noise came from someone arriving home for dinner or a neighbor racing down the road just for the fun of it.

And when I was asleep, the nightmare we were living followed me into my dreams, allowing sleep to come in fitful bunches. As much as I needed the rest, sleep failed to offer a refuge from the storm brewing in my life. To this day, thirty-some years later, I have a recurring dream so vivid, I still wake up in a cold sweat.

When I was five years old, I dreamed that I was lying asleep in my bed when a noise at our kitchen door jarred me from my rest. My eyes opened with a series of blinks to adjust to the night-light slanting through the slats in my closet door; given my heightened fear of the dark, I developed the habit of leaving that soft light on. It served as a comforting friend, should I awaken before the friendly sun filled my window.

Rising from bed, I took my blue bear by the hand as if we were exploring buddies and moved toward my bedroom door. My heart beat out a rapid warning to proceed with caution. Narrowing my eyes, forehead bunched into a knot, I looked down the hall to see what had caused the commotion. I found Mr. Watts standing just inside the kitchen door, illuminated by the pale, yellowed light above the kitchen stove. He said nothing but motioned with his hands for me to come to him. Dressed like an undertaker in a nondescript, charcoal gray suit and wearing his hat, Mr. Watts appeared to have something important to tell me.

I glanced in the direction of my parents' room, found them asleep, and then, defying all logic—since when are dreams built upon logic?—I naively proceeded down the unlit hallway. Without uttering a word, Mr. Watts turned and held open the kitchen screen door. He gestured for me to step outside. For reasons I cannot explain, I didn't feel as if I had a choice in the matter. As a moth is drawn irresistibly to the flame, I felt obligated to go with him regardless of the consequences.

Once outdoors, standing under the darkened sky in my white and pink ankle-length nightgown, I found his car parked in our driveway. Bud Sellers was waiting for us in the front seat. After placing me in back, Mr. Watts eased behind the steering wheel and then backed out of the driveway. I stole a look at our home, where my family slept unaware of my departure. With the safety of my house now out of view, I clutched my bear to my chest and sunk into the cold vinyl seat. I looked through the windshield to see where we were headed.

The headlights failed to penetrate the blackness more than a dozen feet; these shafts of light were absorbed faster than they could be projected as if their twin beams were being swallowed by a black hole. I could see little beyond the hood of the car, which appeared to stretch forward about the look and length of a coffin. Neither man spoke. I couldn't speak, nor did I dare say a word. I had witnessed Mr. Watts's behavior in church, the way he sneered at Daddy during the sermon and the way he stomped out the back door, slamming it until the house of God shook.

I feared this man.

Conversation was out of the question.

As far as I could tell, we were lost. I had no idea where we were, where we were going, or more importantly, why I was being taken for this ride. Fear was my unwanted backseat companion as we traveled an unfamiliar, unlit stretch of winding road in the hills. Like a roller-coaster ride minus the fun, the friends, or the assurance that the ride had been inspected and certified safe for its passengers, we continued upward.

The car sped on.

Leaning hard on the curves, Mr. Watts rocketed into the night way too fast for my racing heart. While Daddy sometimes drove to town with a lead foot, he never traveled as recklessly as this. Although the car windows remained closed, my hair blew into my face as if they had been open, allowing gusts of the night-chilled air to whip my long, chestnut brown tresses into a frenzy.

Driving hard around a bend, still climbing, higher, faster, my chauffeur from hell let go of the wheel. Without warning, Mr. Watts and Bud Sellers opened their car doors in unison and jumped out of the car. Only then did I comprehend the danger awaiting me. With no time to escape, the car became airborne. I sailed over the edge of a cliff, trapped within the metal casket. I tried to cry out, but no sounds escaped from my parched throat.

Now falling like deadweight, I plunged earthward. Like a meteorite ensnared in the earth's gravitational pull, the collision was unavoidable. Panic bored a hole through my chest. Upon impact the car exploded into a ball of fire.

I screamed until my lungs burned.

Terrified and now fully awake, beads of sweat clung to my forehead. Thankful to be alive, I shot upright, yanked off the covers that, like shackles, held me to the bed, then ran to get Momma. I hesitated only long enough just inside my bedroom to make sure Mr. Watts wasn't still standing next to the kitchen door as he had been in my dream.

Face wet with tears, I fell into Momma's arms.

Living with the threats and harassment that produced this nightmare was no simple task. Daddy and Momma tried to comfort me with the words of Proverbs 23:18: "For surely there is an end; and thine expectation shall not be cut off." I believe they meant well. And yet in spite of the Scripture, it was terrifying to anticipate going to bed each night. Closing my eyes, I prayed that all would be well in the morning.

Some nights I achieved peace. Other nights were disturbed by the sound of gunshots, explosions, and police lights splashing red bursts of light against my windowpane.

Living with the uncertainty of what any given night would bring has had a lasting impact on my life. Years later, as a teenager, I had to feed on the Word of God if I was to have any hope of resting at night.

I placed the words of Proverbs 3:24-26 on a sticky note over my bed:

> When you lie down, you will not be afraid; when you lie down, your sleep will be sweet. Have no fear of sudden disaster or of the ruin that overtakes the wicked, for the Lord will be your confidence. (niv)

I'd read those words slowly, deliberately, marinating in its truth until I could savor the meaning within my soul. I'd pray and beg my heavenly Father to be true to His promises.

Only then did I have the strength to close my eyes.

The Lord was, and is, my refuge and my hiding place.

+ + +

In the midst of this turmoil, the arrival of my baby brother was a gift from God. Of course, there was the marvel of a new life in our home, complete with a fresh array of smells that tickled my nose—the baby powder, baby oil, and baby bubble bath. To watch Momma snuggle him, bathe him, feed him, and bundle him up in a feather-soft, blue "keeper" for the night was better than watching TV. And Daniel's presence in the home had a way of taking our minds off the sociopath living across the street.

I've heard people say that the first child is a gift to the parents and the second child is a gift to the first child. This was true of my brother. For the first five years of my life I basked in my parents' love. In some ways I had been spoiled rotten. After all, I was their miracle baby and, as such, enjoyed extraordinary treatment.

I remember how Daddy, with a twinkle in his eye, signaled that he was ready to steal me away to the nearby market for a coveted candy run. There, surrounded by mountains of sugary delights, he encouraged me to fill a brown lunch bag with all of my favorite treats. On the way home, sitting side by side in the front seat of the family car, I'd dig into the bag and unwrap my treasures, one by one, while he told me how much he loved his princess.

Likewise, Momma thrived on brushing my hair, sometimes gathering it into pigtails, other times arranging it with the flair of a seasoned hairstylist. Before sending me on my way, she'd place a colorful bow atop my head as if finishing off a Christmas present. When she wasn't dressing me up, doll-like, she'd make time to sew a gorgeous outfit for one of my dolls with the care of a custom tailor.

In spite of their lavish displays of love, I longed for a brother or a sister. And, while playing with friends was a treat, I now had a real live baby doll to smother with love. I took my responsibility as a big sister as seriously as if I had been assigned with the duty of protecting the crown jewels of England. I'm sure I drove Momma nuts asking to hold Danny a hundred times a day.

Our family was complete—Daddy had his princess, and Momma had her boy. Momma had always had a special place in her heart for little boys. When my cousin Eddie was born ten years before me, Momma looked forward to every trip to see her brother Ed and his wife, Shirley, in Baton Rouge. The sun rose and set on Eddie.

With Danny, Momma had a boy of her own.

After Daniel's birth, Grandma Welch, Momma's mother, came to stay with us for several weeks to help with Daniel, with me, and with whatever cooking and housecleaning needed to be done. I was enthralled with the parade of people stopping by, delivering meals, dropping off gifts, and cooing over Danny. I was so proud that they were coming to see "my" baby brother.

By the time June rolled around, Grandma was long gone, the visitors were fewer and farther between, and life felt as if it had finally settled down into a comfortable routine. Danny was sleeping through the night, and I, too, found sleep less elusive. I was beginning to rest at night because the last explosion to rock our home had been six months prior—an eternity. While thankful for the respite from the bombings, as far as I was concerned, six months were not long enough.

Never would have been better.

The Bible says that, in the spiritual realm there is an enemy, the devil who, like a lion, prowls about seeking someone to devour. You might say we had our own earthbound lion roving the streets of Sellerstown. During the night hours, this tormented creature was pacing, preparing, watching, and waiting for us to let our guard down. As we'd soon discover, on Saturday, June 28, 1975, this cowardly lion would unleash his wrath upon us while we slept.

Under the half-opened eye of the watchful moon, with the clock approaching 1 a.m., a sniper pulled into Mr. Watts's driveway. He parked, leaving the engine running to ensure a fast exit, then slipped out of the driver's door, shotgun in hand. He took up his position beside the car and trained his rifle scope on the initial target. His instructions were simple: Shoot with speed and efficiency and make a clean getaway.

I don't know how much he had been paid.

I don't know how much he knew about his prey.

I doubt the gunman cared that he was about to take aim at the home of a pastor. This was business, after all. Nothing personal. Like a hired gun, he was there to do a job and then move on. The fact that a five-year-old girl and a four-month-old baby were home did nothing to prevent him from embarking on this act of senseless violence.

With just enough pressure to actuate the trigger, the automatic twelve-gauge shotgun launched its solid lead projectile into our faithful sentry, the mercury-vapor light in the backyard. The grounds around our house fell dark and, like a curtain of blackness, concealed the activity of the shooter.

Gun resting against his shoulder, Daddy's car now in the crosshairs of his scope, the shooter fired his weapon four times in quick succession. Hot metal slugs ripped into our family car. Two shots flattened the rear tires, and two plowed into the driver's side rear fender mere inches from the gas tank. By God's grace, the munitions didn't cause the fuel tank to explode. Had that happened, a fireball would have turned our home into an inferno.

It's unknown whether the gunman paused to reload his gun or if he used another weapon. Either way, the shooting continued. With my bedroom the subject of his attack, the gunman unloaded his ammo in my direction as I slept. Bullets carrying the power to send me to an early grave plowed into the brick siding just outside the wall where the headboard of my bed rested.

He fired again.

This time his shots shattered my bedroom window. The bullets flew inches past my head before lodging in the closet between my room and my parents' bedroom. The sound of breaking glass and the barking of a gun woke me with a jolt. Sitting upright in bed, blinking at the darkness, it took several long moments for my mind to transition from sleep to reality. Before I *knew* what was happening, I *felt* something was wrong, but what? Why did the feeling of dread hang in the air around me?

Why was my momma sobbing in her room?

Was something wrong with Danny?

Why had Daddy cried out, "Becky! Stay in your bed!"?

With a squint, aided by my closet night-light, I saw shards of glass strewn about the carpet. But was this unsettling tapestry of Momma's tears, splintered glass, and warnings from my father real or imagined? Was I caught in the middle of another nightmare like the time Mr. Watts came to take me away? As if answering my musings, I heard the fear in Daddy's voice as he repeated his plea, "Becky, don't move! Stay down!"

I'm thankful I had the sense to obey Daddy's command. I don't want to think what might have happened had I stood at that precise moment to seek the shelter of my parents' bed, as I had done many nights before. My body could have been used to stop one of the bullets. Whether or not it was genuinely Mr. Watts's intention to have us killed, or just shaken up, I can't say for certain. I do know, however, it wouldn't have taken much for one of us to have taken a bullet in the chest.

What if Momma had been awake, standing at the crib to change Danny's diaper? Or sitting upright in bed feeding him a bottle? The shot through my window could have tunneled through the flimsy drywall and pierced her heart. What if Daddy had heard me stirring over the initial round of shots and entered my room to check on me? He, too, would have been seriously injured, if not killed outright.

Like a puzzle with a thousand pieces, I struggled to fit together into any meaningful order the troubling thoughts swirling in my mind. Why was Mr. Watts *still* targeting us? Night after night, we prayed that this man would have a change of heart. We begged God to take away his anger, to transform his mind by the power of the gospel message that Daddy preached Sunday after Sunday. After six months of relative calm, with a newborn baby under our roof, we thought maybe, just maybe, Mr. Watts had softened.

And now this unprovoked assault.

In a way, my shattered bedroom window got off easy. It could be replaced. The damage done to our nerves, however, was taking its toll. There would be no quick fixes. No magic pill. No simple solution that could easily mend the broken places in our spirits. To hear my momma crying, her sobs so deep they welled up from the depths of her soul, was almost too much for me to handle as I remained confined to my bed.

How I wanted to comfort her.

How I needed her to comfort me.

Tires squealed outside of my now-splintered window. The roar of an engine seemed to dissipate in the distance. I could only assume that whoever had done this to us had sped off. Daddy, however, watched from the living room window. He stood to the side to avoid harm during the last few shots and watched the gunman bolt from the scene.

At 1:20 a.m., surprised to find the telephone still operational, Daddy called the law and described what he had witnessed. He reported to Wayne Piver, a Columbus County police officer, that the parsonage had been the subject of yet another attack. A male assailant, whose features were unrecognizable in the dark, got into a two-tone light and dark car after he finished firing and raced away.

Patrolman Piver, joined by County Detective Alton Lennon, arrived on the scene and identified five of the spent shotgun shells still lying on the ground in Mr. Watts's driveway. A number of bullet fragments were also extracted from under the carport. With two bullet holes marking his car, Daddy now had a daily reminder of the battle we were in. His devotion to the church came with a price, that much was clear.

But how far would these attacks go?

None of us knew this ambush was just the preamble.

Even though we might suffer from one of these sneak attacks on any given night, my parents were determined to keep life as normal as possible during the day. Daddy would go about his church business and sermon preparations while Momma cooked and cleaned without discussing the scary events in front of me. Speaking of cleaning, Momma loved a clean house. That's an understatement. Momma declared our house a "dirt-free zone." She waged a war on grime with the competence of an army general directing his troop into battle.

Aunt Pat says Momma would catch dust before it had a chance to settle on the table. Her utility room housed an arsenal of cleaning products; bottles of Clorox, an array of brooms and mops, and an assortment of towels awaited to be drafted into the good fight. Although she was petite, Momma applied enough elbow grease to keep her counters polished to a shine.

Momma had a peculiar habit of hand washing her turnip greens, mustard greens, and collard greens in the sink with a few drops of dishwashing liquid for good measure to loosen the dirt. After inspecting each leaf to ensure there were no hidden granules of earth stuck in a leafy fold, she'd run her greens through the rinse cycle in the washing machine.

She was especially thorough when it came to laundering Danny's cloth diapers. Her routine was to wash Danny's diapers in Clorox, then in Tide, and finally put them through an extra rinse cycle. By the time she was finished, a biohazard team couldn't have done a better job disinfecting them. To save time, I'm surprised Momma didn't use Pampers or some other brand of disposable diaper, which had recently become popular. Then again, Momma was a frugal pastor's wife. She had to stretch her resources any way she could; old-fashioned cloth diapers made the most sense.

Sometime around 8 p.m. on Tuesday, July 1, 1975, her work was finally done for the day. She enjoyed a few minutes of tranquil quiet as she sat down with Danny to rock him to sleep. Wrapped in a pillowy-soft, baby blue nightgown and sporting a fresh cloth diaper that had been carefully pinned around his five-month-old bottom, Danny had been fed his last bottle for the night and was out like a light.

Transitioning him from the rocking chair to the cradle, Momma laid him on his tummy in his crib. Although space was tight, his crib was adjacent to my parents' bed and a few feet from one of the two bedroom windows. Although the plan was eventually to give him his own bedroom down the hall, for now this was the most practical arrangement.

I could hear Momma hum a few bars of her favorite song, "Danny Boy," as she eased out of the bedroom. Closing the door softly behind her, Momma then stopped by my bed for nightly prayers. Once again, we prayed for Mr. Watts and for God's hand of protection over us. After we had prayed for several minutes and before I climbed under the covers, I embraced Momma. I buried my head against her neck and squeezed her with all the strength my little arms could muster.

I never wanted to let go.

I was still reeling from the gunshots that had hit our house just three nights before. I needed Momma's assurance that everything would be okay, that tonight nothing bad would happen to me. To her. To any of us. I couldn't shake the feelings of dread that Mr. Watts might strike again. Instinctively sensing the distress coursing through my body, she ran her fingers through my hair and kissed the top of my head.

"Mona?" Daddy was calling from the kitchen.

"I'll be right there, Robert," Momma said just above a whisper. True, Danny was a sound sleeper—most of the time. Even so, she didn't want to wake him by speaking too loud.

"Hold me, Momma . . ."

"I am holding you, darling." I could feel the warmth of her breath tickle my ear like a feather as she spoke. "But I've got to help your daddy put up the food."

"Please . . ."

"Sweetheart, I'll come back and check on you after a little while, okay?" She lifted me onto my bed and snuggled the covers around me.

"Promise?"

With a kiss to my forehead, she said, "I promise."

I didn't let go.

"Becky," she said, cradling my face in her hands. "Do you remember what Psalm 91 says?"

Our eyes met. I nodded. It was one of her favorite parts of the Bible. Momma loved to quote from it whenever I was fearful. Softly and slowly, she spoke the words from memory, "'He shall cover thee with his feathers, and under his wings shalt thou trust: his truth shall be thy shield and buckler.' You'll be fine. The Lord is watching over you." With a smile that melted my heart, she said, "I love you, darling. Now off you go to bed."

She kissed my forehead and then helped me under my covers. Turning out the light, Momma headed to the kitchen to join Daddy, who was preparing a variety of foods for the freezer. I could hear them as they worked at the other end of the small house. I pictured them side by side, cutting and wrapping the fresh fish Daddy had caught and the meat they had bought.

As I'd seen them do before, I knew they'd be cutting and placing the vegetables and fruit purchased at the market or picked from the garden into individual baggies. Since Momma often entertained unexpected guests, she liked to keep her freezer stocked with preportioned options.

The sound of my parents talking and working into the night had a calming effect on me, much like listening to the gentle waves of the ocean caressing the beach. The comforting rhythm of their voices ebbed and flowed until at some point, my eyelids yielded to the tidal pull of sleep. While Danny and I slept at one end of the house and while my parents bustled about like two beavers busy preparing food at the opposite end, three men entered our yard with dynamite in their hands and evil on their minds.

The strategy of this, the third bombing, was to position the charge of explosives near the corner of our house closest to where Danny and I were sleeping—a mere twenty feet from our beds. At 10 p.m., Mr. Watts's three henchmen lit the fuse and then sped away. Like an extended thunderclap, the rumble from the blast could be heard more than two miles away and was felt by neighbors living several doors up the street.

Momma's friend Carolyn Sellers, who lived on the other side of Aunt Pat's house in a single-wide trailer, watched the force of the blast literally rock the peas in the pot on her stove. Turning to her husband, Roger, Carolyn told him, "Don't go out there. That parsonage is plumb blown up. It's not there."

I have no idea why my room didn't suffer damage, aside from dolls and framed pictures being knocked from my dresser. My parents' room was hit hard. The bomb blew out three windows, two in their bedroom and one in their bathroom. The glass, wood frames, and windowsills sailed into the room like spears seeking a target.

In a blur of tears and screams, I fled my room and ran for my life. I found myself outside in the front yard, running in place as if a jolt of electricity were coursing through my nervous system. The palms of my shaking hands covered the sides of my head. My ears throbbed as if someone had taken a rubber mallet and struck my eardrums. When Daddy, running toward me, called my name, his voice sounded muffled, as if I were hearing it in muted tones underwater.

He dropped to his knees and pulled me to himself. I collapsed in his arms. "I'm here, sweetheart," he said, over and over. "It's okay, sweetheart. It's okay."

Through streams of hot tears, I saw Momma across the front lawn heading in our direction. Relieved that both of my parents were safe, I closed my eyes and tried to breathe. I felt Momma join our little huddle; her arms slipped around my waist as she nuzzled the back of my neck with her face. Although she tried to sound strong, her voice was shaky. "Oh, my darling, Becky . . . my sweet, precious darling."

At some point it occurred to me that Danny wasn't with us, but I was too afraid to ask if he had survived the blast. Was that why Momma was sobbing?

Within minutes of the explosion, people from all parts of town flooded into our yard. Momma's friend and singing partner, Eleanor Tyree, and her husband, James, who lived more than a mile away, had jumped into their car and were among the first to arrive at the parsonage.

Eleanor asked, "Where's Danny?"

"I . . ." Momma shook her head side to side.

Eleanor reached out and gripped Momma's arm. "Ramona, is the baby all right?"

"He's still . . . still in his room."

Momma had been so unnerved by the attack that she couldn't face seeing what might have happened to her baby. I think she expected the worst and couldn't bring herself to go inside that bedroom. For his part, Daddy had watched me run out the front door and, recognizing that I might be headed straight into danger, chased after me. Who was to say there wasn't still a sniper outside? Or maybe someone waiting to kidnap one of us? He knew these people were capable of anything, and his first instinct was to prevent anything else from happening to his daughter.

"Don't you worry, Ramona," Eleanor said, "I'll get him." With that, she raced inside. As Eleanor approached the bedroom, she expected to hear Danny crying, wailing in pain. Instead, there wasn't a sound emanating from behind the closed door. She pushed open the door, snapped on the light, and gasped at the minefield of broken glass and torn drapes.

Still no sound from Danny.

How could that be? Was he dead?

After all, his crib, situated under one of the shattered windows, was directly in the line of fire. Eleanor hurried across the room to the baby. In spite of the fact that glass and wood fragments had cascaded into Danny's crib, she couldn't believe that he never woke up. Nor did a single sliver of glass or fragment of wood land on his body, which is a miracle considering that he was surrounded by razor-sharp objects.

Had Danny stirred or rolled over, his tender body would have been pierced like a pincushion in a hundred different places. Chunks of glass could have cut his face, his eyes, his bare arms with ease. Instead, as if an angel had covered Danny with his wings, not a scratch was found on him. Momma had been right when she had recited those words just hours before about God's protection . . . "He shall cover thee with his feathers, and under his wings shalt thou trust" (Psalm 91:4).

With care, Eleanor plucked Daniel from the jaws of the lions' den and carried him to Momma. By the time Eleanor rejoined us in the yard, a full contingent of police officers had descended upon us. Traffic on Sellerstown Road was immediately placed under surveillance. The familiar swirling red and blue beacons lit up the night sky, casting bursts of color against our faces as Daddy and Momma spoke with members of the church who had come to offer whatever help and comfort they could provide.

That's when my daddy lost it.

While talking with friends, Daddy looked across the street and saw Mr. Watts, flanked by several of his thugs, standing at the edge of his driveway. Like a vulture enjoying a feast of death, Mr. Watts was surveying the damage. He seemed to be savoring the tasty chaos and the delicious panic created by the bombing.

A moment later, Daddy's eyes met his.

They stared, unblinking.

Like two rivals facing each other before a gunfight in the Wild West, they stood their ground. Daddy stopped his conversation midsentence. He began to contemplate the unthinkable. In that moment, adrenaline pumping through his being, the old man, the barroom brawler, the ex-Navy fighter, threatened to assert himself. How dare Mr. Watts try to kill his family? Didn't he have the right to defend his home from this deranged man?

Mr. Watts glared back at Daddy from behind his thick black glasses. Still staring, the corners of his mouth morphed into a smile, an evil, demented grin of satisfaction. As if rubbing salt in a wound, Mr. Watts began to laugh at the mayhem he had caused. Taking a cue from their boss, his goons began to chuckle too. The laughing and backslapping were all Daddy could take.

That night, the perpetrator had crossed the line.

With every raw fiber in him screaming injustice, Daddy set aside the biblical call to "love your neighbor as yourself" and the instruction to "pray for your enemies"—themes he had preached from the pulpit for years. Instead, driven by a desire to defend his family, Daddy took off like a charging bull across our yard toward Mr. Watts. Given his size and the magnitude of his wrath, it took several men, including James Tyree, to grab Daddy and hold him back from doing something that most certainly would have landed him in jail.

I had never seen my daddy so livid.

James Tyree was convinced by the look in Daddy's eyes that if he had reached Mr. Watts, Daddy would have unleashed two-and-a-half years of pent-up rage and, quite possibly, have killed Mr. Watts on the spot. While wrong, no one would have blamed Daddy, considering all that Mr. Watts had put our family through.

A few of the church members later said they should have let Daddy go that night, come what may. If necessary, they would have gladly posted bond on his behalf. In their eyes, it was heroic for Daddy to settle the matter with his own hands.

And yet I know Daddy must have had deep regrets for allowing himself to get so close to the edge. He knew the Scriptures well enough to know that his struggle wasn't against flesh and blood but against the devil, the enemy of his soul. After that momentary lapse in judgment, and in spite of what Mr. Watts would do in the future, Daddy prayed he'd never take matters into his own hands.

It takes a tough man to turn the other cheek.

Daddy was troubled over the impact that these attacks were having on us. Like any parent, he wanted his family to be safe. He yearned to protect us, though he prayed he wouldn't resort to brute force. At the same time, as Daddy told a reporter the next day, "I'm no quitter. I will not desert my congregation." Daddy vowed to stand his ground, even if it cost him his life; he wouldn't hesitate "to lay down my life in defense of my church, but the continual danger that is inflicted on my wife and children has to be stopped."

Speaking to another reporter after the third bombing, Daddy explained why he wasn't packing his bags and leaving town: "So many of God's soldiers spend their time retreating. The Bible teaches that when the wolf comes the hireling will flee, but the Good Shepherd will lay down His life for His sheep."

Taking his cue from Jesus' example, Daddy would stand by his congregation until God told him to move on. As such, Daddy would never let Mr. Watts drive him away from serving the Lord in Sellerstown. Daddy told the press, "When the Lord gets ready for me to leave this church, He won't send the message by the devil."

I'm not sure how Mr. Watts felt about that comparison.

I wouldn't be surprised if he was flattered.

After all, his devilish plans were far from over.

CHAPTER 8

# Holding On to Hope

He came close.

Very close. Almost too close.

The threatening letters and menacing phone calls didn't do it. Neither did two home invasions, the weekly harassment during worship services, the sniper shootings, the cut phone lines, nor the first two bombings. None of those acts of intimidation had driven him from serving the people he loved in Sellerstown. But during the sleepless night following the third explosion, a blast that could have claimed the life of his only son, Daddy was toying with the unthinkable. The mental tug-of-war between staying and leaving became stronger.

Mr. Watts was determined.

Mr. Watts was capable of anything.

And Mr. Watts seemed willing to kill his children.

The night of July 1, 1975, changed everything. With his baby sleeping in a crib surrounded by broken glass and splinters of wood like miniature harpoons targeting his helpless body, Daddy was cut to the core. Mr. Watts and his partners in crime had tried to intimidate Daddy by attacking our house back when Momma was pregnant. As she told the press, "They felt like they could get to my husband through me. They had no consideration for my condition." Now this unhinged fiend was going straight for Daddy's son and daughter—and that was beyond the pale.

Hours after the neighbors, the police, and the press cleared from our yard, Daddy still heard the blast in his head, resounding, pounding, driving home the point that Mr. Watts would never give up his campaign of terror. Daddy wanted to be strong. He was convinced that the Lord wasn't telling him to pack our bags and abandon the church—at least not yet. In fact, while praying with Brother Billy Sellers after the sniper attack several days prior to this bombing, he felt the Holy Spirit was saying that those things that had been done in darkness would be brought to light.

That wasn't wishful thinking on Daddy's part. He and Brother Billy had studied the words of Matthew, a follower of Jesus, who wrote, "All nations will hate you because you are my followers. But everyone who endures to the end will be saved. . . . Don't be afraid of those who threaten you. For the time is coming when everything that is covered will be revealed, and all that is secret will be made known to all" (10:22, 26, NLT).

Daddy had taken encouragement from that portion of Scripture and their extended time of prayer. He had been convinced Mr. Watts would be caught and placed in jail. But two days after that precious time of prayer, with three windows blown from their frames and a wife and daughter struggling to hold on, Daddy's resolve felt like sand draining from an hourglass. Time was running out. Dare he hold on to the hope that Mr. Watts would be arrested *before* he struck again?

After all, Mr. Watts should have been caught by now.

How could Mr. Watts evade justice for so long?

Everyone in the community knew who was behind these actions. Granted, the evidence was circumstantial, and Mr. Watts was a well-connected former county commissioner who was, by definition, above reproach—at least in the minds of some people. That meant nothing less than comprehensive corroboration of his hand in these crimes was necessary. Daddy knew Detective Dudley was doing his best to gather rock-solid proof in order to get a full and proper conviction.

That took time.

Maybe more time than Daddy could endure.

Besides, the lawman was just one man with a full workload. What if Mr. Watts struck again, and this time one of us was injured . . . or worse? How could Daddy live with himself? As the pastor, he was truly prepared to die for his flock. He was related to President Andrew "Old Hickory" Jackson, which may explain why he wasn't about to abandon his post. But the thought that his family might be harmed wasn't a price Daddy wanted to pay.

Just when he reached his lowest point, help arrived in full force. The morning after the bombing, July 2, 1975, as if drinking from a fire hose, we were deluged with assistance from every branch of law enforcement in the country: a cadre of local, state, and federal agents poured into our yard.

When it rained, it poured.

At long last, Columbus County Police Detective Sergeant George Dudley received the help he both needed and had requested from the State Bureau of Investigation (SBI), the Federal Bureau of Investigation (FBI), and the Bureau of Alcohol, Tobacco, and Firearms (ATF). And the unannounced appearance of a mobile crime laboratory parked on our front lawn meant one thing: these boys were serious players. They had all the tools necessary to study the evidence at the crime scene. This, in turn, convinced Daddy that the case would be quickly resolved.

Joining the surge of law enforcement officers sweeping for evidence around our house was a U.S. postal inspector who came to investigate the assassination-like attack on our mailbox. His task included scrutinizing the unsigned letters that threatened harm and death. Daddy's spirits soared. Maybe now the role of Mr. Watts in these events would be exposed and justice served.

From Daddy's viewpoint, given this aggressive show of force by the authorities, he would be free to return to his first love—ministering to the people of Sellerstown. For the first time in years, he could set aside thoughts of retreating in the face of persecution to continue the work he felt God had called him to do.

Of all the law enforcement agents on the scene, Daddy was especially drawn to ATF Agent Charles Mercer. I can't say for sure what it was about Agent Mercer that captured Daddy's confidence. Physically speaking, Agent Mercer was no Arnold Schwarzenegger. Unlike the Terminator, Agent Mercer wasn't an imposing man. He had no bulging muscles or steel blue eyes that instilled fear in the bad guys. In fact, Daddy was taller, broader, and more muscular than this ATF special detective.

With the exception of his sea green eyes, Agent Mercer was nondescript. He wore no glasses, no hat, and had no distinguishing features; he didn't sport a handlebar mustache or Elvis-size sideburns. Husky, standing five feet nine, he wore a pressed shirt and pants with a gun strapped to his waist. But his eyes, as mysterious as the ocean, seemed to reflect his emotions and convey his thoughts as clearly as if he were having a conversation. Those who met him felt as if Agent Mercer could "talk" with his eyes even if he never uttered a word.

However he communicated it, this agent had a single focus—getting to the bottom of the case. I think what Daddy must have seen in his eyes was tenacity. Agent Mercer seemed to have a strength of purpose, some driving force that compelled him to get answers. As they spoke, it became clear that this man had the dogged determination of a hound dog who would refuse to give up the chase until justice rolled down upon the perpetrator.

Sharing an office with George Dudley at the Columbus County police headquarters, Agent Mercer quickly set up camp and got whatever he needed from the local police officers, who were eager to help. Daddy's gut feeling about the man after their first meeting was later confirmed when Agent Mercer posted a $10,000 reward to the person who provided information that Mr. Watts was behind the bombings at the parsonage.

Like the welcoming rays of sunlight chasing away a stubborn fog, Daddy found himself basking in more good news the following Sunday. According to the church's bylaws, the members were required to vote on the reappointment of their pastor on the first Sunday of July every two years. In a 60–2 decision, once again the church family overwhelmingly affirmed their desire to retain Daddy as their pastor.

That is, if my parents were willing to stay.

Daddy was honest with the church about the toll these attacks were having. Yet he promised to stay the course. Head held high, supernaturally calm in the face of his trials, he assured the packed church his message wouldn't change, nor would he be intimidated from fulfilling his calling. His words reflected what he would soon tell a reporter: "We battle fear from time to time, even though we are spiritual people. Then, too, we feel that there's no force that can destroy us." He was honest that Momma, in particular, had some reservations. Living in the valley of the shadow of death isn't for the faint of heart. Daddy admitted, "Her initial reaction was more emotional than mine, but after that initial reaction, she's ready to fight along with me."

He added, "I stand flat-footed and preach the truth. I don't sugar-coat it. We feed the flock of God. I always had a certain amount of backbone, so we're just stonewalling it here." Another development that Sunday gave my parents the necessary hope to press on. Concerned about our safety, the church voted to hire an armed security guard to patrol the grounds around our house at night. That safeguard provided a certain peace of mind. Maybe, just maybe, there would be an end to the violence. And maybe, just maybe, we could sleep without the fear of awakening to yet another attack.

I suspect Mr. Watts was steaming in pew number seven.

He had done so much to chase my family away. And if we weren't leaving voluntarily, Mr. Watts probably figured the church would see the wisdom of removing this man who, like a lightning rod, attracted unwanted negative attention to their fellowship. By his calculations, the church should have been sufficiently primed and ready to vote Daddy out of office and, in turn, seek a less "controversial" pastor to lead them. But what Mr. Watts failed to calculate was the deep bond Daddy and Momma had cemented in the early days of their ministry in Sellerstown.

I'm surprised he missed this connection.

From the moment Daddy set foot in Sellerstown, he made it his mission to reach the unreachable and teach the unteachable. He provided a welcoming place where love and laughter were offered in generous servings regardless of who you were or what you had done in the past. If you weren't in church on Sunday, on Monday he'd put on his boots, find you in the fields or at your place of business, and personally check on you. If you were sick, he'd pray for you and say, "See you in church next Sunday."

Take James Tyree, for example.

A cattle farmer by trade, before he met my father, James had no use for church, primarily because there were those in the church who had no use for him. His mother, Betsy, had told James that he was going to hell for all the years he had lived like a heathen, which, no doubt, had something to do with his love of cigars and alcohol. He'd be the first to admit that his affinity for alcohol drove him to drink just about anything he could get his hands on.

To say that James enjoyed smoking cigars would be an understatement; they were his constant companion. Unless he was eating, sleeping, or in the shower, he had a stogie in his mouth. While the Bible doesn't specifically teach that smoking is a sin, in Betsy's book it was one of those outward signs of "heathen" behavior.

But more than these "sins of the flesh," there was another reason why James was going to hell, or so his mother believed. James had been divorced. Compounding his "sin" was the fact that he had remarried. Betsy didn't believe in second marriages. Living under a cloud of condemnation by his mother, convinced that he was beyond the reach of the Cross, it's not surprising that James avoided going to church.

Shortly after Daddy arrived in town, he caught wind of James's story—a story that was not too far from that of his own journey. Rather than write James off as a lost cause or a modern-day leper, Daddy slipped on his work boots and pursued James while he was out tending to his fields. I have no idea how Daddy developed his approach to pastoring. Somehow, somewhere along the way, he knew that to be effective in growing the church, he had to walk among the people, meet them on their turf, and accept them the way they were.

As he worked side by side with James, Daddy's goal was to befriend this man. He knew he had to earn the right to be heard if the walls around James's heart were ever to come down. On a number of occasions they spent hours digging holes to construct a post-and-wire electric fence. Daddy would say, "I'll be over in a little while," and then arrive at the work site before James. His enthusiasm to serve was infectious, although at first James wasn't quite sure how to size up the new preacher. As they labored, Daddy told James about his path to faith in Jesus—how he, too, had tasted the wild life, watched his first marriage dissolve, drunk heavily, and been disinterested in the things of God.

This wasn't what James had expected to hear. The tattoo on Daddy's forearm, an indelible embarrassment left over from his Navy days, wasn't what James expected to see. And the unconditional love and lack of condemnation he experienced from the "preacher man" wasn't something he anticipated feeling, either. To James, Daddy was more like a brother than a pastor. Their lives had such a surprising amount in common, James liked to say, "We were clicking on the same clock."

Naturally, when Daddy went on to explain that his story didn't end with the drinking and skirt chasing, James was all ears. The moment God had changed Daddy's heart, he became a new man. Pausing long enough to make eye contact, his shirt matted with sweat and dirt, Daddy told him, "Brother James, God can do the same thing for you that He did for me." With that, Daddy invited James to church the following Sunday. He was convinced that no one—not even James—was beyond the saving grace of Jesus.

James came.

So did his wife, Eleanor.

Like a thirsty man drawn to water, James came forward that morning in response to Daddy's invitation to receive Jesus. At the end of the sermon, standing at the altar while Momma played "The Old Rugged Cross" on the organ, James gave his heart to the Lord. It wasn't long before Eleanor, who had likewise lived under her mother-in-law's condemnation, came to faith.

In the months and years following his conversion, James became one of the head deacons in the church, typically sitting on the platform while Daddy preached. And while they worked closely on church matters, the bond of friendship they shared spilled out into the week—sometimes in hilarious ways.

Like the time James invited Daddy to earn some extra cash on a job in Clinton, not far from Sellerstown. Daddy's construction skills would come in handy, and our family needed the cash, so he agreed. Always one to pull a joke, James arrived with five other men to pick up Daddy in a black hearse. With care, they backed the hearse down the driveway and parked it close to the house adjacent to the carport. They thought Mr. Watts was probably doing backflips when he looked out the window and saw a hearse across the street. You know, he thought his dream had come true; the pastor was finally gone. Daddy and James laughed so hard imagining that they might have pulled a fast one on Mr. Watts that they almost had a wreck on the way to the job.

Together, Daddy and James nurtured a sense of community within the church family, with plenty of fishing and hunting trips and church picnics. Outdoor activities were a way of life for those in the fellowship. And when James would go fishing with Daddy, the playful banter between them was always part of the action.

James typically sat in the back of the boat to steer while Daddy cast his line from the front. On one occasion, trying to keep a straight face, James ran the front of the boat into the trees, prompting Daddy to say, "Um, Brother James, can you back up a little?" James burst out laughing so hard over teasing the pastor, his face turned red. Being a good sport, Daddy laughed too. The bond of brotherhood between Daddy and James ran deep.

More than that, these early seeds of friendship, which had been sown in James as well as in the hearts of those in our church, set the stage for the people's unwavering allegiance and commitment to their pastor. The devotion they shared was such that they'd be willing to lay down their lives for each other.

Mr. Watts knew this.

Not only had he witnessed James's conversion and the impact of Daddy on the church, but two of Mr. Watts's own sons, Lee and Elwood, responded to the gospel message that Daddy preached. Both had asked Christ into their hearts and, over the years, like James, found a real friend in Daddy. Elwood even traveled with Daddy on an out-of-state camping and fishing trip. Such a bond of friendship with his own sons easily could have infuriated Mr. Watts.

I'm sure Mr. Watts wondered how his own family could enjoy the company of his enemy. And now, after the overwhelming vote to retain Daddy as pastor in spite of the persecution, Mr. Watts watched in disbelief as "his" church slipped further from his fingers. Carrying out three bombings in one year hadn't been enough.

Pacing and planning, watching and waiting, Mr. Watts appeared to be biding his time while the various branches of the law put Sellerstown under their collective microscope. After the heat of their scrutiny had passed, Mr. Watts struck again.

I played.

In spite of the attacks, or perhaps because of them, during the summer of 1975 I lost myself in a make-believe world of activity. Those who knew me as a child knew I was equally happy playing the part of a tomboy or a prissy little girl. I loved playing with Barbies about as much as I enjoyed grabbing the waist of my best friend, Missy, as we rode on the back of her motorcycle through the strawberry fields adjacent to Mr. Watts's house. She was fearless of him, even though she knew what he was capable of doing. Naturally, I had to be fearless, too. Four years older than me, Missy got her first motorcycle at age seven. That summer, Missy was nine and I was five.

Riding together, both of us barefoot and without helmets, we'd zoom through the fields to the woods to build a fort. We lived in the country, where nobody checked on such things as underage children riding a motorcycle. Besides, it was our street, and we pretty much did what we wanted. When we'd get to the woods, we'd set up camp, burn sticks and leaves, munch on whatever snack we brought from home, and then brush our teeth in the stream. We'd sit there and talk for hours.

I'm not sure how it came up, but as we sat together by the stream not long after the third bombing, Missy wondered why I was unusually sad. I told her that my dog, Tina, had been missing for several days. That's when Missy broke the news to me. She said she had heard that Mr. Watts had poisoned Tina and buried her remains in his tobacco barn.

I found that news almost too much to handle. I had heard that Mr. Watts had poisoned other dogs on my street before—often using enough poison to kill a horse, according to the veterinarian who conducted an autopsy of one victim. But little Tina? Why would Mr. Watts want her dead? It's not like Tina was a serious watchdog who might alert us to the presence of an intruder. Was Mr. Watts really such a coldhearted man that he'd kill Tina just to spite us?

Wanting proof that Mr. Watts had been so heartless, we hopped on Missy's motorcycle and headed to his barn. Although it was the middle of the afternoon, long shadows swallowed the rows of drying tobacco leaves in sheaves of darkness. The thin shafts of light angling rays of sunshine through the slats of barn-wood siding did little to illuminate the cavernous belly of the barn. We realized that, without a flashlight, finding a freshly dug grave would be difficult.

With our toes in the black dirt, fearful that we might be caught trespassing, we worked quickly to identify any signs of a grave. The creaking and groaning of the aging structure freaked us out. Still, we inched forward, studying the earthen floor just inside of the door. Before our eyes fully adjusted to the dim light, I walked into an overhead cobweb straining under the weight of dust. My heart catapulted into my throat. I stifled a scream, wanting to appear brave to impress Missy, even though I had been ready to leave before we had arrived. At the same time, I just had to know whether or not my Tina was buried here. We pressed further into the near darkness.

Afraid of being discovered, we retraced our footsteps after several fruitless minutes of searching in the shadows. I knew that, even if we had found Tina's final resting place, there was no way I could confront the man who had robbed me of one of the sweetest parts of my life.

With the barn being our only clue as to where Tina might have been buried, we gave up the chase. In my heart I accepted the fact that Mr. Watts's barn marked Tina's gravesite. I looked back one last time as Missy and I zipped down the dirt road. I knew I had to find a way to forgive Mr. Watts for yet another transgression.

The summer marred by Tina's death was also the summer I got "married" several times. When I was in my girlie mood, I'd wrap a towel around my head like a make-believe wedding veil, pick some of Momma's best flowers—which always got me into a heap of trouble—and then set out to find Billy Wayne, my five-year-old groom-to-be. I think Billy Wayne played along with my fantasy wedding plans because he had a crush on me, as I had on him.

Sometimes we'd pretend to get married in my backyard. Other

times I'd find Billy Wayne playing at his house and would conduct the ceremony there. Anywhere was fine with me. But the most fun was when I'd drag him to church, where we'd find Daddy working and ask him to marry me and Billy Wayne. Trying not to laugh during this solemn moment, Daddy would pick up a hymnbook—pretending it was a Bible—and then go through a ceremony with us.

One day when Daddy got to the "You may now kiss the bride" part, I looked over at Billy Wayne's freckled face and said, "Billy Wayne, take that sucker out of your mouth so you can kiss me!"

Billy's eyebrows shot up so high, they almost collided with the top of his head. His eyes exploded into two round saucers of fear. Having played along with this ridiculous playdate long enough, he shook his head left to right as if to say no and then ran out of the church as if the devil were in hot pursuit. I called after him, "Wait, Billy Wayne, wait! Come back here this instant!"

I don't think his cold feet at the altar stopped me from asking him to marry me the next day. My grandmother thought the fact that I wanted to get married all the time was so cute that she took the time to make a miniature wedding dress with a veil for me. Now that I had the real thing, I put Momma's towels back and got married in style.

As I continued to grieve the loss of Tina, Daddy tried to comfort me with the thought that there would be an armed night guard watching our home. Although I never told him, I had developed a habit of lying on my right side in bed to give me an easy view of my room. I knew that if I rolled over and faced the wall, I'd be giving an intruder the advantage of a surprise attack.

I knew I had to be prepared for anything.

The uncertainty of not knowing if and when we'd be struck with another bombing was bad enough, but not being able to get immediate relief by looking around to be sure no one was standing in my room terrified me. Making matters worse, my imagination worked overtime after Tina's death. Having concocted so many scary "what if" scenarios, I found myself wrestling with the same question every night:

*Will I be here in the morning?*

Then again, I knew the violence Mr. Watts planned could hit us while I was awake, too. It had happened during December while we were enjoying Christmas with friends. And, it occurred again on September 16, 1975. I remember that rainy night all too well. My grandparents on Daddy's side were visiting us from Alabama, so I was allowed to stay up late. Huddled around the television, laughing and enjoying one another's company, we were oblivious to the impending blast.

At 9:20 p.m., about an hour before the night guard arrived, a fourth explosion rattled our home. The dynamite, attached to a pole six feet above ground, was set in the soybean field behind our home. Thankfully, we were physically unharmed, although the bomb ripped up a ten-foot square of the field.

Perhaps the scariest part was the timing of the bomb and the knowledge that the law hadn't been able to stop the attacks. As Daddy told the press, "You can see how closely they are watching us. If they can find one hour of darkness when there is not a watch, they'll hit us. We've had every agency you can get. These people are still at large."

Having experienced a taste of Mr. Watts's wrath, Daddy's parents tried to get him to resign and move home. No doubt that was part of Mr. Watts's revised strategy. If the church wouldn't release their controversial pastor, maybe Daddy's kin would apply enough pressure to break Daddy's resolve if Mr. Watts struck while they were guests in our home. In spite of their pleas to leave, Daddy didn't feel released from his calling to Sellerstown—and said so. He would stay and fight the good fight on his knees.

Knowing Daddy's mother, my grandma Erma Ruth Nichols, as I did, I knew that pacifist approach wouldn't sit well with her. Frankly, I was surprised she didn't grab a frying pan and go over to Mr. Watts's house, knock on his door, and let him have it. That was the way she had expressed herself before she found Jesus. Grandma was a strong woman, so strong she gave birth to seven children at home without the benefit of anesthesia—except for when she gave birth to Daddy, who weighed more than eleven pounds. If Daddy wouldn't leave, Grandma was the sort of woman who believed he should do whatever was necessary to protect our home.

On the other hand, when it came to retaliating for this fourth bombing in a year, I remember my grandfather, William Franklin Nichols, arguing, "That man's not worth the powder or lead it would take to kill him. He's worthless. Don't waste a bullet on him. He's nothing more than a sorry good-for-nothing anyway."

Not that Daddy would consider revenge—killing or otherwise. Daddy had faced that fork in the road before. Thanks to his friends who restrained him from taking matters in his own hands after the third bombing, he didn't want to risk being sent to jail himself. Instead, Daddy wanted to lead the Sellerstown community with a life that exhibited biblical forgiveness, not vigilante justice.

I'm sure Daddy imagined that our prayers would be answered and that Mr. Watts would wave the flag of surrender. Or that at least we'd wake up one day and see a For Sale sign in the front yard of Mr. Watts's house, indicating he was fed up and was moving on since we had no plans to surrender. Neither option materialized. It's probably a good thing that Daddy didn't know what Mr. Watts had planned next.

CHAPTER 9

# Hearing Voices

The voices of despair beckoned.

Spewing nothing but falsehood, a chorus of ominous voices began to haunt Daddy day and night. The sinister utterances, which harmonized with the agenda of hell itself, resonated within his head and told him he would be destroyed. His mission was over. He was a failure. He would never win. These champions of fear and paranoia, like weeds threatening to choke off the life of every good thing around them, said he would lose everything he had worked for in Sellerstown.

He yearned to silence the voices.

In his heart, Daddy knew they were all lies.

And while they were nothing but vacuous fabrications from the pit to be ignored, as the voices persisted, so did Daddy's spiral into a depression. He would walk through the house confessing out loud the words of 2 Timothy 1:7, "For God hath not given us the spirit of fear; but of power, and of love, and of a sound mind." Nevertheless, he became obsessed with each car that passed by the parsonage. Every time one approached or he heard footsteps outside, he would race to the windows to see what mischief might be imminent. If we happened to be gathered in a room at night with the lights on when Daddy heard these sounds outside, he would hush everyone. He'd ask us to turn off the lights, stay away from the windows, and remain quiet until he checked out the situation.

After all, the question haunting Daddy wasn't *if* Mr. Watts would strike again. The question was, *when* would the next attack occur? Night after night, as the deep orange sun sank into the horizon, Daddy dreaded the ominous feeling that tonight might just be the night when a string of anonymous midnight callers would waken him from his sleep . . . or that his home would be bombed again . . . or that one of his children or his wife would be harmed.

Whether Daddy cared to admit it, the campaign of terror was taking a heavy emotional toll. Although Daddy refused to abandon the church, his nerves were shot. During the fall of 1975, the voices of discouragement reverberating in his head battled for dominion over his heart. Daddy found himself fighting a depression so severe that, rather than lingering after church services to greet and visit with worshipers, he'd slip out the side door and take refuge at home. Daddy even stopped visiting door to door, as had been his custom over the years. Instead, he remained in bed for hours day after day.

What he needed were words of peace and comfort—not the voice of confusion. What he longed for was God's assurance that all would be well with his soul, that his family would be safe, and that the persecution would come to a swift and just ending. With the determination of a drowning man clinging to a life preserver, Daddy clung to the words of Psalm 28:1-4, in which King David, no stranger to persecution, wrote,

> Unto thee will I cry, O Lord my rock; be not silent to me: lest, if thou be silent to me, I become like them that go down into the pit. Hear the voice of my supplications, when I cry unto thee, when I lift up my hands toward thy holy oracle. Draw me not away with the wicked, and with the workers of iniquity, **which speak peace to their neighbours, but mischief is in their hearts.** Give them according to their deeds, and according to the wickedness of their endeavours: give them after the work of their hands; render to them their desert. (emphasis added)

Daddy had reason to hope that, indeed, everything would work out. He was encouraged to witness ATF Agent Charles Mercer digging deep into the case, like a hound dog on the hunt of truth. He was heartened on September 30, 1975, two weeks after the fourth bombing, when Agent Mercer served a federal warrant to search the home of Mr. Watts.

Perhaps the end was in sight.

Perhaps Mr. Watts would be brought to justice.

However, Daddy's disposition darkened when Agent Mercer, following the search of Mr. Watts's property, told the press, "The search warrant is merely a tool that we work with, and by no means does it reflect an accusation on anyone." Daddy was convinced Mr. Watts was behind the two years of oppression. How, then, could Agent Mercer downplay Mr. Watts as a suspect? Why was it taking so long to gather the evidence proving his guilt? How much longer would Daddy have to fight the good fight under a constant cloud of fear?

Like a pendulum swinging back and forth on a grandfather clock, Daddy's mood swings that fall were as regular as time itself.

One minute he was trapped in the doldrums; the next minute hope abounded. At one moment, Mr. Watts appeared to have the upper hand. The next moment, progress would be made on the case, giving Daddy the strength to press on.

For instance, because the drama in Sellerstown had been so widely reported and had so horrified most residents, North Carolina congressman Charlie Rose requested a summary of the acts of terror directed at our home and church from the FBI and ATF agents. This was good news. Perhaps there was enough pressure building on the case that it would be resolved sooner rather than later . . . if only Daddy could squelch the voices predicting defeat.

Meanwhile, there was more good news to brighten Daddy's outlook. An aide to then-governor Jim Holshouser gathered newspaper clippings from which he determined that action was needed. On October 16, 1975, the governor publicly offered a $2,500 reward for information leading to the arrest and conviction of the person or persons responsible for these acts of terrorism in his state.

But it wasn't long before the internal voices forecasting Daddy's doom renewed their strength. Their fiendish chant soared once again, this time just after 7 p.m. on November 6, 1975. That's when Mr. Watts initiated a fifth explosion. While our house was unharmed, the foundations undergirding Daddy's heart began to crumble. Maybe the voices were right. Maybe he or his family wouldn't make it out of Sellerstown unharmed. Maybe he should quit.

Perhaps the most disturbing aspect of this attack was the fact that a hired armed guard, Leo Duncan, was on patrol when the detonation took place. Worse, Mr. Watts was speaking to Leo Duncan in his driveway at the precise moment of the blast. Evidently Mr. Watts had lured Leo away from his post, leaving our home unguarded long enough to strike again.

+ + +

Momma was a strong woman.

A steel magnolia before the phrase was coined.

She was graceful yet strong on the outside, soft and tender on the inside. And yet she found it difficult to watch her husband struggling to hold it together in the wake of the fifth bombing. She, too, was reaching the end of herself and needed an oasis to recharge from the front lines. Although she didn't want to be apart from the love of her life, Momma knew the love they shared could stand the distance. After celebrating Daddy's birthday on November 11, 1975, Momma packed the car and took Danny and me to Bogalusa to be with her family.

At age five, I had no say in the matter.

Granted, being with my grandparents was always a highlight. And yet, I was such a Daddy's girl that being apart from him bothered me almost as much as if I'd lost my right arm. Driving away from home that afternoon, knowing that I wouldn't hear Daddy's voice in the morning or smell his aftershave when I wrapped my arms around his neck, a gray cloud of sadness settled on me. I'm sure the feelings were mutual.

Momma thought this was for the best, so off we went.

On November 13, 1975, two days after Daddy's birthday, he received a real gift of encouragement. A federal grand jury was assembled in Raleigh, North Carolina, to explore the preliminary evidence gathered in the case. Subpoenas for eight people were issued, including orders for Horry Watts, Bud Sellers, Wayne Tedder, and Daddy to appear before the grand jury.

Under normal circumstances, this should have muzzled the persistent voices inside of Daddy's mind. However, his yo-yoing between hope—that the case would be resolved—and despair—that Mr. Watts was too slick, too skilled, too adept at evading justice—began to catch up with Daddy. And no doubt, after Momma, Danny, and I left Daddy at home, he probably stayed up all night, sitting in a chair near the window to monitor the street.

I'm sure he must have thought that any restraint Mr. Watts exercised while the family was home—which wasn't much—would evaporate the moment we were gone. With Daddy home alone, he probably figured there was nothing stopping Mr. Watts from unleashing his full fury. That, of course, would explain why Daddy didn't sleep at night and, instead, slept so much during the daytime.

On Sunday, November 16, 1975, a highway patrolman found Daddy incoherent and slumped over the steering wheel of his wrecked car. He had crashed in Newton Grove, North Carolina, some eighty miles away from home. After preaching at our church in the morning, Daddy had been scheduled to speak at another church's Sunday night service. He never made it. No doubt Daddy had fallen asleep at the wheel. The accident required Daddy to be transported by ambulance to Columbus County Hospital, where he was treated in the emergency room. Daddy was to appear before the grand jury the following morning. Due to the personal crisis, he never had a chance to testify.

Several days later, Momma sensed something was wrong with Daddy's mental state. The unsettling experience happened during a phone call she placed to him from Bogalusa that week. Danny was sick, and Momma had asked Daddy to pray for their son. But when Daddy began his prayer, he started to pray for someone unrelated to the need at hand. He sounded incoherent, confused.

After the call, convinced that Daddy was suffering a much deeper depression than she had imagined, Momma left Danny and me with her mother and traveled back to Sellerstown with Daddy's sisters Aunt Dot and Aunt Martha. The three women packed up Daddy, planning to whisk him away to his parents' home in Mobile, Alabama.

As they loaded Daddy and his luggage in the car, Mr. Watts strolled into his front yard. Like a vulture anticipating the death of a wounded animal, Mr. Watts smiled and gloated and all but rejoiced at the broken man he saw across the street that afternoon.

In a moment of brutal honesty, Aunt Dot confessed to me years later what she was feeling as Mr. Watts appeared to relish Daddy's broken condition. She said, "I've never been a violent person, but at that moment I wished I had been able to put my hands on a gun and make Mr. Watts pay for what he had done to my brother." Mustering their willpower, the women ignored Mr. Watts as they finished packing the car.

On November 20, 1975, Daddy was admitted to the University of South Alabama Medical Center. After submitting Daddy to a heavy battery of physical and psychological tests, the doctors were convinced of two things. Medically speaking, Daddy's heart had been damaged from stress. In their view, any other man would have had a heart attack from such extreme pressure. The second prognosis was that Daddy had had a complete nervous breakdown and was exhausted.

He needed immediate bed rest.

He needed prayer. He needed a break from the voices.

The doctors wanted to offer hope yet remain realistic about the extent of his condition. They told Momma, "It will take at least three weeks to come around, and then he will not be out of the woods." Momma told the doctors she was shocked that this had happened to a man who had been a tower of strength for his family and for the church. In their professional opinion, Momma said, "They told me this is what happens when the base of the tower crumbles."

Daddy, heavily sedated, was admitted to Charter Hospital, the psychiatric wing of the University of South Alabama Medical Center, where he stayed for six weeks until his insurance ran out. Because of

Mr. Watts, three holidays were stolen from us due to Daddy's breakdown. Hospitalized, sedated, and alone, Daddy missed Danny's first Thanksgiving, Christmas, and New Year's celebrations. Rather than experience the joy and happiness that I had enjoyed, my brother's childhood, although he was just nine months at the time, was shortchanged.

For their part, the church showered us with thoughtful expressions of love and faithful prayers. Upwards of sixty get-well and Christmas cards poured in as the church family prayed for our quick return. One child sent Daddy a Humpty Dumpty card in which she wrote, "My prayers will always be with you. And you mean *everything* to me."

Ironically, even Mr. Watts signed and mailed a get-well card in which he'd expressed hope that Daddy would experience "more happiness than you have ever known!" Whether he wrote that out of guilt or a twisted attempt to deflect criticism, I don't know. Somehow, receiving a card from Mr. Watts felt about as appropriate as someone bringing a beer keg to one of our church picnics.

When Daddy was strong enough to return to Sellerstown, he still wasn't operating at full capacity. His bullet-riddled car, the one he had wrecked several months prior, needed far too many repairs. Since we didn't have the money, the generous church family voted to purchase Daddy a new 1976 Buick—which drove Mr. Watts mad. They also approved, and paid for, a single-wide trailer. This home away from home was placed on the farm of James Sellers out in the Beaver Dam community, just a few miles away.

The church leadership wanted to give us a refuge at night, well away from Mr. Watts's immediate scrutiny, while the lawmen did their job. Even better, this new location was adjacent to a neighbor who had excellent guard dogs. Any attempt by Mr. Watts or his men to approach the trailer with ill intent would arouse a round of barking loud enough to raise the dead.

Admittedly, our getaway was not a secret. Nor did it stop Mr. Watts from harassing us. I remember watching him drive past the trailer, slowing his car to glare through the windshield, just to let us know he knew where we were living. He was livid that the church spent money on this shelter for us. Aside from the cost, he had to be miffed that he could no longer keep tabs on us during his nightly prowling.

I remember as evening approached, we'd pack up as if we were going on vacation and return to that little haven, make dinner, and then settle in for the night. The next day we'd return to the parsonage to conduct our lives and the church business. For me, the novelty of living in our new "home" wore off pretty fast. In my view, it wasn't fair that Mr. Watts got to stay in his house with his personal things while we lived like gypsies out of suitcases.

There was such an injustice to it.

Didn't we have a right to live in peace like other families? Shouldn't we, too, be able to lay our heads down on our own beds and feel safe through the night? I admit I *was* sleeping better. For that, I was thankful.

The phone rang. As Daddy had done numerous times before, he reached for the receiver not knowing whether a friend or foe would be on the other end of the line. It was just as likely to be a call for help from one of the parishioners as it might be another crank call.

"Hello?"

When the caller spoke, his words were muffled as if smothered in fabric. Once again Daddy strained to understand what was being said. As before, without identifying himself, the anonymous man groused, "You're a thorn in a friend of mine's side . . . and the best thing you can do is leave the community."

Daddy waited. Would there be more to the threat this time? When the caller fell silent, Daddy said, "God bless you, son."

The phone went dead.

+ + +

Mr. Watts, Roger Williams, and Charles "Wayne" Tedder were huddled in the house directly across the street from the parsonage. The phone from which the call had been made sat on the table between them. Mr. Watts, the owner of the residence, had asked Roger to make the call and insisted that Roger cover the mouthpiece with a handkerchief as he spoke. Wayne watched as Roger did as he was told.

Wayne, like Roger, was another one of Mr. Watts's brute squad who took frequent trips on the wrong side of the law. Much of Wayne's life had been a cocktail of bad judgments and even worse behavior, mixed with a history of pill popping and heavy alcohol consumption. Wayne was willing to do whatever Mr. Watts required, primarily due to his own indebtedness to the man.

Like a wayward fly, Wayne was stuck in Mr. Watts's web with little chance of escape, and he knew it. At one point Wayne privately confessed to Roger, his cohort in crime, a desire to stop taking orders from Mr. Watts, saying, "I've just got to get out of it. My nerves won't take any more."

After the call was finished, Mr. Watts retrieved the handkerchief, tucked it into his pocket, and then withdrew a twenty-dollar bill. Even though it was payment for services rendered, when Mr. Watts "asked" for something to be done, Roger knew Mr. Watts was not the sort of man to be crossed. The last thing Roger needed was to be in his crosshairs. Handing the cash to Roger, Mr. Watts said, "You're a good ole boy, and we're going to get along just fine."

Mr. Watts, like a seasoned military commander in the heat of the battle, was directing a private war against the young Navy veteran turned pastor. This call was just the latest maneuver to provoke and unsettle us. All that was left for Mr. Watts to do was to watch. And wait.

And, if necessary, strike again.

By God's grace, from November of 1975 until August of 1976, the better part of a year, we savored what amounted to a cease-fire. Though our family continued to receive occasional threats over the phone, there were no more bombings. No shootings. No cut phone lines. To be candid, I'm not sure how Daddy or Momma would have coped had there been a string of attacks during that year. God knew what we could handle. The Good Shepherd knew we needed that season of refreshment to restore our souls in green pastures.

Daddy had been welcomed back by a church eager to be reunited with their beloved pastor, and he returned to the business at hand as best he could. For her part, Momma resumed her work with the Spiritualaires, an eleven-piece music and singing group she founded in 1970, not long after she and Daddy began to serve in Sellerstown. Although Momma stopped traveling with the band after Danny was born, she was actively involved in rehearsing and arranging their music.

Virtually every weekend the group was booked to conduct "sings" at churches throughout North Carolina and the neighboring states. With the men dressed in red jackets, white shirts, and blue ties, and the women sporting handmade navy blue and white dresses, the Spiritualaires was, in many ways, one of the pioneer music groups to debut on the contemporary Christian music scene.

To facilitate their heavy travel schedule, James Tyree made arrangements to purchase a 1948 Greyhound Silverside bus. The oil-burning tan and white bus was nicknamed "Old Lizzy" because it was older than anybody on the bus. He had the exterior of the aging bus painted with the band's name accented with a series of musical notes.

Week after week, the singers, often with their children in tow, would load the electric organ, piano, drums, and lead and bass guitars and then pray they'd make it to the next location. The Spiritualaires relied upon love offerings rather than tickets, and the group recorded two albums that were sold at their events. After each concert, they took the opportunity to offer an altar call for those who needed prayer or wanted to invite Jesus into their hearts.

Early in their music ministry, Daddy would travel with the band on occasion—a practice he had to quit due to stress and the need to prepare for his sermons on Saturday. Even though Daddy no longer accompanied the band, he remained supportive of their musical outreach—as long as the team was back at their posts on Wednesday night and both services on Sunday.

The unifying nature of the Spiritualaires was yet another reason the church family remained united in the face of Mr. Watts's persecution. They lived together, sang together, and experienced a precious bond of friendship. Ironically, the Spiritualaires had rerecorded Dottie Rambo's song, "One More Valley," which promised that after enduring "one more valley, one more hill . . . you can lay down your heavy load." Little did they know that in the summer of 1976, Daddy and Momma would be entering the valley of the shadow of death with a series of attacks that would further test their resolve and faith.

August 1, 1976, was an insufferably hot Sunday in Sellerstown, with temperatures topping ninety-one degrees. The sweet, robust smell of tobacco leaves drying in the nearby barns, carried on the wings of a gentle breeze, filled the air. People arriving for the evening service found spaces to park their cars on the grassy front yard of the church. We didn't have a paved parking lot; the casualness of leaving vehicles on the natural grass just seemed to fit the intimate, welcoming feeling worshipers enjoyed.

Inside the sanctuary, Momma was stationed at the organ and played a medley of favorite hymns as the faithful packed the church. Trading looks with Daddy as the clock inched toward 7 p.m., she transitioned into the call to worship to start the service. When Daddy took to the pulpit, he seemed to preach with a renewed strength of purpose. He was in his element, teaching the Word of God to those eager to learn.

That evening, Mr. Watts returned to his old tricks, igniting the sixth explosion across the street from the parsonage. I think the blast was his way of letting the church community know that he hadn't given up—not by a long shot. By detonating this bomb while church was in session, he wanted everyone to know he was still in control and a force to be reckoned with.

A month later, in early September, when his series of threatening letters, shootings, and bombings had still failed to drive us away, Mr. Watts waved the promise of a pile of cash under the nose of one of his henchmen. Roger Williams was summoned to the home of Mr. Watts. Facing the former county commissioner, Roger listened as Mr. Watts vented. Mr. Watts groused once again that Daddy was a thorn in his side. "I've tried so hard to scare him out but it don't seem like he'll leave," Mr. Watts said, adding, "We've done everything we know to do."

That's when Mr. Watts presented Roger with a tempting offer to make some serious cash.

The deal was simple.

Use your car to run the pastor over.

Make it look like an accident.

There's $100,000 in it for you if you succeed.

As before, Mr. Watts was the mastermind who preferred to leave the dirty work to others. He peeled five one-hundred-dollar bills from his wad of cash and placed the crisp bills on the table. You know, just a little gift to whet Roger's appetite for the big payday. Something to show he meant business.

Roger snatched up the money and tucked the cash into his pocket. Intrigued by the plan, Roger wasn't entirely ready to act. This, after all, was a really big deal with serious consequences. Mr. Watts was asking him to kill the popular pastor, and he wanted to know what would happen if he were somehow implicated in the death. Roger wasn't a wealthy man. If he faced charges, he wouldn't be able to hire a good lawyer to keep him from life in prison.

Mr. Watts told Roger not to worry, saying, "If you make it look like an accident, I don't think you'll be caught. But if you are, there is plenty of money, plenty of it, for your defense and for doing that for me." With a pat on the back as Roger turned to leave, Mr. Watts said he'd be in touch. For reasons unknown, Mr. Watts had second thoughts and never activated his plan.

Instead, on Wednesday night, October 13, shortly after our family received a death threat, Mr. Watts and Bud Sellers ignited yet another bomb in our driveway. This, the seventh powerful explosion, could be heard two miles away. At the time, sixty people were gathered in the church for the midweek service; the other youngsters and I were meeting at Aunt Pat's house two doors away from the church. An armed parishioner stood guard to ensure our safety. We, too, were shaken by the blast.

While a contingent of police and ATF agents cordoned off the area to investigate the explosion, Daddy spoke with the press. Daddy was grateful to report that nobody had been physically harmed—although there was a close call. Upon hearing a shotgun go off, a member of the congregation stepped outside to patrol the area. Not seeing any reason for alarm, he returned. Had he remained outside, he could have been injured by the blast. Daddy admitted, "We're all sort of shaken," but reiterated that he had no plans to quit. "We just intend to carry on and take more precautions when we have night services."

I don't know whether Mr. Watts read the paper and noticed Daddy's public refusal to quit. If he had, that might explain why five days later, on October 18, Mr. Watts struck for the eighth time. There was no way he'd let this country preacher beat him. If Daddy refused to go, then Mr. Watts would just have to turn up the heat by detonating an explosion in the field behind our house. Although we weren't spending nights at the parsonage, I believe Mr. Watts was trying to drive home the point that he was still dead serious: We would leave Sellerstown walking, crawling, dead, or alive.

Three weeks later, on November 10, 1976, gunshots pierced the otherwise peaceful evening and shattered the security light illuminating the church lawn. Minutes later, Mr. Watts and his sidekick Bud Sellers struck again, igniting a bomb that exploded during the middle of our Wednesday night church service.

Billy Sellers, one of Daddy's loyal and dear friends, narrowly escaped harm. Speaking to the press, Billy said, "I was sitting on the back pew [when] a shotgun blast was heard. I walked outside to see what it was and didn't notice that the light had been shot out. If I had, I might have wandered outside to check it out and might have been blown up when the dynamite exploded. I went back in the church, and the dynamite exploded just as I got back inside."

Following the blast, three men from the church, E. J. Sellers, Billy Sellers, and Barry McKee, rushed outside and searched the fields around the church property. They found and caught a man, Wayne Tedder, a friend of Mr. Watts, hiding in a nearby field with a shotgun in his hand. The gun was the weapon used to shoot out the night-light on the church grounds. The suspect, who owed Mr. Watts some money, was held until the police arrived.

Catching Wayne Tedder red-handed was encouraging. And yet, Daddy's fragile nerves were rattled, pushing him closer to yet another mental breakdown. He wasn't alone. The effect of the bombing unnerved the entire community. Robert Sellers said, "This thing's got to come to a close. Little children are scared to death, running around shaking, and the people are getting tired of this thing. You can't even so much as rest in [Sellerstown]." Eddie Sellers agreed, adding, "You have to leave home to get a nap. It's gettin' so we expect it every night."

The pressure was on.

We weren't the only ones feeling the heat.

Mr. Watts, having initiated four bombings in as many months that summer and fall, knew the law and an organized citizen patrol were watching Sellerstown like hawks. Special Agent Charles Mercer was asking tough questions and pursuing every lead. One misstep and Mr. Watts would be exposed—and he knew it. Needing to do something to divert unwanted attention from himself, Mr. Watts devised a plan. He just needed to call in a favor from one of his minions to carry it out.

On Thanksgiving Day, November 25, 1976, police answered a call for help at the residence of Mr. Watts, who reported that someone had taken several shots at his house. The bullets from a high-powered rifle had penetrated the exterior wall just below his front window. What Mr. Watts failed to report was that he had paid a man to shoot at his home in order to make himself look like a victim, the same way he had mailed himself a threatening letter.

+ + +

Recognizing that entertaining guests in the trailer at Christmastime wasn't an option due to space limitations, my parents decided to move back to the parsonage just after Thanksgiving. I had mixed emotions upon hearing that news. Although I was happy to be home, I had felt safe in the trailer and wanted to feel the same level of comfort in my own bedroom. And yet knowing that Mr. Watts was, once again, pacing outside my window, watching us through his thick, eye-distorting glasses, I found falling asleep a challenge.

I was okay being home during the day, mind you. Mr. Watts never attacked us in broad daylight. But when the sun went down, my fears soared. Getting into bed was next to impossible. How could I close my eyes and fall asleep with the knowledge that Mr. Watts, a man who hated us, just might choose to assault us in the dead of night?

Momma didn't seem to share my anxiety. I watched her display a strength and confidence that prompted me to ask, "Momma, what are we gonna do if there's another bombing? What if I die?"

Stroking my hair, offering me a tender smile, she'd say, "Honey, it's okay. You know why? Because to die is to be together with Jesus where nobody can hurt you."

In my mind I understood her point: If the worst thing happened—namely, that I was to die in my sleep—I'd be okay because I'd be in heaven. But getting my heart to go along with what I knew in my head seemed as impossible as climbing Mount Everest.

Much to my surprise, for several precious weeks after moving home, Mr. Watts left us alone. For a short time, it looked as if we'd be able to enjoy Christmas without a further incident.

Now *that* would have been quite the gift.

On Sunday night, December 12, 1976, a cold rain and thick fog moved in, yet it failed to put a damper on the congregation's attendance. Every seat in the sanctuary was filled as Daddy preached on the topic of fighting the good fight of faith. His text was 1 Timothy 6. Midway into his message, the building shook as Mr. Watts bombarded us with his tenth destructive device.

Ten bombs in two-and-a-half years.

Six targeting our home.

Four aimed at the church.

Daddy could only take so much. For the next two weeks, he was hospitalized for mental distress. Our Christmas was ruined.

Our loved ones begged us to leave. Grandma Welch called Momma weekly, trying to convince her to move away, whether that was home to Bogalusa—or Mobile—or just about anywhere but Sellerstown. Grandma was beside herself, fearing that the attacks would never end. On the other hand, the church yearned for us to stay. My parents, torn between the pleas of the family and the call they felt upon their lives to this community, believed the situation had to get better.

And the devil in pew number seven remained committed to his crusade to drive us from Sellerstown . . . "crawling or walking, dead or alive."

CHAPTER 10

# Black Thursday

The visitor came.

In the spring of 1977, Daddy was home when a sharp knock on the front door echoed through the house. There was nothing unusual about guests stopping by the parsonage unannounced. In a way, our home doubled as his office. People with church or personal business often dropped by for an impromptu meeting. Although Daddy didn't recognize the caller, he greeted the man with a warm handshake and invited him into the den.

By all outward appearances, the man looked as normal as anyone you'd meet on the street, although the look in his eyes had the intensity of a hawk. He wore no mask, nor was he dressed in a white, hooded robe. And while he didn't sport the white cross encircled in red, the symbol of the Ku Klux Klan, the man introduced himself as the personal bodyguard of the Grand Wizard of North Carolina.

As they took their seats, the man explained the reason for his visit. With his commanding knowledge of the facts, he demonstrated that he and the Klan were fully aware of the events unfolding in Sellerstown. The Klan felt that the constant persecution we were suffering was wrong, and furthermore, he said everybody knew who was behind these attacks.

I'm sure Daddy must have felt a degree of inner conflict as he listened. On one hand, the harsh prejudices and practices of the Klan were the polar opposite of the love of Jesus he preached, not to mention the saving love that defined his life. And yet Daddy must have felt some degree of gratefulness that this outsider cared about our situation.

But the man didn't come to just offer sympathy.

He came with a radical offer to help.

Before stating his proposition, the man said, "Mr. Watts is never coming to justice." Evidently, he knew about Mr. Watts's connections within the "good old boy" political system. He must have known that someone as powerful as Mr. Watts could pull whatever strings were necessary to evade a conviction forever. But the Klan, as he was quick to point out, had contacts and manpower. Sitting a few feet from Daddy, the man leaned forward and laid out his proposal.

"We're ready to take him out," he said without a hint of sarcasm. There was nothing in his body language—no wink, no smirk—nothing to indicate the offer was a joke. This man was dead serious. "Nobody has to know," he said, adding, "Just give us permission, and it can all be over once and for all."

The thought that there would be no more bombings, shootings, home invasions, threatening phone calls, midnight stalking, or interruptions in church must have been appealing to Daddy on some level. The idea that he and his family would finally be safe from the resident madman was almost too good to imagine. How different his life would be if Mr. Watts wasn't in the picture! If he just gave the word, the cloud of fear that followed him every waking hour would be gone.

But to have the man "taken out"?

Killed?

I can't say for certain, but I wouldn't be surprised if Daddy, weighing this extreme proposal, pictured in his mind's eye the temptation of Jesus by Satan. While alone, hungry, and vulnerable after a forty-day fast, Jesus was tempted by the devil, who promised Him the world if Jesus would simply bow down and worship him. Just as Jesus resisted the temptation to take a shortcut to glory, Daddy would have no part in killing Mr. Watts.

"I appreciate this," Daddy said after a moment to process his thoughts. "But that's not the way we do things. Yes, we're frustrated. Yes, the process is taking its toll on us and on the community. But we're dependent on God to take care of Mr. Watts for us."

+ + +

Spring gave way to summer without another explosion rocking our world. In fact, Mr. Watts took a break from his string of bombings in 1977. The reasons for his cease-fire are unknown. Perhaps the reason for his restraint was the ever-watchful eye of Special Agent Charles Mercer, who left no stone unturned in his investigation. Or perhaps it was the $10,000 reward offered by Agent Mercer for information linking Mr. Watts to the bombings.

It might have had to do with the fact that Mr. Watts was having difficulty leveraging his wealth to buy off the police. On one occasion, for example, Mr. Watts initiated a ninety-minute casual conversation with Deputy James Coleman and County Police Chief Jesse Barker. Mr. Watts spent most of the time describing how much money he had amassed and wanted these officers to know he was "well off." Without offering a bribe outright, the implication had to have been clear. Evidently, they didn't take the bait.

Their investigation wasn't for sale.

The yearlong suspension of hostilities—at least those involving guns, home invasions, and bombs—was a welcomed relief. However, Mr. Watts still sat in pew number seven each Sunday morning making faces at Daddy. He tried his best to cause a distraction by coughing, sucking his teeth, squirming in his seat, and tapping his watch.

To an outsider, the actions of Mr. Watts during church might have appeared eccentric at worst, the ludicrous yet harmless actions of someone who wasn't right in the head. But to those who knew the man, it was evident that Mr. Watts wasn't a changed man. He still paced at night. He still glared at us with a smoldering disdain that, like hot lava, would inevitably surface.

Somewhere, somehow, he'd strike again.

It was just a matter of time.

Even so, as the months rolled on without an attack, life, at least for me, settled down into a more peaceful, uneventful rhythm. I rode motorcycles with Missy, played in our secret fort in the woods, and occasionally hung out with Billy Wayne. Admittedly, now that I had finished first grade, I discovered Billy Wayne had cooties. He was, after all, a boy, and all boys had that dreaded disease, which is why I stopped trying to marry him. No longer in a hurry to get to the altar, having lost the interest in sealing our "vows" with a kiss, I was open to new ways to pass the time.

One hot, summer afternoon, Daddy was working around the house, and Momma was taking a nap with Daniel. I was bored, which can be dangerous when you are seven years old and the adults are preoccupied. Spying the yellow school bus used to pick up people for church, I got a crazy idea. Don't ask me where the thought came from or why such a notion struck me as okay. It just did.

I decided it would be fun to make mud pies on every seat of that bus. It would be my own giant kitchen on wheels with plenty of room for all the pretend flavors I could cook up. Retrieving the water hose from the side of the house, I got busy creating fresh mud pies on Becky's Bakery Bus. With the care of a pastry chef, I carried the mud to each seat, shaped it into a pie, and then cut it into individual servings with my knife—a stick. As I worked, I decided two pies per seat sounded about right.

You know, one for each passenger.

Just as I was finishing my preparations, Daddy came by to see why I had been so quiet for so long. When he approached, I was standing outside the bus, proud of my accomplishment. He looked at me, the water hose, and the mud on my hands, shirt, and shorts. Then his eyes drifted toward the open door of the bus. Without saying a word, he walked up the stairs and into the bus to find out what I had been up to. I tagged along behind, waiting for his words of praise.

As he walked down the aisle, studying each seat without comment, I began to realize what I *wasn't* hearing. There was no "Wow, Bec, this is great!" or "Your mud pies sure look yummy." Instead, I received the what-in-the-world-have-you-done look followed by a speech explaining why my bakery wasn't such a good idea. He didn't need to raise his voice for me to get the picture that he was displeased with my handiwork.

While I had experienced a string of horrors at the hands of Mr. Watts, I realize now that the thing I feared most in life was the thought that I might do something to cause my father to stop loving me. I think Daddy sensed this. And although I was sent inside to clean up while he took the hose to spray down the interior of the bus, he never gave me the impression that his love for me had been dampened.

I was his little girl, and he still loved me.

For her part, Momma, the practical joker in the family, wasn't too happy to see me coming into her "germ free" house covered in mud. Like a drill sergeant, she marched me down the hall to the bathroom for a good fingernail scrubbing and bath. And yet, like Daddy, I didn't get the sense that she loved me less for making such a mess. I was grateful that neither of my parents held a grudge or chose to shame me for what I had done. Their unconditional love for me outweighed my childish choices.

They even laughed about my amateur cooking later.

The unconditional love my parents displayed toward me was just a reflection of the kind of people they were. Their Christlike love was also the primary reason why they were persistent in forgiving Mr. Watts, even though they had been under fire year after year. Indeed, Daddy and Momma were cherished by the folks in Sellerstown because my parents extended grace and kindness—without judgment or shame—to all with whom they came in contact.

Their commitment to the church remained rock solid, much to the puzzlement and dismay of my grandparents. The weekly disruptions instigated by Mr. Watts in church, along with the ongoing late-night, anonymous phone calls to our home, kept all of us on edge. They viewed Mr. Watts like a hot-spring geyser; his disdain for us bubbled beneath the surface from a deep well of hatred. They feared his rage would eventually reach critical mass and, without warning, explode.

On Monday, March 20, 1978, just days before Easter, Grandma Welch called Momma, begging my parents to leave Sellerstown and return to the safety of their hometown. Grandma, trying to sound optimistic, said Daddy could always start a new church plant or help with an existing, struggling church. She told Momma, "Please get out of there. I can't take it anymore. I'm worried sick. Your daddy and I will pay your moving expenses."

Momma put her foot down. Sellerstown was the only home Daniel, now three, and I had ever known. For the better part of a decade they had grown deep roots in the rich soil of Sellerstown. Momma and Daddy loved their home, their church, and the farming community. Picking up to settle somewhere else wasn't an option. In no uncertain terms she told Grandma Welch, "Mother, I will live and die here. We are not leaving!"

You see, Momma had just told Grandma Welch that she had taken a dear friend, Sue Williams, under her protective wing and wasn't about to abandon someone in need. Grandma viewed this as an unwelcome development and a new danger to our family. Momma saw offering shelter to Sue as a ministry opportunity. Sue, a petite woman with a shy, graceful smile, was one of Momma's closest confidants from church. They had formed a sisterhood over the years; Sue leaned on Momma's shoulder during the breakup of her first marriage, and Sue had been there to support Momma during the threats and assaults on our home. Like an extended member of our family, Sue had vacationed with us on several occasions, including the Cherokee trip when I'd panicked at the staged train robbery.

Their friendship was a gift to each other.

And now, Sue was in dire straits.

Just days before Grandma's call, Sue stopped by our house to see Momma. Sue was desperate. She told Momma that her husband, Harris Williams, a thirty-five-year-old alcoholic given to drunken rages, was physically abusing her again. This time she barely escaped. Momma knew about Harris and his previous trouble with the law. She was well aware of his criminal record, which included a conviction and imprisonment for assaulting Sue.

Whenever Harris would become violent, he was quick to express sorrow that he had hurt Sue. While sorry, he apparently was unwilling or unable to shape up. Even Daddy had reached out to Harris on several occasions in hopes that Harris would be receptive to the life-changing power of Jesus. His words must have fallen on deaf ears.

As Sue poured out her heart to Momma, it was clear that Harris had fallen back into his old pattern of hard drinking and subsequent bad behavior. The last few days living with him had been unbearable—several nights before Sue came to see Momma, Harris had threatened her again.

She, in turn, went to Harris's probation officer on the morning of March 23 and asked him to take out a warrant against her husband. Like tossing gasoline on a fire, her request made matters worse for Sue. When Harris learned she had called the law on him, his rage intensified and he made additional threats. Sue had nowhere to turn—except to Momma. Upon hearing the details of Sue's plight, Momma didn't hesitate to invite Sue to move in with us. She told Sue to bring a few things along with her baby, since Sue had made arrangements with her ex-husband to take care of her other sons. We'd find a way to shelter them for as long as was necessary.

This was no casual suggestion. There was an urgency to Momma's invitation. An insistence. An awareness that Sue was in grave danger, probably more than she fully recognized at the time. Momma said our home would be a temporary refuge until Sue could get things straightened out. I'd say that was ironic, considering how the parsonage had been the focal point of ten recent violent attacks.

Grandma Welch wasn't the only person concerned about our safety. On Wednesday afternoon, March 22, Momma, who had been making some extra cash selling houseware gifts, stopped by Aunt Pat's house to deliver her order. For a few minutes the two lingered on Aunt Pat's front porch to talk. Aware that Sue was now living with us, Aunt Pat said, "You know, Ramona, I'm not sure how safe it is to have Sue in your house with Harris's problems."

Momma acknowledged her concern but said she felt led to help Sue any way she could. After all, Momma lived by the words of Jesus in Matthew 25 when He said, "For I was hungry and you gave me something to eat, I was thirsty and you gave me something to drink, I was a stranger and you invited me in. . . . Whatever you did for one of the least of these brothers of mine, you did for me" (NIV). In Momma's view, supporting Sue in this small way was really an opportunity to serve the Lord.

Maybe it was the caring nudge of Aunt Pat suggesting we'd be safer without Sue living in the parsonage. Perhaps it was the desperate plea from her mother to move to the safety of their home. Whatever the reason, that same evening during the midweek church service, Momma felt compelled to take a public stand against anxiety and fretting over what *might* happen to her and her family in Sellerstown.

With a bright, beaming smile that seemed to chase the shadow of fear from the sanctuary, she read Psalm 91:

> I WILL SAY OF THE LORD, HE IS MY REFUGE AND MY FORTRESS: MY GOD; IN HIM WILL I TRUST. SURELY HE SHALL DELIVER THEE FROM THE SNARE OF THE FOWLER. . . . THOU SHALT NOT BE AFRAID FOR THE TERROR BY NIGHT; NOR FOR THE ARROW THAT FLIETH BY DAY; NOR FOR THE PESTILENCE THAT WALKETH IN DARKNESS; NOR FOR THE DESTRUCTION THAT WASTETH AT NOONDAY. . . . BECAUSE THOU HAST MADE THE LORD, WHICH IS MY REFUGE, EVEN THE MOST HIGH, THY HABITATION; THERE SHALL NO EVIL BEFALL THEE, NEITHER SHALL ANY PLAGUE COME NIGH THY DWELLING.

Before concluding her comments, Momma told the congregation, "I believe God will protect my family. All of us should have faith that God will do *His* perfect will in our lives. Besides, what He allows to happen is out of our hands." With that, she took her seat.

It would be the last time Momma spoke in church.

The events which were about to unfold the following night would change our lives forever.

By all indications, Thursday, March 23, 1978, would be an exciting day. Lunch box in hand, I headed off to school, anticipating the celebration of Easter just around the corner. Being as fond of candy as I was, having an insatiable sweet tooth, I couldn't wait for the Easter egg hunts to begin. Toss in plates brimming with homemade goodies and the chance to dye our eggs with colorful splashes of creativity, and I was eager for Easter to arrive.

As I left home, I knew Momma would be busy during the day preparing the special music for church, and Daddy would linger at his desk perfecting his Easter Sunday sermon. When I returned home, Momma had a fresh-baked pie cooling on the kitchen counter; the aroma of dinner simmering on the stovetop filled the air. About five o'clock, we took our places around the dinner table.

Sue and her baby joined us for supper in what was to be the unofficial beginning of our Easter celebration. Although Sue was on edge because of the threats from her husband, she did her best to enter into the joy of the occasion.

Daddy, seated at the head of the table, glanced at Momma and shared a smile that seemed to say, "Thanks, honey, for all of your hard work." Daddy was poised to give thanks for the meal as Momma, standing beside her chair, finished filling my Charlie Brown glass with iced tea. In order to make room on the table, I took the tea pitcher and placed it on the counter by the sink.

I returned to my seat, but before I could sit down, I heard someone yank the screen door open by the carport. It wasn't surprising when guests arrived unannounced since we lived with an open-door policy. Friends often stopped by for a visit—even during mealtimes. Momma and I exchanged a quick look, expectant, wondering who was coming into the house.

I immediately recognized the visitor.

Harris Williams.

He had caught us completely off guard while we were relaxed and in the middle of family time. At age seven, I had had my share of trauma. Almost out of instinct, the caution in my heart caused it to collide with my chest. I cannot say why. Something about his sudden appearance didn't feel right. He appeared tired, yet focused, a man on a mission. In the silence, the room felt as if a force for evil had violated its four walls.

Sue, with her baby sitting on her lap, sat closest to the intruder. A look of shock and panic crossed her face. Even though he hadn't said a word, Sue knew Harris's demeanor was not a humble one. He hadn't stopped by to mend fences with her. He wasn't there to seek forgiveness for the most recent beating.

Daddy, still seated, spoke first.

"How are you doing, Harris?"

His neck stiffened, his jaws clenched.

"Not too damn good."

Daddy slid his chair back and stood up, but he didn't approach the man, at least not at first. The last thing Daddy wanted was to provoke a confrontation. About twelve feet separated the men. "If you are going to curse in this house," Daddy said with a surprising calmness, "you can leave our home right now."

Harris was in no mood to be crossed.

He was quick to fire back.

Literally.

With the focused determination of a killing machine, Harris reached for a .38-caliber pistol tucked in his waistband, concealed underneath his shirt. Pulling out the deadly weapon, Harris took aim and shot my daddy in the right shoulder. I watched in helpless disbelief as the hot flash of light leaped from the gun. The deafening blast mixed with our screams. My ears burned as if touched by a hot poker. Although not the target, Sue started screaming at Harris, begging him to stop.

I stared at my wounded daddy in complete shock. This couldn't be happening. Not here. Not now. But it was. The stain of fresh blood splotched its way across the front of his white dress shirt. Fast. Too fast. He was losing a lot of blood. The warmth behind his eyes seemed to drain, replaced by a mixture of bewilderment and pain. I knew what I needed to do. I was taught that whenever shots were fired, I was to seek cover. Yet I froze, unwilling or unable to act. Fear crawled over me like a swarm of fire ants.

Escape was out of the question. Harris, armed with three guns and eighty-three rounds of ammunition, stood between us and the door to safety. And while Daddy's hunting rifle hung on the wall behind the attacker, there was no way to reach it.

Daddy, unarmed, turned and took three steps *toward* the assailant as if driven to defend his family any way he could. Having played football years ago, maybe Daddy thought he could tackle and disarm the assailant if he could just get into position. Seeing the flash of determination in Daddy's eyes, Harris yelled, "I told you to back off!" That's when the gun thundered again, spewing a host of hellish yellow sparks from the black steel barrel.

The second shot shattered Daddy's left hip, knocking him to the floor. With Daddy's six-foot-three frame sprawled on the ground like a lifeless giant, Harris turned and pointed the weapon toward Momma. Standing by the kitchen table and in front of the washing machine, she was unarmed; she held no knife, no gun, not even a chair to throw in her defense.

She cried out, "Jesus! Jesus!"

The gunman stood seven feet from the woman who had given me life, who, for almost eight years, had clothed me, fed me, and nurtured me. The one who filled my life with laughter, love, and lessons on forgiving others just as we had been forgiven by Jesus. None of that history mattered to this man. Without hesitation, with a cold indifference to her precious life as our mother, he fired a single bullet to her chest.

The lead projectile clipped Momma's heart. She staggered backward, clutching at her wound. The moment the bullet pierced her heart, my heart shattered too. With the sound of the gunfire still echoing in the room and the pungent sulfur stinging the air, Momma managed to turn and stumble out of the kitchen while Sue, having jumped out of her chair, attempted to defuse her husband's attack.

Momma's unsteady footsteps receded down the hallway. As I would soon discover, she wasn't attempting to get away. In a thousand years she would never abandon her family. Rather, at the risk of taking a shot in the back, Momma was driven to get to her bedroom to call for help. The phone, our only lifeline, rested on her nightstand.

Within seconds of the shot, our training kicked in.

My brother and I, frantic and numb with disbelief, dropped to the floor, taking refuge under the kitchen table, not that the tablecloth would hide us for long. It was our only option. With streams of searing tears free-falling from my eyes, I choked back a wave of sobs. I wanted to be a brave girl. And yet, stealing a look at my daddy through the chair legs, I knew there was nothing I could do for my parents.

At least maybe I could protect my brother.

That's when it dawned on me that he wasn't there.

+ + +

The house was quiet.

The screaming had been replaced by an eerie silence. After shooting Daddy and Momma, Harris marched Sue and their baby down the hall and held them hostage in my bedroom. About the only thing I could hear was the heaving of my heart within my chest and my labored breathing as I struggled to fill my lungs. Huddled on a chair beneath the table, I shivered with fear. Where was Danny? Somewhere during the commotion he had wandered off. How did I miss that?

Was he in the bedroom with Harris?

Was he, too, a hostage?

My head hurt with the implication. And what about my momma? Was she alive? Why hadn't she come back? Maybe she fell unconscious. I saw how Daddy was struggling to stay alert. To be sure, she needed help, but how? Daddy couldn't move. I was too terrified to abandon my hiding place. My tears formed a puddle on the floor beneath me. Looking at the bloodstains on Daddy's shirt, I managed to ask a question just above a whisper.

"Daddy, are you going to leave us again and go into the hospital?"

With his back resting against the lower kitchen cabinets, arms hanging useless at his side, he said, "Yes, but it will only be for a little while, sweetheart."

Daddy's kind, reassuring voice had always been able to comfort me. I wanted to believe he would be okay, but he looked bad. I wanted to think help would arrive to save us before it was too late. But how? It was doubtful that anyone would have heard the shots—other than maybe Mr. Watts across the street. He, of course, would be the last guy on earth to come to our aid.

This was what he wanted.

He spent years trying to drive us away.

Why would he lend a hand now?

I was about to ask Daddy another question when I heard movement in the hallway. At the risk of drawing attention to myself, anxious to learn whether or not it might be my brother, I inched my head out from under the table. A flood of relief and panic hit me at the same time: Daniel stood there looking as if he were lost in his own home, which was understandable, given the hellish ordeal he had just witnessed as a three-year-old. He had found his way back to the kitchen. I was relieved that he wasn't a hostage, yet afraid he might be spotted if he remained out in the open.

With a wave of my hand, I whispered, "Danny, you've got to get under the table with me." I placed a finger to my closed lips, signaling for him to remain perfectly quiet. Without hesitation, he followed me under the table and then curled up on the cold linoleum floor. He appeared dazed; his eyelids were wide-open as if held in place with toothpicks.

"Where did you go?"

A hushed moment passed between us. I could almost hear the second hand on the clock above the sink ticking off the seconds. Poor little man, he had no idea what was happening or why. Which is not to say I had a handle on things. I didn't. Far from it. Nothing made sense. How could it? One minute we were having dinner; the next minute both of my parents were clinging to life.

Daniel blinked and then said, "I saw Mommy." Having spoken the words, he closed his eyes and fell asleep.

"How's Daniel?" Daddy asked, keeping his voice low. Evidently he had noticed Danny's return to the kitchen yet couldn't see his son's face.

"He's asleep."

"Good. I was praying he would be."

With a wince that distorted his face into a knot, Daddy tried to shift his legs on the floor. I'd never seen him so fragile, helpless, and unable to spring into action and take charge. The man who hung the moon in my world, who lit the stars with his smile, now struggled for each breath. I wanted to avert my eyes. Would I watch him take his last breath? If so, then what? In the past, whenever we were attacked, I depended on him to tell me what to do next. I needed him to do the same now . . . if only he could hold on.

"Are you in pain, Daddy?"

"No. I'm fine, sweetheart."

I wasn't sure if he was just saying that to make me feel better or if he was numbed by the shock. Neither of us spoke for what seemed like an eternity as he drifted in and out of consciousness. The house remained silent. We were on one side of the house while Momma, Sue, and her baby were on the other end with Harris. When Daddy finally regained a moment of clarity, he asked me to do the impossible.

"Bec?"

"I'm here, Daddy."

"I need you to check on Momma."

"Me?"

"I can't move, honey. You've got to be brave. You've got to go down the hall and see if she's okay."

"But—"

"Can you do that for me?"

I didn't have the capacity to comprehend this jarring shift in responsibilities any more than I could explain why anyone would barge into our house with deadly intent that afternoon. Such knowledge was uncharted territory for my young mind, as foreign and unfamiliar as the dark side of the moon. What choice did I have? I didn't want to cause my daddy more pain with my hesitation. On the other hand, I wasn't keen on the idea of being anywhere near the gunman. Surely he could appreciate that fact. And yet I was the only option he had.

As I turned to leave, Daddy's husky, six-foot-three frame remained crumpled on the kitchen floor. I had never seen him so vulnerable. Make no mistake, Daddy was not a wimp. He was a man's man. From the time he was a boy, he'd excelled at fishing and hunting. I had tasted the venison he'd brought home. When it came to construction, be it painting, building, or remodeling, his hands could manipulate just about any tool with the artistry of an Old World craftsman. Having excelled in football in high school and, later in life, having served in the Navy, Daddy knew how to handle himself in any situation.

Except for this one.

Reluctant to leave my covering, I made slow, deliberate movements away from the kitchen. I willed myself to place one foot in front of the other. My shoeless feet, treading on the thin, brown tweed carpet in the hallway, made no sound, for which I was thankful. The narrow hall, about thirty feet in length, seemed like a dark cavern waiting to swallow me whole. The overhead light remained off, and I had no plans of turning it on for fear that it would betray my presence.

I paused for a long second to listen.

At the far end of the darkened hallway, on the right, my parents' bedroom door stood ajar. A glow from the setting sun tumbled through the curtains flanking the bedroom window. Like a lighthouse with a dirty lens, the meager illumination led me as I started toward Momma. Directly across the hall from my parents' room, I could see that my bedroom door remained shut, presumably with Harris and the hostages locked inside. It was also entirely possible he was lurking in the hall bathroom, Daniel's room, or the living room—all of which had doors leading off the hall.

Although I heard no sound, I assumed the gunman was in my bedroom. A thin shaft of light escaping beneath the door suggested such was the case. If so, would Harris yank open that door as he had done in the kitchen minutes before, see me standing there, and then finish what he had started? If the grown-ups in my life didn't stand a fighting chance against him, I was under no illusion that somehow things would be different for me.

Everything inside of me beckoned me to turn back.

And yet I had to press on. I had to get to Momma.

I passed Daniel's room and, with a turn of my head, didn't see anything out of place. Pushing onward, I drew up parallel to the hall bathroom on my right. The space was empty—although the shower curtain was drawn and might have concealed someone hiding. I took several tentative steps forward, stopped, leaned my head around the corner of the opening to the living room on the left. Nothing.

Ten steps farther and I reached the end of the hall. My face flushed with renewed anxiety. I'd have to turn my back to my bedroom to enter my parents' room. That would give Harris a clear advantage. He could take me out before I knew what was happening.

The look on Daddy's face, which had pleaded for answers, pushed me beyond my fears long enough to do what had to be done. At my parents' bedroom doorway, I paused once again. This was the room where I had sought shelter whenever Mr. Watts bombed our home, a place of refuge where I had spent many frightful nights in the safety and comforting arms of my parents. Now it was the last place I wanted to be.

The room blinked into focus.

The scene didn't make sense at first.

My mother's body was prone on the floor, halfway under the bed, legs protruding. I stepped closer. That's when I heard a busy signal from the phone. Momma, after grabbing the receiver, had crawled under the bed to call for help. As I got down on my knees beside her, I saw Momma's blood staining the floral bedspread. I extended my hand and, holding my breath, touched her leg. Was she still breathing? Would she be all right? I had no idea how severely she had been wounded.

"Mommy? . . ."

No response. Had she heard me? I dared not raise my voice above a whisper. I leaned closer for another try.

"Momma?"

When she didn't answer and didn't move, I wasn't sure what that meant. Was she unconscious? Was she in shock? Was she . . . dead? Whatever the case, there was really nothing more I could do. I didn't have the physical strength to pull her out from under the bed. And I couldn't call the law since Momma had the receiver with her somewhere under the bed.

I tiptoed back down the hall and resumed my position under the table in the kitchen. Daniel was still asleep. A weak, expectant look eased across Daddy's face.

"How's Momma?"

"I called her name, Daddy . . ."

I choked out the rest of the message, ". . . but she wouldn't answer me."

Daddy's eyes closed.

His chest heaved as his head fell back against the cabinet with a thud. Tears rolled down his face and mixed with the blood on his pants. The anguish in his reddened eyes sprang from an inner wound so deep, so profound, Daddy looked as if his heart might burst. The news about Momma was too much to bear—the musical girl with the giant pink curlers piled on top of her head, the woman who had captivated his soul from the moment they met, now lay unresponsive.

He had been powerless to protect her.

He was powerless to save her.

He must have felt as if he had failed her. Like a spike through his heart, that reality hurt more than the pain inflicted by his two bleeding gunshot wounds.

I remained quiet while he composed himself. He finally spoke.

"Becky—"

"Daddy?"

"I need you to get help."

"Me?"

I'm sure Daddy could see the fear in my eyes. I was just a kid in the second grade. I was no match for the madman barricaded within our house. "But how?"

"You've got to be a big girl . . . you've got to run as fast as you can to Aunt Pat's house . . . tell her to call the law."

"But—"

"I'm counting on you, sweetheart. . . . I know you can do it. Please—hurry." He offered me a faint, reassuring smile and then drifted out of consciousness.

That's when I slipped out the side door.

That's when *I ran.*

CHAPTER 11

# Unanswered Prayers

I had to run until I could run no more.

Although I wanted to charge down Sellerstown Road to Aunt Pat's house, the harder I ran, the slower I seemed to travel. The thought that my little sanctuary of dolls, toys, and keepsakes was now the temporary living quarters of a man bent on death overwhelmed me. With a turn of my head, I studied my bedroom window, looking for any signs of movement.

Could the armed man see me running for help?

If so, he had a clear shot at me from that window. I knew the damage this monster was capable of inflicting. I had witnessed his destructive handiwork minutes before. If he had watched me escape, I knew beyond a shadow of a doubt he both *could* and *would* take me down in an instant. My steps slowed at the thought. My legs felt as if they were slogging their way through an invisible muck, hindering my forward progress.

Trapped in a sluggish nightmare, longing to reach the safety of Aunt Pat's, I risked detection and pressed on as best I could. Our homes were separated by a freshly planted cornfield. The rows of tilled soil stretched about the length of a football field. Running that distance with the burden I was carrying felt as if I were traveling to the other side of the world with more baggage than I could handle.

The instant my toes set foot on the edge of her property, I cried out.

"Aunt Pat! Aunt *Paaaat*!"

I continued to yell her name as I charged down the driveway toward her home, feeling a mixture of relief and panic; I was glad to be out of harm's way yet alarmed at the thought that my family was still under siege.

The conflicting emotions tore at my heart until I thought it would tear in half. I wanted to be safe, but I wanted the same thing for Daddy, Mommy, and my little brother. I stopped short of the door, hands on my knees, gasping for breath like a runner at the end of a race—except there wasn't a prize or people cheering, just a struggle to form the words I needed to say.

Aunt Pat scrambled out the side door.

"What's wrong, Becky?"

Winded, gulping air by the bucket, I managed to get out the words, "Aunt Pat! Call the law! My daddy has been shot. . . . Momma has too!"

"Lord have mercy!" Her eyes jumped wide open, as large as saucers, as the words registered.

"Becky, are you sure?"

"Yes, ma'am, he's been shot twice . . . in the shoulder and leg . . . by Harris Williams. You've got to call the law!"

Aunt Pat turned and scampered inside. Snatching up the phone with trembling fingers, she called our house as quickly as she could spin the lazy dial on her rotary phone.

Busy.

She tried again.

Still busy.

Swallowing air as if I had just completed a marathon, my lungs burned, my legs stung, and my eyes flooded. Aunt Pat's daughter Missy, my best friend though older than me by a number of years, raced to my side. She had been playing in the yard and heard my cries for help. Being a tomboy, and therefore, unafraid of most anything, Missy said we had to do something—*anything*—to help my family.

Drawing upon her strength, driven by a deep desire to know that my family was going to be okay, I agreed. I started to head back to the scene of the crime with Missy at my side. We didn't get farther than the ditch just before the cornfield. Aunt Pat burst through the side door. With a flurry of frantic hand motions, she beckoned us to return, yelling, "Come back! Come back!"

We hustled back across the yard and fell in line behind Aunt Pat as she dashed across the street to her mother-in-law's house. Once inside, while blurting out the details of what had transpired, Aunt Pat called the police. Help was on the way. At least that much was good news. With the law notified, we returned to Aunt Pat's house to begin the waiting.

Though my feet were at rest for the time being, my mind knew no such peace. It churned with questions. Would Daddy and Momma be okay? They had to be okay, didn't they? How fast could the ambulance get there, anyway? How serious were their wounds? And what was that awful Harris doing in my bedroom with the hostages? What further damage did he have planned? What if the law didn't arrive fast enough in our sleepy corner of the country to catch him and stop whatever else bad he wanted to do?

Oh, how I wished I knew how Daddy and Momma were doing.

It would take hours to get answers.

+ + +

I trembled.

Darkness settled over Sellerstown in long shadows as the fast-approaching evening wrapped the sky in a blanket suitable for the night. Having run to Aunt Pat's seeking help for my parents, still shaking from the horror of what had transpired moments before, I shivered as if chilled by the night air, although sweat soaked through my shirt. I had an unquenchable thirst to know if Daddy and Momma would be okay and feared for the safety of my brother, too.

What if Danny woke up and wandered down the hall in search of me? What if Harris heard him walking around and decided to take my brother hostage too? I had to do *something*, but what? I toyed with the thought of trying to sneak back to our house again.

Then again, what could I do? I was no match for Harris and had no illusion of confronting him. For all I knew he had already finished what he had started. If so, there was no point putting myself in his sights. I decided to stay put.

Yet pacing between rooms at Aunt Pat's served no purpose either. I was distressed by the fact that my family was trapped in that house and I had no choice but to stay put. They were my world and everything I loved . . . if only there were *something* I could do for them.

I peered out the window.

Another wail from an approaching police cruiser signaled more help was on the way; its flashing lights splashed the exterior of our home in an eerie array of blue and bloodred hues, mesmerizing me. The ambulance parked in our driveway, rear doors open, added to the light show with strobelike bursts of colored light. The press, like ants at a picnic, crawled over our lawn, looking for juicy morsels to feed the masses.

Squinting, I scanned the growing crowd of concerned neighbors and onlookers. Was Mr. Watts somewhere in that group? Would he dare show his face on this of all days? Or was he, like a vulture, enjoying a bird's-eye view of the chaos from his picture window? For the better part of five years he had hoped and worked for a moment like this.

In a way I'm glad I didn't learn until later that Mr. Watts was, in fact, standing with some of his hoodlums in the middle of the street alongside our house. Fueled by the raw emotions surging through my body like bolts of lightning, had I seen Mr. Watts that night, ten men would have had to restrain me. No doubt I would have darted across the yard and pounded my little fists of rage against his chest. I would have yelled until my lungs burned, "Why us? Why couldn't you just leave our family alone? What did we ever do to hurt you? Who gave you the right to pick on us?"

The television cackling away in the corner of Aunt Pat's living room caught my attention. In a surreal, mind-numbing moment, I was drawn to the screen. I found myself watching and listening as the news crews, just down the street from where I was standing, began broadcasting their live coverage of the hostage situation at *my* house. I moved closer toward the television, holding on to hope for some good news. I clung so tightly to the hope—Momma and Daddy were okay—that I had to remember to breathe.

The reporter said the police were talking to Harris.

The reporter said Harris wasn't budging.

The reporter said Daddy was in the ambulance.

When the reporter announced that a woman had been shot and

killed, my heart rocketed to the bottom of my throat. I felt the walls around me close in. Which woman? Momma—or Sue? Something in my heart wanted to believe that even though Momma had not answered me earlier, she would survive her wounds if she received help in time. I desperately wanted my mother to be alive. I needed her to be alive. I didn't know how I could go on if she was the one who was dead.

At the same time I felt conflicted, torn within as if my heart had been pulled in two directions. I sure didn't want Sue to be dead. If Harris had shot Sue during his standoff with the police, that would mean her boys would be without a mother. While I would have been thrilled to know Momma was alive, I didn't want any of us to be without a mother. It would be several torturous hours before I'd have an answer.

At 6:09 p.m., as I would later learn, Lieutenant Alfred Hayes of the Columbus County Police arrived at the parsonage with his partner, Lieutenant Herman Price. Lieutenant Hayes maneuvered his patrol car into the driveway and then pulled onto the side yard to the right of the house where two armed men, E. J. and Billy Sellers, stood beneath the pine trees. The officers stepped out of the car, hands on their weapons, and approached with caution.

After a quick round of questioning, Lieutenant Hayes learned these vigilantes were not a part of the attack. Having heard about the assault on their pastor through the grapevine, these church members had arrived faster than the law and were discussing what they might do to rescue my parents. Lieutenant Hayes thanked them for their efforts but sent them out of harm's way.

When Lieutenant Hayes knocked on the carport door, Daddy

managed to invite him inside, his voice strained as he spoke. The officer discovered my brother still sleeping under the table and Daddy, his shirt covered in blood, sitting on the floor exactly where I had left him. He approached my daddy.

"How badly are you hurt?"

Giving no thought about himself, Daddy said, "Please, check on my wife. She's in the back of the house . . . she needs your help more than me."

"Yes sir, but—"

"Don't worry about me. Just be careful," Daddy said. "Harris is back there, too. He's got a gun . . . and his wife and son are with him."

Lieutenant Hayes knew he had to act fast. He had an injured man on the floor, a vulnerable child who might get hurt should there be a confrontation with the shooter, a hostage situation, and an injured woman who might or might not still be alive. Time was not on his side. If there was a fighting chance to save my mother, he knew he had to get to her quickly. And yet with a gunman at large, acting rashly could be deadly.

The door to the kitchen opened again, and Lieutenant Price entered. Lieutenant Hayes instructed him to take Danny out of the house while he moved toward the hallway. With my brother now safe, Lieutenant Hayes knew the next order of business was to address the hostage situation. Taking up a position at the opening to the hallway, he called out.

"Harris?"

"Yes?" He spoke through the closed bedroom door.

"Harris, come on out and let me talk to you."

I'm sure Harris's mind was scrambling to sort out his options. Should he try to escape before the house was crawling with police? If so, how? And where would he go? When Harris shot my parents, he had crossed a line. At some point in time, he'd eventually face justice.

If he didn't attempt to escape, how long could he remain barricaded in my bedroom? When he finally spoke, he made a not-so-veiled threat of more tragedy.

"Back off! There's two more lives at stake in here."

Lieutenant Hayes tried to defuse the situation. "Just come on out, Harris, and let's talk about it."

Pressure. Too much pressure. The reality of what Harris had done was sinking in as he talked things out with Sue. There was no way to take back the bullets and undo the nightmare. Looking at his wife and infant son, surrounded by my dolls and toys, Harris stalled for more room to think.

"No. Don't rush me," Harris said. "Give me a little more time."

Lieutenant Hayes advanced down the hall, taking up a safe position in the doorway leading to the living room. He remained out of range in the event Harris opened fire down the hallway. He called out again.

"Harris?"

"Yes?"

"Is everybody with you okay?"

"Yes . . . but . . ."

"But what?"

"Check on Mrs. Nichols—the preacher's wife."

"Where is she, Harris?"

"She is in the bedroom across from this bedroom." Harris must have seen Momma on the floor in her room after he walked down the hallway to lock himself and the hostages in my bedroom.

"Listen, Harris. Just come on out, okay?"

"No, I'm not coming out just yet." A pause. "Please go and check on her and see if she needs some help."

Whether it was out of real concern for my mother or a ploy to get the lawman in his sights, Lieutenant Hayes didn't know. He wasn't about to take chances, at least not yet.

"Harris, come on out. Throw your gun out and come on out. I'm not going back there."

"I won't hurt you if you don't try to come in this room," Harris said.

A long moment passed between them. Lieutenant Hayes turned and saw more backup entering our home. Lieutenant Dudley and Officers Sanford Hardee and Wayne Piver arrived to provide backup within the house. Outside, several dozen law enforcement personnel took up positions around the parsonage to secure all exit points.

When Lieutenant Hayes didn't immediately respond to him, Harris said, "Don't come to this room. Go to the other room."

Now that the lieutenant had protective covering by fellow officers, he ventured into the hall and advanced to my parents' bedroom. When Lieutenant Hayes turned on the light, he found Momma lying facedown, her head and shoulders still wedged under the bed in the same position as when I had last seen her; the telephone handset remained underneath her chest. He observed a splotch of blood on the back of her dress, and since Momma was unresponsive, he checked her vital signs.

He had arrived too late.

The police turned up the heat.

With no chance of helping Momma, my brother safely ushered away, and Daddy in transit to the hospital, one of the officers cranked the thermostat governing the furnace as high as it would go. If Harris wouldn't come out on his own, they hoped to sweat him out. For the better part of three hours, Harris remained fortified in my bedroom with the curtains drawn. Throughout the standoff, Harris told the police he would come out but then failed to comply with their requests to surrender.

Ten times . . . twenty times . . . almost thirty times Harris repeated his intention of coming out peacefully. Several hours into the ordeal, at eight o'clock, his lawyer arrived and attempted to convince Harris to give himself up. As nine o'clock approached, Lieutenant Hayes tried again.

"Harris?"

"What?"

"Come on out, Harris. It's over."

"Don't come near this room! I told you I'll come out when I'm ready."

"We have no intention of making a move on you."

"I mean it. Don't make me do any more than I've already done!"

There was that threat of more harm again. Lieutenant Hayes tried to calm him down.

"We're not here to hurt you, Harris."

"Then why are there so many police?" Evidently, Harris pulled back the drapes long enough to observe the swarm of police activity in the front and side yards from my bedroom windows.

"All we want to do is to prevent any further trouble, Harris. We have no intention of leaving, and like I said, I promise we have no intention of making a move on you."

Silence.

"Harris, we are prepared to stay as long as it takes. We've sealed off all roads within a one-mile radius."

Drenched in sweat, parched from the sweltering heat, in need of fresh air, Harris decided he had had enough.

"Okay . . . I'm coming out."

"Listen carefully, Harris. I want you to crack open the door and push out your guns."

A minute passed. And then another.

Four minutes later, the door creaked open. One by one, Harris slid his guns down the hall. It was over. Lieutenant Hayes, flanked by three other officers, placed Harris under arrest, handcuffed him, searched and emptied his pockets, and then took Harris into custody. Although Sue was sobbing, she and her baby were safe.

For that, I'm eternally grateful.

+ + +

Momma was gone.

I first heard the news from the TV. And while Aunt Pat confirmed it, I didn't believe what I was hearing. The edges of my ears burned as if touched by hot coals. Wanting to know for myself that they weren't mistaken, frustrated that nobody was giving me any details, I snuck out the back door of Aunt Pat's home with Missy at my side. Once outside, barefooted, heart hammering within my chest, we broke into a hard run through the cornfield separating our homes to avoid being caught.

I just had to see Momma.

It would have been difficult to make our way had it not been for the swirling lights on the rescue vehicles. Beacons of red and blue lit our path. We jumped the ditch by the road, crossed the street, and continued our run behind my house. In the near darkness, we slowed to a fast walk and then rounded the corner to the side yard leading to our carport. My lungs blazed within, matched by the burning in my legs that felt as if they were about to buckle beneath me.

We walked the last few yards and stopped at the edge of the carport a few feet from the ambulance. The screen door to the kitchen was open. We arrived at the precise moment three rescue-squad members were backing out, slow and steady, carrying a body on a stretcher covered in a white sheet. As they navigated the steps, the reality hit me with the force of a tornado. The report was true. One woman had been shot and killed.

Yes, Momma was really gone.

There was nothing I could do to help her now.

+ + +

The street cleared.

With the shooter safely behind bars and the crime scene secured, the sea of reporters and police personnel flooding into the community hours before now receded into the night almost as quickly as it had arrived. A disquieting stillness settled on Sellerstown Road. I felt lost, helpless, and disoriented.

As a seven-year-old child, I wasn't fully sure what death meant. Momma was no longer in my life, but where had she gone? Aunt Pat hugged me and assured me that Momma was in heaven, but I wasn't sure why God needed her more than we did. My uncertainty was complicated by the fact that I had no idea when I'd be able to see my daddy again and wondered whether he, too, would be leaving for heaven soon.

That dreadful, traumatic night, Aunt Pat tucked me into a bed at her house. While I was thankful for her love and care, the fact that my mother wasn't by my bedside only served to drive home the point that she was gone. As I fell asleep, I hoped the events of the day were just a bad dream. I wanted to believe that when I awoke the next morning, we'd be together again as one big, happy family.

When the sun filled the sky, my hopes for a brighter day faded. Momma was gone. Sitting at Aunt Pat's breakfast table with Danny, I felt paralyzed. I wanted to be brave, to smile, to act as if everything were normal. The best I could do was to go through the motions of eating. Anxiety stabbed at my heart until there was nothing left to feel.

Momma was gone.

+ + +

The phone rang.

Hands covered in flour, Aunt Dot placed the rolling pin to the side and then bustled across the kitchen to answer the phone. Another ring. Although not a clean freak like Momma, she wiped her hands on her apron, careful to avoid dirtying the receiver. She had been busy baking Easter pies with Grandma Nichols, Daddy's mom, when the call came.

"Happy Easter!" she said, although Easter was still a few days away. Aunt Dot cradled the phone against her shoulder as she worked. Her kitchen was filled with the delightful aroma of baked goodies.

"Is this Dot?"

"Yes—" The way the caller had said her name, she sensed something was amiss.

"It's James Tyree."

While not normally a man of few words, this time James, the head elder of the church, got directly to the point. There was no way to sugarcoat the reality of what had transpired.

"There's been a shooting . . . at the parsonage."

A jolt of lightning rattled my aunt's heart. Her mind filled with questions. Shooting? Who was shot? Robert? Ramona? One of the kids? When? Why? Was it a hunting accident, or was Mr. Watts somehow involved? She knew things had quieted down in Sellerstown. While her brother still struggled with emotional distress, by all appearances the threat of physical harm had ended a year ago.

Now this.

As if reading her mind, James said, "I'm sorry; Ramona didn't make it."

Words failed her. A cold numbness chilled her to the bone. Ramona? Dead? Impossible. The room seemed to spin. She reached for the kitchen counter to steady herself.

"Brother Nichols was shot, too."

She heard the words, but they almost didn't register. Robert? Like being punched in the gut, she felt the wind knocked out of her. James added, "He doesn't know yet that Ramona is dead. You and Martha gotta get up here."

Grandma Nichols studied Aunt Dot's face during the phone call. As she watched Aunt Dot's cheerful expression suddenly turn dark as if a black cloud had moved through the room, Grandma kept asking, "What is it? What's happened?" Aunt Dot was too unnerved to speak. She handed the phone to her mother. Grandma Nichols listened, speechless, as James repeated the horrifying news.

Her son had been shot. Twice.

He was in intensive care.

It was too early to know if he'd make it.

Her daughter-in-law was dead.

The report was too much to bear. Grandma Nichols was overwhelmed with grief. When she saw her mother was too hysterical and emotionally drained to move, Aunt Dot peeled the phone from her hands and finished the conversation with James.

Aunt Dot and Aunt Martha, Daddy's sisters, took the first available flight. James Tyree picked them up at the airport and, as they raced to the hospital, filled them in on the details—at least the parts that were known so far. Upon arrival, they found the front entrance to the facility a literal sea of humanity. Well-wishers from the surrounding area converged upon the parking lot, hoping to get inside for an opportunity to see Daddy. The press did too. Dodging cameras and microphones and reporters looking for a scoop inside the lobby, they made their way to the chaplain, who, in turn, briefed them on Daddy's condition.

Surgery was needed.

His condition was critical.

He had lost a lot of blood.

His doctors didn't believe Daddy was strong enough to hear the news that his wife was dead. Aunt Dot and Aunt Martha would be permitted to enter his room on the condition that they didn't upset him with the horrible news.

They were ushered into the intensive-care unit, where they found Daddy resting. His large frame filled the bed. Seeing him lying still, his face as pale as the hospital sheets, was almost too much for them to handle. As kids, he had always been there to protect them; now they had to be there for him.

Aunt Dot approached her brother, fighting back a surge of emotions. Sensing someone was present, Daddy opened his eyelids to half-mast, as if still he lacked the strength to open them fully. Rolling his head to one side, it took a moment for him to recognize his sisters.

"I'm sorry you have to keep coming here for me."

Aunt Dot moved close to his bedside. Slipping her hand into his, she applied a soft, tender squeeze. As brother and sister, they were cut out of the same parental cloth. She'd do anything for her sibling. "It's no trouble. We want to be here, Buddy. Mom and Daddy are coming up too."

A faint smile appeared, then faded as quickly as it had surfaced, pulled down from the surface of his face by an unseen undertow of pain. "How are the kids?"

"They're fine, Buddy," she said, offering another reassuring squeeze of her brother's hand.

"Where are they? You sure they're all right?"

"They're with Pat. Everything is okay."

That was a bit of a stretch. How could everything be okay ever again? Aunt Dot knew we had just witnessed the murder of our mother. She knew we were shaken to the core of our beings, stung with disbelief. And yet she knew she had to appear strong.

"What about Ramona?" His forehead wrinkled into a knot, as if bracing for bad news. He searched her face, clinging to the frayed strands of hope. When she didn't answer immediately, he asked more directly, "How is she?"

That was a tough one. It was the question Aunt Dot didn't want to answer. At least not now, not when he was about to undergo surgery. Fighting back a sudden surge of emotion that threatened to betray the truth, Aunt Dot said, "Buddy, we came straight to your room." While technically accurate, she had sidestepped the grave reality.

"After we leave here," she added, "we're going to check on Ramona, okay?"

Like a dark cloud, a worried look crossed his face. The muted chorus of equipment monitoring his condition, humming and occasionally beeping in the corner, was the only sound breaking the near silence between them.

"Buddy, just relax," she said. "I'll check on Ramona."

"You come right back and let me know—" he said, gripping her hand with a sudden surge of strength. She managed to smile, although she really wanted to cry. Aunt Dot chose her words carefully.

"We're putting you . . . and her . . . in God's hands."

On Saturday, two days after the shooting, Daddy was wheeled into surgery. Hours later his surgeon informed us that the operation had been a success. Daddy would need three weeks in the hospital to recover. After that, he would be on crutches for several months. In spite of the positive prognosis, the metal pin used to repair his hip would cause Daddy to limp when he walked—a permanent reminder of this traumatic chapter of his life.

After Daddy pulled through the surgery, his doctors, the chaplain, and family members gathered around Daddy to inform him that his bride didn't make it . . . his best friend and soul mate had gone to be with the Lord. Now Daddy would have to continue his journey in this life without the woman he cherished.

A blank stare settled on his face as the reality sank in. His hollow eyes betrayed the fact that his mind was racing back to happier times—like the evening they met in Bogalusa . . . their first date in the coffee shop . . . the day they stood proudly at the altar to exchange vows just weeks after meeting . . . the children they begged God for when they couldn't conceive . . . the souls they ministered to across the country. He had lost the companion who had stood by him through the blackest nights. She had been his faithful partner in ministry—he in the pulpit and she at the organ supplying the sound track of praise for the service.

They were such a great team.

While a twenty-inch scar marked the location of the incision, there was no outward sign of the scar left on his broken heart upon hearing the news that the love of his life was gone. Stricken with a grief so profound, so overwhelming, Daddy wept bitter tears. While the wounds to his body would heal in time, he knew nothing would erase the memory of that fateful day. Daddy later said that during his season of intense mourning, the Scripture came to him, "Sorrow not, even as others which have no hope" (1 Thessalonians 4:13).

My mother's brother-in-law, Walt, was there when Daddy was told about his wife's death. While there's never a comfortable time to raise the subject, Walt carefully asked Daddy what he wanted to do with Momma's body. Daddy said, "After the funeral in Sellerstown, take her home to Bogalusa." His precious Mona would be laid to rest where they first met.

I can only imagine what Daddy felt in that moment. As much as he had wanted to protect his wife and children, he had been powerless to do so. As I would later witness, guilt over his inability to keep Momma out of harm's way tormented Daddy for years to come.

When I was finally permitted to see him later that day, Daddy's face brightened as I entered the room. I pulled myself onto the hospital bed beside him, careful to avoid jarring his injury. While I was still dealing with my own loss, I wanted to be strong for him. I put on my best smile and said, "Mommy's in heaven now."

With his big hands, Daddy pulled me to himself, tight. He buried his head against my neck and cried softly. He lingered in that embrace for what felt like an eternity, almost as if he were afraid to let go for fear of losing me, too. Through his tears Daddy whispered, "I know, Becky. I know."

I was at a loss for words. While Momma had been the sun in our universe, she wasn't coming back. Nothing I could do or say would fix things for Daddy—and for Danny and me. Life would never be the same without Momma illuminating our home with her sparkling spirit. And yet we knew that, if life were to go on, it had to be without her. One day we'd see her again in heaven. But the waiting is always the hardest part. In a way, Daddy's embrace expressed these things without words. He'd miss her every day. So would I.

I still do.

With the possible exception of Mr. Watts and his foot soldiers, the entire Sellerstown community, along with our family and friends around the country, were devastated by the tragic news. There were two opportunities for them to say good-bye to Momma in Sellerstown. A memorial service was also held in Bogalusa. Due to his injuries, Daddy was unable to attend any of them. I'm sure it haunted him that he didn't get to see her one last time this side of heaven.

A wake, which drew hundreds of people, was held at the Peacock Funeral Home in Whiteville on Saturday night. A memorial service followed at our church on Sunday afternoon, March 26, 1978. Of the three hundred or so people who signed Momma's guest book after the Sunday service, the name of one couple jumped off the page when we looked through the book later: Mr. and Mrs. Horry Watts. Frankly, I'm amazed that Mr. Watts would show his face. He probably thought he had to attend, or his absence might make him look like he had been involved in some way.

Once again, I'm glad I didn't see him. I was sitting in the second row with Aunt Dot. I'm not sure how that encounter would have gone had I known he was back there in pew number seven—no doubt in his usual spot. This time Mr. Watts didn't smack his lips, clear his throat, point to his watch, or make faces to disrupt the proceedings. He probably was too busy privately rejoicing that his dream of getting us to leave Sellerstown, "crawling or walking . . . dead or alive," was coming true before his eyes.

I wasn't all that surprised that the sanctuary was filled to overflowing. Momma's coffin, positioned ten feet from me, remained opened throughout the service. It was Easter Sunday, yet this wasn't how I'd expected to spend the holiday. Everything about the moment felt unreal. The day that was to be a celebration of Jesus' resurrection had now turned out to be the day I laid my mother to rest. My mind drifted, trying to make sense out of the situation.

Just a few days before, Momma had been practicing her special Easter music at the organ. Now she lay in a casket, unable to lead us in the celebration of Christ's resurrection. Likewise, two days prior I had watched Daddy at his desk perfecting a sermon for the occasion. Now he lay still in a hospital bed, incapable of bringing us the Good News.

The room came back into focus as the Spiritualaires, the singing group Momma had founded, took the stage. Standing around the casket of the woman they loved, they began the memorial service with a rousing rendition of "On the Other Side of Jordan." I have no idea how they managed to sing so beautifully under those circumstances.

Clara Cartrette, a reporter who had faithfully chronicled the horrendous drama in Sellerstown for years, was on hand and captured the moment during that song this way: "Hands were raised in glory that the pastor's wife, who was so loved and such a shining light and inspiration to those who knew her, had gone to meet God."

When the Spiritualaires finished, Daddy's assistant pastor, Mitchell Smith, stood at the podium and offered these words: "It would appear that we're here in defeat, but we're not; we're here in victory! We have hope beyond this life. Ramona has found this hope, and we rejoice that there is victory for a child of God."

Later in the service Rev. Sam Whichard, a visiting pastor from the Fayetteville area, compared Momma to Phoebe, whom the apostle Paul commends in Romans 16:1-2. He said, "Ramona was a servant of the church, dedicated to truth and self-sacrifice. Like Phoebe, she shared the sorrows, hurt, problems, and burdens of others, offering hope to the hopeless and help to the downcast. Ramona cast over this community a fragrance we'll never forget—of faithfulness and dedication." His words were punctuated with amens from the congregation.

I can't say when, but at some point I found myself struggling to stay awake. I was exhausted, both physically and emotionally. As my eyes drifted shut, I leaned over and fell asleep with my head on Aunt Dot's lap. I'm not sure how long I slept, but I awoke in the uneasy dream that had become my life.

Thankfully, Danny was spared the emotional upset that might have come from seeing Momma lying in the casket. Aunt Pat was kind enough to keep him during the funeral, even though that required her to sacrifice a chance to sing at Momma's funeral with the Spiritualaires as well as the opportunity to tell her good-bye. In a way, Aunt Pat did Momma one last favor by taking care of her son; the best thing for Danny during this traumatic episode of his life was to remain on some sort of a schedule. He needed to be in a quiet place taking his nap rather than surrounded by hundreds of people looking at him with worried, tear-stained faces.

After the service, when people looked at me, I saw sadness in their eyes. Those who greeted me did their best to comfort me, saying things like, "Your mother is in heaven now," and "Your mother was such a saint," and "You know your mother gave her life for her friend." Several told me I should be proud of her.

I know they meant well.

I appreciated their hugs and warm words.

I just couldn't comprehend that she wasn't coming back. Nor could I shake the feelings I'd had when it was my turn to look inside the casket. My first thought was that Momma wouldn't like the way her hair had been fixed. I'm not saying they did a bad job, but Momma was always so particular about her hair.

Standing alone, peering into the coffin, I wrestled to make sense out of everything. Momma just lay there with a peaceful expression on her face. I wanted to reach in and, with a tender nudge, say, "Wake up, Momma. It's time for breakfast"—the way Danny and I had done so many mornings before. But Momma wouldn't be preparing our breakfast or any other meal ever again.

She wouldn't be the one getting me ready for school or walking me out to meet the bus with a big smile on her face. I'd never see her "I'll see ya later" wave of the hand again or be enveloped in one of the big hugs she gave me when I returned home from school. She wouldn't be kneeling at my bedside at night to say prayers with me anymore. And, while I knew someone else would fulfill these motherly duties, she wouldn't be my momma.

After the memorial service, one of the neighbors, Johnnie Sellers, my momma's friend, came over to me with tears streaming down her face. She said, "Your mother and I were getting ready to plant a garden together." Then she slowly walked away in shock, unable to believe or accept the fact that this had really happened.

Neither could I.

CHAPTER 12

# Eight Men and Four Women

After the press, the police, and the well-wishers had departed, there was the matter of Daddy's recovery. The doctors had implanted a long, metal pin into Daddy's leg, requiring him to remain in the hospital for the better part of a month. While he recuperated, my grandparents, Aunt Dot, Aunt Martha, and Aunt Daisy returned to live in our home. Out of respect for my parents—and to avoid sleeping in the room where Momma had died—they removed the mattresses from the beds and slept in the living room on the floor.

When Aunt Pat invited Danny and me to stay at her house, I hugged her hard enough to squeeze the air out of her. For obvious reasons, there was no way I'd set foot back into the parsonage so soon after the attack—if ever. The memories were too intense, too fresh, and too painful for me to deal with; the thought of ever living there again felt creepy.

Granted, friends from church did what they could to clean up the house in anticipation of our return. The food that Momma had lovingly prepared for our Easter feast, left untouched due to the attack, had been removed. The bloodstains on the kitchen floor where Daddy had fallen, as well as those on the carpet and bedspread in my parents' bedroom, had been scoured clean. Even so, there was nothing they could do to scrub away the memories that hung in the air like dark phantoms.

I don't remember ever going back to my room, where Harris had held his wife, Sue, and baby hostage. While I have only a vague recollection of the immediate aftermath of the attack due to the trauma I experienced, I doubt I would have felt safe trying to fall asleep in my princess suite. And with Daddy lying in a hospital bed somewhere across town and with Momma gone, I felt as alone as if I had been orphaned.

Day by day I'd wake up wondering whether this would be the morning when I'd hear Momma humming a favorite tune while preparing breakfast in the kitchen. I wanted and needed her desperately to be there for me. I had lost a part of my heart when she died. Now, nothing seemed real. Indeed, the events of the next several weeks ran together in a blur of raw emotion.

When Daddy was finally released from the hospital three weeks after he had been admitted, we packed our belongings and flew to Mobile. For Daddy, part of the healing process required him to gain some distance from the home where his bride had been gunned down. Spending time recuperating with family would be good medicine.

The trip south, however, proved to be taxing. When we arrived at the airport and boarded the plane, we were seated near the back because Daddy had to be carried up the rear stairs in a stretcher. Watching six men, one each in front and back and two on each side, struggling to maneuver him up the steps was unsettling. This giant of a man, who had carried me in his arms countless times before, was unable to simply walk up the steps like everyone else.

Besides, it felt wrong to be going on a trip without Momma. I could see other kids on the plane, laughing and having a wonderful time together with their mommies and daddies. Why couldn't it be the same for us? The more I thought about the fact that life would never be the same, the more upset I became.

Aunt Dot did her best to keep things pleasant on the flight. She tried to fill the role Momma would have played, buckling Daniel and me into our seats while answering our questions. It was, after all, only the second time I had been on an airplane. Sensing my discomfort, she attempted to distract us by pointing to the activity outside the window as the ground crew bustled about.

Despite her efforts, my nerves were stretched thin. Once airborne, things went from bad to worse. The whine of the jet engines was extremely loud, which put me further on edge. They sounded as if they were ready to explode; if that happened, I knew we'd crash. Nauseated from worrying, without warning I threw up all over my seat and myself. I was so scared and embarrassed.

The flight attendant and Aunt Dot tried to clean up my clothes and settle me down. Since our baggage had been checked, I didn't have a change of clothes with me. They did the best they could to wipe away the mess. It bothered me the entire flight that my outfit had blotches all over it. Momma had always taken pride in our things being clean, and now here I was a total mess . . . emotionally *and* physically.

What was happening to me?

If only I could wake up and find that life was the way it used to be.

I think the most difficult part for me was knowing that this was more than a trip south; it was an attempt to start over . . . without Momma. Once we landed in Mobile, I knew I'd be facing a new home, a new church, and a new school that fall. The thought of scaling such a mountain of change was overwhelming. My world as I knew it had been scrambled beyond recognition, and I approached the future with profound apprehension.

The summer of 1978 was hard on me and my brother. Adjusting to life without Momma and without friends was no small task for two high-energy kids. I missed the bike rides with Missy to our secret fort in the woods. She was my confidant, and now she, too, was gone. Thankfully, my grandparents and Aunt Dot were our primary caretakers. We were blessed to have such a loving family surrounding and supporting us at this time. Still, I had to deal with the reality that my life would never be the same.

During that first summer without Momma, Danny and I went to see her family in Louisiana. Grandpa and Grandma Welch had been devastated when they heard that their precious daughter had been killed. Making matters worse was the fact that she was shot right in front of their grandchildren.

Momma's brother, Ed, and his wife, Shirley, along with Momma's sister, Sue, and her husband, Walt, were shocked and enraged that their sister's life had been snatched from them. The Welches were a close-knit family, and now one of them was gone. Danny and I were all that was left of Momma.

As we walked through their front door, my grandma could not contain her emotions any longer. She wrapped her arms around us and cried from the depths of her broken soul, from that place in a mother's heart where love knows no end. She said she didn't understand why my mother had prayed so hard to have children and yet God had allowed her to be taken away from them.

I had some of the same questions.

The piano that Momma had played for so many years sat in the living room, untouched and silent. Her fingers would never again grace the keyboard to entertain family and friends. Its music was replaced by the sound of our grandmother crying. Wanting to be strong for her, I tried to remember all the things people had said to me at Momma's funeral. Maybe some of those words would bring comfort to her and Grandpa.

During our visit, Grandma Welch took us to the cemetery to see Mother's grave. Danny and I sat on the little white bench placed there by my grandparents. The grave site was beautiful. The black marble trim and the white rocks that surrounded it made me think Momma would be pleased to know her parents had put so much thought into remembering her.

Momma's gravestone had an oval-shaped picture of her smiling on it. To see the smile and twinkle in her eyes brought me comfort. It was as if she were telling me that she was happy and safe with Jesus and that no one could hurt her or threaten her ever again.

As I had feared, I felt as nauseous the first day at my new school as I had on the airplane. Walking to my third-grade class, knees threatening to buckle beneath me, the unbearable thought of a new teacher and classmates was more than I could take. If I could just make it to my desk and sit down, maybe I'd be okay.

I had to fight the sensation of throwing up again.

It didn't take long for the gossip to spread through the hallways. I'd overhear the other students at school whispering things like, "Did you know she actually saw her mom get shot?" . . . "Yeah, and did you know her mother died?" . . . "I heard her dad was shot, too. Poor kid saw the whole thing."

Beyond the rumors and knowing glances, there was the practical matter of my schoolwork. Momma had always helped me with my homework, and now she was gone. Daddy was on a regimen of painkillers and nerve medication, so there was little he could do to tend to my needs.

I didn't want to be at this school. I didn't feel as if I fit in. I was the "new kid"—the outsider from North Carolina. The other kids all knew each other, and I had no motivation or desire to break into their well-established circles.

The best part of the school day was when Grandpa Nichols picked me up from school in his old green truck. Riding home with Grandpa was a safe place. I knew he understood my pain, and I had no fear that he was whispering behind my back. As I opened the door to the truck and threw my schoolbag on the floor, he would greet me with a warm smile while extending his hand, which held his daily treat: a peppermint. At least my school day ended with something sweet—candy and a quiet ride home.

When we'd get home, Daniel would be there waiting for me to return from school. He was the only thing that didn't change in my world. Daddy was different now. He was a broken man. He seemed lost and disoriented. That is why I especially loved being with my little brother, except for the fact that he kept asking for Momma. His pleas were especially difficult at night.

You see, Daniel slept in my bed after the shootings. I would sleep on my side with my left arm draped over him until he fell asleep. I was an eight-year-old trying to comfort a three-year-old. Many nights he cried for Momma. I was frustrated that I had no easy answers for him. Back when Momma was alive, he was so attached to her that he would scream when she walked out of the room after putting him to bed. Now she was gone, and there was no way he could be with her no matter how hard or how long he cried.

I tried my best to console him during those restless nights. I'd say, "Danny, Momma's in heaven. Don't worry, we'll see her when we get there." That wasn't good enough. He'd say, "Then I want to go to heaven *right now* and see her. I want Mommy!" After a while he'd settle down, whimpering his way to sleep. This went on for some time. Then he started wandering back and forth between Daddy's room and mine. After several months he decided to stay with Daddy—I guess he felt safer with at least one parent.

I don't remember when Daniel stopped crying for Momma. In a way it was a relief because it hurt me to see him asking for her. But it was deeply painful for me, too. I was old enough to understand that she wasn't coming back, at least not in this lifetime. I knew I had to say good-bye to Momma, our town, my friends, and my childhood.

In August 1978, five months after the shooting that claimed the life of my mother, Daddy and I headed back to Sellerstown for the murder trial. I had such mixed emotions about returning. I was thrilled that I'd get to see Missy, Aunt Pat, and some of my old friends, but I dreaded the thought of staying at our old home under the watchful eyes of Mr. Watts. Thankfully, we were invited to lodge with Eddie and Johnnie Sellers, who lived up the street from the parsonage.

On Sunday, August 6, Daddy preached his farewell sermon at the Free Welcome Church in Sellerstown. The church family had been supporting us since the shooting, and while Daddy appreciated their generosity, he knew it was time to move on. He was encouraged to see the church thriving in his absence, and after he finished his message, he formally resigned as their senior pastor.

On Monday, August 7, the murder trial began. The proceedings were held before the Superior Court of Bladen County in Elizabethtown, North Carolina, and lasted for five days. The twelve members of the jury were selected on Monday and Tuesday; eight men and four women plus two alternates would sit in judgment of this dark chapter in our lives.

The jury was seated on Wednesday afternoon. They would ultimately have to decide whether Harris Williams was guilty of three things:

felonious breaking or entering with the intent to commit the felony of assault with a deadly weapon with intent to kill, inflict serious bodily injury, or the felony of murder

assault with a deadly weapon with intent to kill or inflict serious bodily injury

murder in the first degree

When asked by the judge how Harris Williams would plead, his attorney, Ray H. Walton, entered a plea of "not guilty" on all charges.

Since Daddy and I were the first two witnesses scheduled by the state, we had been summoned to appear at the courthouse that afternoon. Approaching the two-story brick building, I felt as if I were Dorothy approaching the great and powerful Oz. My heart started to flutter inside my chest as I climbed the eight concrete steps up to the glass front doors.

Once inside, it took a second for my eyes to adjust to the dim overhead lighting. Long, cold corridors with marble halfway up their walls stretched out into the distance. Although my shoes weren't red ruby slippers, they echoed against the polished terrazzo floors as we walked to the elevator. We rode to the second floor, where we were directed to sit on an uncomfortable oak pew outside of courtroom number 219 until the bailiff called for us. Daddy took the stand at 3:25 p.m. When finished, he sat just behind our lawyers.

From my viewpoint, waiting was the hardest part of testifying. Sooner or later, just on the other side of the twin oak doors leading to the courtroom, I'd have to face the man who shot my momma. Swinging my legs back and forth like a pendulum, I tried to work off some of the nervous energy building inside me.

While I wanted to give a good testimony for Momma's sake, I dreaded the prospect of being in the same room with the shooter. I didn't relish the thought of him looking at me while I answered questions. In spite of my growing anxiety, I knew it would be a first-class disaster if I got sick, as I had on the plane.

At 4:10 p.m. the bailiff ushered me into the stuffy courtroom packed with about a hundred adults. The judge sat in a high-back chair to my right, flanked by two flags. Although he appeared sympathetic as he looked down on me from his mahogany perch, I didn't have one friend there to lean on for moral support. Not my brother. Not Missy. Not even Billy Wayne. This, of course, was no place for children.

Settling into the witness stand, I caught a glimpse of Daddy sitting in the front row. With a wink, he smiled at me. My heart leaped. Drawing strength from his presence, I forgot about my fears. Sitting upright like a doll in my red and white pinafore, I folded my hands and rested them on my lap.

When District Attorney Lee Greer approached me, I felt as if I could actually hold it together long enough to get through the proceedings. I had met Mr. Greer before the trial for a briefing and found him to be genuinely heartbroken over our situation. In a way he was like a kind, grandfatherly figure. I trusted him.

After being sworn in, Mr. Greer said, "Now, Rebecca, you see that thing in front of you there? Honey, if you will speak into that, I think perhaps everyone can hear you. Get that close to your mouth. Little lady, what is your name?"

"Rebecca."

"And what is your last name?"

"Nichols."

"And, Rebecca, how old are you?"

"I'm eight."

"Do you go to school?"

"Yes."

"Honey, what grade are you in?"

"The third."

"Do you make good grades in school?"

"Yes."

"Do you go to Sunday school?"

"Yes."

"Do you go every Sunday?"

"Yes."

"How about church?"

"Yes."

"Rebecca, do you know who Jesus is?"

"Yes."

"Who is Jesus?"

"God's son."

"Rebecca, do you know what a lie is?"

"Yes."

"What is a lie?"

"It's . . ." I looked at the ceiling to search for the right words.

"It's what?"

"It's not the truth," I said with a smile.

"Well, is it a bad thing to tell a lie?"

"Yes."

"All right. Rebecca, now, I show you this pipe here," he said, holding out his well-worn red pipe for me to examine. "If I said this pipe was gray or was black, would I be telling the truth?"

"No."

"If I said the pipe was red, would I be telling the truth?"

"Yes."

"Then if I said this pipe was black, what would I be telling?"

"A lie."

"Now, Rebecca, why shouldn't one tell a lie?"

Although that was an easy question, I didn't answer at first. I knew perfectly well why we shouldn't lie. I mean, my daddy was a pastor, and I had spent my life in church. But this wasn't a church service. Somehow talking about church stuff in a courtroom didn't make sense to me.

Mr. Greer smiled as if thinking about another way to ask the question. He cleared his throat and said, "Did they teach you in Sunday school that to tell lies is a bad thing?"

"Yes."

"What did they say it is to tell a lie?"

"Wrong." I knew it was also a sin, but I wasn't clear how much the lawyer wanted to know about sin.

"Wrong?"

I nodded.

"All right. Now, if little boys and girls tell the truth and mind their parents and are good, if they die where would they go?"

"To heaven."

"And if little boys and girls are bad and tell lies and are mean, when they die where would they go?"

"To hell."

"All right, honey. Now, do you know Mr. Williams?"

"Yes."

"Where is he?"

+ + +

They told me I would be safe.

They told me just to tell the truth.

And in my pretrial briefing, they told me I'd have to identify my mother's killer. The time for that had come. But now, with Harris Williams sitting beside his lawyers at a table not more than twenty feet from the witness stand, how could I be sure I was really safe?

What would prevent him from coming after me?

Then again, I had to tell the truth. Biting my bottom lip, I summoned the resolve to identify the man who took everything I loved away from me—even if it might provoke him to anger. I pointed diagonally across the room. As I did, the faces of the jury focused on the defendant. Harris looked up, and our eyes met for a long moment before he diverted his gaze.

I remembered to breathe.

"All right, honey. Now, did you see him on March the 23rd?"

"Yes."

"Where did you see him?"

"At my house."

"And do you live with your daddy?"

"Yes."

"And that's Rev. Nichols, isn't it?"

"Yes."

"When you saw Mr. Williams, what was he doing?"

I hesitated. In a way, that was a difficult question to answer. The events of that day flooded into my mind in such a painful swirl of pictures, I didn't know where to start. Sensing my misgivings, Mr. Greer tried a different approach.

"Where did you see him at your house?"

"When he walked in the door."

"Was the door closed when he walked in?"

"Yes."

"Did you see him do anything?"

"Yes."

"What did you see him do?"

"I saw him pull out a gun."

"Pulled out a gun, did you say?"

I nodded.

"All right. Now, what did you see him do with that gun, if anything?"

"Shoot Daddy."

"How many times did you see him shoot your daddy?"

"Two."

"After he shot your daddy, did you see him do anything else with that gun?"

"Yes."

"What did you see him do?"

"Shoot Mama."

"Where was your mother when she was shot?"

"She was standing close to the dryer."

"Did you later see your mother in the house?"

I nodded.

"Where did you next see your mother after she was shot?"

"In the bedroom."

"In the bedroom. All right, honey. Where was she in the bedroom?"

"Underneath the bed."

"Was your mother lying down?"

"Yes."

"How close did you get to her?"

"I got close enough to touch her."

"Was there any blood on her?"

"I didn't see none on her."

"Did you see any anywhere else?"

"Yes."

"Where?"

"On the spread."

"On the spread. All right. Now, after you saw your mother lying there, what did you do then?"

"I went back down the hall."

"When you went back down the hall—" Mr. Greer said, but stopped and then turned to the judge.

"Your honor, this particular question is purely for corroboration of what her daddy had said." The judge motioned for him to continue. He asked, "Did your daddy say anything to you?"

"Yes."

"What did he tell you to do?"

"He told me to run down to Aunt Pat's house and tell her to call the police."

"Did you do that?"

"Yes."

"Now, is Pat your aunt?"

"No. I just call her Aunt Pat."

"When you went to Aunt Pat's, did you say anything to Aunt Pat?"

"Yes . . . I said, 'Aunt Pat, Daddy has been shot by [Harris] Williams. Mama has, too, but I didn't get no answer out of her."

After his final question, Mr. Greer offered me one of his warmest smiles before taking a seat near Daddy. I could tell by the way his eyes sparkled around the edges that he thought I'd done a good job on the witness stand. I was briefly cross-examined and then escorted from the courtroom, thankful to be out of the spotlight and relieved to put some distance between me and the monster who had stolen my mother's life.

+ + +

During the weeklong trial, the state called eleven witnesses while the defense summoned seven. Daddy sat in the front row every day that week, head half-bowed as if in prayer, listening to the proceedings. When asked by the press about his feelings, Daddy said, "I would like to see justice in this trial. I don't have the attitude of seeking vengeance for what this man has done, but I feel that violent people should be confined or dealt with according to the law to protect society."

Grandma Welch, who constantly fought back tears throughout the court case, admitted that being in the same room with the man who took her daughter from her was grueling. She told reporters, "It's so hard to look at him, knowing his finger pulled the trigger." It had to have been especially difficult for her to listen as the defense made the case that Harris was intoxicated and therefore should receive leniency.

On Thursday, the shooter, Harris Williams, was summoned to testify. When his attorney called him to the stand, Harris hesitated. Although he had shown no emotion throughout the trial, evidently he had last-minute misgivings about offering his testimony. After privately consulting with his lawyer at the defense table, Harris rose and took his place before the court.

Their strategy was simple: make the case that Harris had been drunk, that he had no intent to harm anyone, and that he had no memory of the actual shooting and therefore the murder wasn't premeditated. The heart of their case rested on the fact that Harris had consumed a large quantity of alcohol—upwards of two and a half gallons of whiskey over several days—and that he thought highly of my parents; he didn't wish them any harm and was deeply sorry about his actions.

On Friday, both sides rested their cases.

Assistant District Attorney Mike Easley was the first to offer his closing argument to the jury on our behalf. For twenty-two minutes, he recapped the facts of the case—how we were eating dinner, how Harris barged into our house armed with three guns, and then how he shot my parents after exchanging words with Daddy.

As to the matter that Harris was drunk, Mr. Easley said, "Lt. Hayes stated there was nothing unusual about Harris in the morning or evening, no odor of alcohol. . . . Ptm. [Patrolman] Randy Williamson rode all the way to the jail with Harris and said there was no odor of alcohol. He talks about being irrational—he knew where he wanted to go to get that .38-caliber pistol. He wanted that gun that day."

Holding the murder weapon for the jury to see, Mr. Easley said, "This is the one he used to propel two bullets into the preacher and one into his wife. He shot three times and hit three times. That's a pretty good aim for somebody who's supposed to be drunk."

Regarding the character of Harris, Mr. Easley told the jury, "He is a violent and dangerous man and oftentimes mean—he likes to drink, play with guns, slap women, and beat on children. He says he's sorry. Reckon he was sorry when he hit the sixty-nine-year-old magistrate on the head with the cinder block?"

Attorney Easley was referring to a prior incident involving Harris for which he had served eighteen months in jail. "He went there with over sixty bullets and three pistols. Do you think he was going there to have dinner?"

Mr. Easley picked up one of the other weapons and then added, "This is a short-barrel pistol—you can't hunt with it. It's not a target pistol; there is only one purpose—to shoot someone. He'll tell you any poppycock he can because he stands to lose. He says he can't remember; is that a good enough reason? He says he's sorry. You tell a state trooper you're sorry you were speeding and see if he doesn't write you a ticket."

Mr. Easley concluded, saying, "If he had a defense, he would use it. He doesn't need a lawyer, he needs a magician. He's grabbing at straws and has an imaginary defense. Don't ignore the facts. This case has the most overwhelming evidence you'll ever see. Let the people know you will not tolerate this type of conduct."

Defense attorney Mr. Walton approached the jury and for the next fifty minutes attempted to soften the picture of his client. Regarding the whiskey, he said, "I wish it were possible for the stuff to be eradicated. Harris has a drinking problem, and he has some other problems." He added, "Harris went there drunk—absolutely and completely out of it. Only a person who was could do what he did. . . . Do you suppose he went there for the purpose of killing Mrs. Nichols? She was his best friend. Did he go there with the intent to kill his best friend?"

I'm glad I wasn't in the courtroom during his closing argument. To suggest that Momma was Harris's "best friend" was an outrageous claim. Momma hardly knew the man. Sure, she cared for Harris and wanted to see him get the help he needed. But it was his wife, Sue, who was close to my mother. Harris had only been interacting with my parents for about eight months.

Our lead attorney, Mr. Greer, also gave a few closing remarks to the jury. Speaking from the heart, he said, "I ask my God that I never convict an innocent person. There is so little doubt as to what has happened. When Harris opened the door without invitation, he had an intent to commit a felony, which he did. On the murder, he had the witness of a small child, and it's been said that from the mouth of babes come the truth. From Rebecca came the truth. I have worked with many small children as witnesses, but never one better than Rebecca."

As for the sentiment that Harris was sorry and would "trade his life for that good woman and for the suffering of Mr. Nichols"—as his lawyer had told the jury—Mr. Greer said, "All the tears he might shed will not bring Ramona back to her husband and children. The deed is done. Remorse or tears or feeling sorry will not bring her back. Harris was wrong in what he's done. He should have thought of the consequences before he had begun; if you have compassion for him, remember he's the man who took a mother away from Rebecca and little Daniel."

Judge Robert A. Collier spent forty-five minutes briefing the twelve members of the jury about the decision that lay before them. They, in turn, spent two hours and twenty minutes before sentencing Harris to life in prison for second-degree murder plus fifteen to twenty years for assault with a deadly weapon with the intent to kill and inflicting serious bodily injury on Daddy.

Harris had been tried and convicted. I sensed that Daddy was thankful for the sense of closure it afforded him, yet no amount of justice would ever bring Momma back to our family. With the trial behind us, we said our good-byes to our loved ones in Sellerstown and then returned to Mobile.

Two years later, however, there'd be another trial.

This time it would be Mr. Watts who faced charges.

## CHAPTER 13

# Putting the Devil on Trial

I wanted to forget. I wanted to remember.

I had difficulty doing either.

A tug-of-war between equally compelling needs raged within me. In the years immediately following Momma's murder trial, I desperately wanted to forget what I had witnessed when she was gunned down in our kitchen. I longed to erase the mental picture of seeing her body sprawled under the bed. I needed to stop thinking about her lying in the casket, cold and lifeless.

And yet I wanted to cling to every precious detail of my mother. Her touch. Her smile. Her embrace. Her laughter. Her love. I needed *her*. Now that she was gone, I counted the hours, wishing for each new day to come quickly to an end. As far as I was concerned, the faster the better. Every day that passed would separate me further from the events I had experienced; the greater the distance, the more I'd be able to leave behind the sting of Momma's death.

I just didn't want to leave *her* behind.

It was the little things that seemed to rub salt in my wounded soul. Like the time I was shopping with Aunt Dot at the grocery store when I heard a little girl calling after her mother in the next aisle. My ears stung, and my heart ached at the sound of that precious word—*Mom*. In that moment, I was reminded that I would never again be able to call out for my mother and expect a response. Still, I refused to allow the memory of her to fade away.

The days without her seemed unbearably long. She had been my anchor, my guiding light. She had brought me into this world. We were supposed to spend a lifetime together. Momma was going to teach me about purity, modesty, conversational etiquette, and how to be comfortable in my own skin. She had promised to teach me how to play the piano, too. We were supposed to fight over shoes, clothes, and jewelry like all mothers and daughters do.

None of that would happen now.

A number of months after Momma died, I panicked. I was in my room cleaning on a Saturday afternoon, our usual cleaning day. As I removed the pictures, hairbrushes, and decorative items from their assigned places on my dresser, I thought of Momma and how passionate she was about cleaning. One moment I was cleaning, and the next instant I was mourning the loss of my mother.

What's more, I was borderline hysterical because I couldn't remember the soft, almost musical-like sound when she spoke; that tender, calming voice praying over me at bedtime; or the quality of her whisper as she tucked words of affection into my ear while settling me down for the night. Try as I might to get it back, the distinct timbre of her voice eluded me. I closed my eyes tight to block out any distraction, and yet I wasn't able to recall the way she said "I love you" anymore.

Lying in bed at night was especially difficult for me. The memories of us living in Sellerstown and the fear that prevented me from falling asleep back then would flood my mind. When the nightmarish thoughts became too much to bear, too loud to silence, I'd get out of my bed and wander to Aunt Dot's room for comfort—just as I used to seek the shelter of my parents' bed.

There I'd put into words the sadness filling my heart over the loss of my mother. In her gentle way, Aunt Dot would wrap her arms around me and listen to my woes with the patience and love of a saint. As we sat side by side on the edge of her bed, I could smell the scent of the lotion she used in her nightly beauty regimen lingering in the air. The fragrance was familiar—Oil of Olay—the same cream Momma used. Somehow God had given Aunt Dot a mother's love for us, even though she had no children of her own.

Although she sacrificed her sleep on numerous occasions, Aunt Dot never complained or demonstrated resentment that I was unloading my burdens on her. Instead, she empathized with my sadness and assured me it was a normal part of the grieving process. She said this lifetime was as short as the blink of an eye. Before I knew it, I'd be together with my mother again, and this time we'd be together forever.

Aunt Dot pointed me to Revelation 21, which says,

> I heard a loud voice from the throne saying, "Now the dwelling of God is with men, and he will live with them. . . . He will wipe every tear from their eyes. There will be no more death or mourning or crying or pain, for the old order of things has passed away." He who was seated on the throne said, "I am making everything new!" Then he said, "Write this down, for these words are trustworthy and true." (vv. 3-5, NIV)

That eternal perspective continues to melt away my sorrow; it gives me something to look forward to when the feelings of aloneness creep up on me, even today.

+ + +

Just as Aunt Dot helped me grieve, my grandparents doctored my wounded heart as best they could. Through pictures and stories, they reminded my brother and me of Momma's love for us. They encouraged us to trust God and to remember that our purpose in life didn't stop because He had called Momma home. Momma lived in such a way as to bring the Lord glory, they said. That was her goal; ours should be the same. While their words brought hope and comfort, no one could replace her.

After losing Momma, the main consolation in our move from Sellerstown was the fact that nobody was shooting at us anymore. The midnight phone calls had stopped. I could peek through my bedroom curtains anytime—day or night—and not see Mr. Watts stalking back and forth, shaking his fist in our direction. Even the cloud of fear that another bombing might happen eventually lifted.

In that respect, during the two years following Harris's trial, we lived peacefully. The main shadow hanging over us was the damage that had been done to Daddy's nerves. He had lost the love of his life, his companion in ministry, the mother of his two children.

His church was gone.

His friends were gone.

His dreams were gone.

And now, by all appearances, he was slowly losing his mind. At times I watched helplessly as he would talk to people who were not in the room. I remember sitting at the dinner table when Daddy experienced one of his flashbacks. As if being transported in time to the day of the shootings, he completely lost touch with reality. Without warning he jumped out of his seat, knocking several dishes off the table in the process. With a fire in his eyes he shouted at the unseen gunman until my grandfather took hold of him and settled him down.

There were countless days when my grandparents sent Daniel and me outside to play while they tried to calm Daddy after a flashback. Even though I was a child, I knew it would take much more to soothe Daddy's troubled spirit. He needed to be healed, and I had faith that God would make Daddy better. I took markers and paper and drew signs, which I placed over his bed, that read, "Jesus, please heal my daddy." I rode my bike around our yard, praying for Daddy, believing one day soon we'd have a normal life, a life free of Daddy's "episodes."

Granted, Daddy appeared normal some of the time. He had seasons where he'd seem like his old, wonderful self. I drew a lot of comfort from those harmonious intervals. He loved to grill outdoors for company and interact with them like in the old days. He'd jump off the diving board into the pool with a "bomb" dive that splashed almost all the water out of the pool. He was even a guest preacher in various churches every now and then. The good times gave us hope that one day, if we didn't give up, Daddy would be completely healed.

For my part, I did what I could to help Daddy parent Daniel—not that Daddy needed me to do so. I figured if I anticipated Daniel's needs as Momma used to do, though, I might take some of the pressure off him. When Daniel struggled with his emotions over Momma's death, I'd put my arm around him or hold him and remind him that we always had each other and we still had Daddy. And I made sure I kept track of where Daniel was going and what he was doing. If he needed help getting dressed or was hungry for a sandwich, rather than bother Daddy, I stepped in and lent a hand.

Even so, Daddy's moments of normality seemed to pass by far

too quickly. Inevitably, another setback would occur. Sometimes he would wake us up during the middle of the night in order to go on a trip. With his suitcase packed, he informed us that he had a revival to preach, and we had to get going right away. Having awakened everyone, determined to hit the road, he started rummaging through the entire house searching for the Bibles and car keys we had stashed to prevent him from wandering off.

Daniel and I unpacked his bags, and after reassuring him there was no scheduled meeting, we'd finally return to our beds. We would get only a few hours of sleep some nights before the alarm sounded for school. Tired and worn out, we'd get dressed, go to our classes, and try to concentrate. Although we pretended that our lives were normal, a question always lingered in the back of our minds: *Will Daddy be there when we get home from school? Or will he be in the hospital again?* This was especially unsettling for me as a twelve-year-old preteen, a concern that shadowed me for the next two years.

Daddy's fragile condition was severe enough to require heavy medication—even an extended hospitalization of six months. Because of the death of Momma and the years of harassment at the hands of Mr. Watts, Daddy's mental state had been thoroughly scrambled. The endless hours spent answering the phone, only to hear the breathing of a maniac, or peeking out the window every time a car passed the parsonage, created an anxiety that wreaked havoc on his nervous system.

I'm sure his condition was complicated by second-guessing. He had to have wondered about the wisdom of staying in Sellerstown when friends and family had pleaded, begged, and prayed we'd leave before harm was done. Should he have listened? Had he been stubborn? Had this been some sort of contest of wills: Daddy vs. Mr. Watts? Or had the voice of God really confirmed in his spirit that he should not abandon this congregation?

What if he had taken their advice and left?

Momma would still be alive, that much is certain.

But would leaving to save our own skins have been what the Lord wanted? Didn't Jesus say to take up our cross and follow Him? Did we get a say in where Jesus took us? By definition, a cross, as Daddy knew, was suffering even unto death. The Scriptures don't paint a rosy picture for those who follow the Lord. Daddy knew full well that Jesus promised, "In the world ye shall have tribulation." That's part of the deal, part of what happens when living in a fallen world. And yet Daddy also knew full well that Jesus promised His followers hope, saying, "Be of good cheer; I have overcome the world" (John 16:33).

In spite of what Daddy knew to be true in the Bible, his constant questioning about his decision to stay acted like a stage-four cancer. The speculations devoured his inner being, reducing him to a shell of his former self.

As a young girl, I vacillated between good and bad days. I still had my daddy, but he wasn't the man I had known. Sure, some days the fog cleared, and I experienced the intimacy and love I had once known. Most days, however, were close to insufferable. I wished I could have unzipped the darkness and the depressive atmosphere at home and crawled out to where there was light. I longed for fresh, breathable air and a new cup of hope to quench the years of dry prayers. The other cups of hope had spilled each time Daddy was taken away to the hospital, which left me wondering if there would ever be any refills.

Walking alone to the bus stop on cold school mornings, watching the air as I breathed in and out, I remember thinking that this could *not* be my life . . . not my *real* life. I had been born to wonderful parents, and now they were gone. Momma was dead, and Daddy was gone into sort of a living death, a zombie-like, disoriented state of being.

For me, losing them was such a burden; at times as I walked to the bus, it felt as if I were carrying another person on my back. I didn't appear to be bent over, but my heart was weighed down with a heaviness that made even the short trek to the bus stop seem to take forever.

Worse, the thoughts echoing in my head felt as if they were so loud everyone at the bus stop could hear them. Even so, I'd smile and say hello to maintain the illusion that everything was just fine with me. No one knew the effort that charade took just so I could carry on with a "normal" school day.

Making matters worse was watching my daddy go in and out of hospitals. That was especially hard on me. I wanted to be with him, but it hurt to witness his condition. His clothes had a disinfected hospital smell, not the familiar scent that I had loved about him. At times when we visited him in the hospital, I'd find him unshaven and his eyes reddened and glossed over from the medications.

His face, tired and drawn from one too many sleepless nights, seemed to lack color. We'd take him outside and sit at a picnic table so he would get some sun. Our conversation was somewhat stilted due to the sedatives. He'd answer questions in clipped phrases, like a vending machine dispensing one treat at a time.

None of these changes in Daddy's countenance prevented me from sitting right beside him for the entire visit. I sat so close you couldn't squeeze a dime between us. My brother and I would take turns sitting in Daddy's lap, as if he were Santa—only better. I'd hug him, kiss him, and love him as if there were nothing wrong. I just hoped, prayed, and waited for him to be healed. I knew God could glue back the pieces of his shattered life.

When it was time for us to leave, I'd offer him my brightest smile. I'd wrap my arms around his neck one final time and say, "Good-bye, Daddy." That, however, didn't sit well with him. He'd shake his head and say, "Honey, please say, 'See you later,' not 'good-bye.'" I think the thought that he might never see his children again weighed on his heart.

More than once after leaving the room, I overheard Daddy telling my grandma Nichols, "Mom, I'd rather have a dozen cancers in my body than have to suffer with these severe nerve problems. If I'm not going to get any better, I'd rather for the Lord to take me on home. I can't take it any longer. It's like hell on earth. Please, Mom, pray for me this way."

At the same time, I knew that Daddy had a rock-solid faith that he could be healed by the power of Jesus. He knew there was no sickness or brokenness beyond God's repair. Jesus was the Great Physician. Daddy had preached about the healing power of the Lord, had prayed for others who had been sick, and had watched the Lord heal them. If it was God's will, he, too, could be made whole again.

In spite of the ongoing physical and mental anguish, Daddy never gave up on his faith in God. I overheard Daddy talking to his mother, Grandma Nichols, in the kitchen, saying, "These tormenting spirits can touch my body, my mind, and my emotions. But they can't touch my born-again spirit." Indeed, he loved God more than life itself.

I'd hear Daddy walking through the house, confessing the Scriptures "My peace I give unto you" and "He hath not given us a spirit of fear, but of power, love, and a sound mind." He spoke emphatically, using his hands for emphasis, as if preaching. He'd quote, "The thief cometh but for to kill and steal and to destroy, but Jesus came that we might have abundant life" and "He came to bind up the brokenhearted."

At times Daddy appeared to be basking in the grace of God to continue the good fight of faith. On his good days, he'd stop taking his medicine and call a friend who struggled with problems of his own. Daddy would pray with him, offer words of Scripture and encouragement, and essentially serve as a lifeline to this fellow traveler. Nothing encouraged Daddy more than bringing hope to the hopeless.

Sometimes I heard Daddy crying out to the Lord in prayer, repeating that he had forgiven Mr. Watts and that he wanted Mr. Watts to become a changed man through the power of Jesus. Interestingly, I never once heard Daddy complain that Mr. Watts had escaped justice. He didn't badger God with endless "Why, God?" questions about the suffering Mr. Watts had caused our family. Neither did Daddy rejoice when he learned about a breakthrough regarding Mr. Watts's role in the Sellerstown bombings.

On June 5, 1980, two years after the murder trial, Grandma Nichols, Daddy, Danny, and I took a trip from our home in Alabama to North Carolina. I think Grandma thought it would be a good idea for us as a family to reconnect with our old friends from Sellerstown.

I couldn't wait to see my friend Missy, whom I'd always admired as I would a big sister. I was now ten, and Missy was fourteen. Even though two years had passed since I last saw her, we picked up as if I had been gone just a few days.

One afternoon, we stood in front of her bathroom mirror, laughing at the sight of our green facial masks plastered from chin to cheek. For a moment, the distant memory of a more peaceful, playful time in our shared history was reflected in the two sets of eyes staring back at us. Even though life was different for us now, our friendship felt as familiar and comfortable as a pair of favorite shoes.

I had the same warmhearted reunion with Aunt Pat. After a hug that spoke volumes, she raked my hair with her fingers, cupped my face between her tender hands, and just shook her head. I sensed she was marveling at the young woman I was becoming. She said, "You look so much like your precious mother, Becky." My heart swelled. In a way, it felt good to know I was able in some small way to bring joy to those who knew, loved, and missed Momma.

After we had arrived and settled, Daddy bought a local paper to read with his coffee. Daddy read that ATF Special Agent Charles Mercer never stopped pursuing Mr. Watts's involvement in the bombings.

According to the newspaper account, Mr. Watts had been indicted by a federal grand jury, was arrested on June 9, and immediately made bail by posting a $200,000 bond. He had been charged on two counts: first, conspiracy to detonate a destructive device in the series of Sellerstown bombings; second, conspiracy to violate our freedom of religion as protected by the First Amendment and our civil rights of life, liberty, and property as guaranteed by the Fifth Amendment to the United States Constitution.

Through his lawyers, Mr. Watts entered a plea of not guilty. Not surprisingly, he had retained four of the best lawyers money could buy. The attorney for Bud Sellers, R. C. Soles, was a state senator. For the better part of eight months, this team of skilled barristers bombarded Federal Judge Earl Britt with a virtual barrage of motions and objections. Among those motions was a request to omit any evidence not originally presented to the grand jury. This move prevented the prosecutor from pursuing evidence linking Mr. Watts to any events of wrongdoing after November of 1975—including the shooting of my parents. Finally, on February 2, 1981, the trial of Mr. Watts began.

Daddy, the first to testify, flew back to North Carolina to face in court the devil who previously had occupied pew number seven in church. It would be the last time the two men saw each other. When asked by the press about his reaction to the news that Mr. Watts had been indicted, Daddy described the mental torture he still experienced years later. "I have to take tranquilizers, and I just got out from a six-month stay in the hospital. The wounds to my body have healed, but I can't put that time out of my mind," Daddy said.

Grateful to see the wheels of justice finally moving forward, Daddy added, "I have been waiting and praying those Fed boys would see this thing through. I feel a great sense of relief that this thing is finally going to court. I try not to think about it, but it wakes me in my sleep. You can't blink away a thought in the dark." No wonder Daddy roamed through the house in the middle of the night.

Daddy's testimony spanned two days. Ironically, the trial went through Valentine's Day. I'm sure Daddy's heart had to have been aching as he sat there in court without his valentine, reliving the painful past he had once shared with Momma.

Mr. Watts was prosecuted by Assistant U.S. Attorneys Ted Davis and Wallace Dixon, who pulled together upward of one hundred witnesses to make their case. At their request, the witness list had been sealed until trial to prevent harassment of their witnesses.

Even with that precaution in place, Gail Claude Spivey, one of the government's witnesses, told the judge that he had been threatened by members of the defense team. He testified that he had been approached and was told, "If you're not very careful, you could get blown to pieces." He added, "I leave this courtroom with great fear." That appeared not to be an unwarranted concern; his house had been burned down shortly after receiving the warning and just before he had taken the witness stand.

The government's star witness was Agent Charles Mercer, who had done a thorough job accumulating evidence over five years. According to one report, Attorney Davis painted Mr. Watts as "a rich and powerful man in Columbus County who was stripped of his powers in a church he was not even a member of [who] plotted to run the pastor and his family out of the Sellerstown community."

Fifty-four witnesses were ultimately called by Attorney Davis, who, like a skilled surgeon, stitched together seventy pieces of hard evidence as he sewed up the case against Mr. Watts. Layer upon layer, Attorney Davis laid the foundation and built a rock-solid wall of evidence for the jury to consider.

For the better part of three weeks, Attorney Davis methodically walked the jury through the threatening phone calls and letters, the series of shotgun blasts and bombings. He presented dynamite fuses, photos of craters in the yard and bullet holes in our car, and the results of telephone traces from calls made to the parsonage. He rounded out his case by interviewing detectives, ballistic experts, and specialists in forensics.

One of the most damaging pieces of evidence was a government witness who claimed under oath that Mr. Watts had offered him $100,000 to kill my daddy by running him over with his car. Mr. Watts had told him to make it look like an accident.

That dramatic testimony must have been the final straw. Mr. Watts stunned the court when he abruptly changed his plea from "not guilty" to "nolo contendere," which in Latin means "I do not wish to contend," to the two counts related to our family's situation. Not wanting to risk a jury verdict, with his revised plea Mr. Watts threw himself on the mercy of the court.

During the sentencing phase of the trial, Bob Burns, one of the attorneys for Mr. Watts, pleaded leniency for his client. He told the judge that the Mr. Watts he knew personally for some forty years wasn't the man as described in this case: "The picture painted of him from the witness stand is not the H. J. Watts I've known. I have found him to be a peacemaker. . . . I have known him as an honest and kindhearted man. Without exception in transactions with him, there has been no question of what is right and wrong; I have found him ready and willing to do the right thing."

Mr. Watts was a peacemaker?

Mr. Watts was a kindhearted man?

Does a peacemaker mastermind five years of terror against a pastor and his family? Where's the kindheartedness in publicly ridiculing my father during a worship service while smearing his reputation by calling him an adulterer behind his back? How could a man with these alleged qualities even dream of detonating a bomb outside the window of a house where an infant is asleep?

To help make his case that the Mr. Watts personified during the three-week trial wasn't really a scheming, evil man, Mr. Burns produced forty Columbus County residents. While thirty-five of them stood when called upon in the courtroom to acknowledge their support, five others took the stand to testify on record to the upstanding character and reputation of Mr. Watts.

Attorney Ed Williamson followed his cocounsel's address to the court, adding that Mr. Watts's "plea admits to you and the world his wrongdoing and his presence and manner show his remorse. He deserves mercy. The things he admits should never have been done."

Mr. Watts didn't "admit" to using violence and threats to harass our family.

He pleaded *no contest*.

The evidence against him had been so overwhelming that even a blind man could see Mr. Watts would be hard-pressed to gain a favorable judgment. He made a calculated decision hoping that his friend, the judge, who had represented him in years past, might somehow go easy on him now.

For his part, attorney Ted Davis, who successfully prosecuted the case, urged the court to remember the severity of the harm done by Mr. Watts. "When the Reverend Robert F. Nichols came to Sellerstown in 1969, he was six feet three inches tall, weighed 230 pounds, and was in excellent physical and mental condition," Mr. Davis said in his closing address. "Today, he is still six feet three inches tall, weighs in excess of three hundred pounds, and is in terrible mental and physical condition."

Davis continued, saying, "The bombings, shootings, harassment, and threatening phone calls have left him a shell of his former self, the result of this malicious treatment. He was run out of his position and was forced to go back to Alabama to escape the living hell he endured and to shield his children from the events of this trial. They walked in fear of being shot or bombed, and nothing can erase the horrifying fears they endured. We'll never know the horrifying fears Ramona Nichols endured, not knowing if they would be killed. All of this pain is the result of one man's jealousy."

After all was said and done, Mr. Watts, the man who stalked our family for five years, received what amounted to a hand slap on the wrist from Judge Britt. After commending Agent Charles Mercer for "a thorough and relentless investigation," the justice said, "Passing sentence is the worst job about being a judge, and it is extremely more difficult when people involved are people you know very well."

You could almost see that the fix was in.

He continued, "Attorneys Burns and Williamson have spoken of their knowledge of Mr. Watts, and I, too, have known him for years. R. C. Soles and I represented him in an official capacity when he was a county commissioner in a lawsuit involving taxation. I have had the opportunity to get to know some of his family and do some legal work for them. All of these things make it weigh heavier on my shoulders."

Given that history with Mr. Watts and his family, you'd think the judge would have recused himself due to the possible conflict of interest. He added, "I agree [with Watts's attorneys] that the Horry Watts pictured in this case is not the Horry Watts I knew, but I have to deal with the Horry Watts in this case. . . . The severity of the offenses committed easily dictate maximum punishment of all charges, but the severity of the offenses is not the only factor the court should consider. The person involved is, of course, the most important thing."

Judge Britt concluded, "The sentence will be the maximum sentence, but that will not be the ultimate. I will send you to the institution to find out what is in the best interest of society and H. J. Watts." As ordered by the judge, Mr. Watts underwent sixty days of "mental, physical and psychological testing in Butner Federal Correctional Institution." Probably the most disturbing aspect of the judgment to me was what Judge Britt considered to be the "maximum" sentence for targeting our family:

Count one: $10,000 and five years in prison
Count two: Five years in prison to run concurrently with the first five-year sentence

I should point out that at the same trial, Mr. Watts was also tried and sentenced to an additional ten years for conspiracy to bomb two other people as well as for using the postal system to deliver threatening letters to them. Taken together, Mr. Watts was facing fifteen years in prison and significant cash fines.

Upon hearing the judgment, Mr. Watts became visibly emotional. He removed his thick, black-framed glasses to brush away his tears. I don't know what prompted the outburst of emotion. Mr. Watts rarely displayed any feeling around us other than anger, rage, or spite. I have my doubts that his tears flowed from a repentant heart. If anything, I suspect they were a product of embarrassment.

As mentioned earlier, Mr. Watts knew a thing or two about

correctional facilities. In 1972, as a county commissioner, Mr. Watts helped facilitate the planning and building of the Columbus County Law Enforcement Center—a state-of-the-art jailhouse. His name, along with the other commissioners', was engraved on a sizable placard that had been affixed adjacent to the entrance of the prison.

Ironically, this slogan was splashed in large type on the wall of the prison: RESPECT FOR LAW IS THE BEGINNING OF WISDOM. That was nine short years before this event. Mr. Watts had to have been mortified to learn that he, of all people, was now heading to jail. In spite of his money, power, and his squad of lawyers, the unthinkable had happened.

He had lost.

At age seventy-five, the man who wasn't accustomed to losing was now a convict. Rather than toss the case out on some technicality, his longtime associate and friend, Judge Britt, did the sentencing. The thought that his residence would be a prison cell somewhere within the federal penitentiary system—not his beloved stretch of Sellerstown Road—had to have been humiliating.

On March 11, 1981, justice prevailed.

Mr. Watts was finally placed behind bars.

CHAPTER 14

# Life Is Hard, but God Is Good

The tide turned.

In spite of the good news that Mr. Watts was to receive some measure of justice for his behavior, the years he had spent persecuting our family wounded Daddy to the depth of his soul. While Daddy had his good days, in the wake of the trial he went from better to worse. He suffered from paranoia and constantly battled taunting voices inside his head. His condition, we were told, was aggravated by extreme sleep deprivation. These vestiges of Mr. Watts's hounding led to bizarre behavior and ultimately to a severe nervous breakdown.

Even when Daddy was sick, I loved to be with him. I came to accept the fact that he would break down at times. In my view, he was still my daddy in spite of the challenges to his mental state. His hugs never changed; they were engulfing, warm, and safe.

When I was fourteen, we were advised that Daddy might benefit from a stay in a special faith-based institution that dealt with those who had similar struggles. I understood he had to go.

Right before Daddy was to leave, Danny and I had an opportunity to say good-bye. Other times when Daddy had been taken to a hospital, we'd come home from school, and he'd already be gone. No good-byes. No hugs. No last prayer together as a family. So this was a treat to get to send him off. When Danny and I arrived home from spending some time with friends, the house was quiet. The shades had not been drawn open to let in the usual light that made our home feel warm and welcoming, perhaps because Daddy felt safer knowing strangers on the outside couldn't see in.

I found Daddy sitting upright in his brown cloth recliner in the family room. He sat as still as a statue. He wore his normal attire, a short-sleeve, button-down shirt, khaki pants, and brown slippers. When I searched his face, I could barely see the brown of his eyes due to the redness that surrounded them. He had a distant look on his face as if he were somewhere else.

I didn't hesitate to climb onto his lap.

Though I was fourteen, I hadn't outgrown the security I felt from sitting on his lap. I reached to wrap my arms around him for one last hug, but the hug wasn't returned as usual. I said, "I love you, Daddy," but he sat like a prisoner sworn to silence. During that brief encounter, I got the feeling that he was looking through me rather than at me. In the past he'd make eye contact when speaking to us; now he appeared tired and broken.

I knew I couldn't stay long. The car was packed and ready for the long road trip ahead. I held his huge hand and once again said, "I love you, Daddy. . . . I'll see you soon." Just then, and much to my surprise, he said, "I love you, Rebecca." He didn't make eye contact as he spoke. He didn't need to. The words were enough. It was such a gift to me for God to allow him to step back into reality—if just for a moment—to let me know that his love for me had not drifted away along with his mind.

After I slipped off his lap, Danny came and hugged Daddy, but at age nine, he just said his "I love yous" and turned around to leave. There was no point in waiting for a conversation. It wasn't going to happen. Daddy was too tired and heavily medicated. As Daddy left for the trip, I hoped and prayed that this hospital visit would be a short one.

I didn't see the storm coming.

There had been no alarm, no forewarning, nothing to prepare me for the news that would send me reeling for years. I was completely blindsided. On October 5, 1984, my world was blown apart. The tornado of grief hit on Friday while I was attending school. My teacher called me to her desk and, with a look on her face I couldn't quite make out, told me I was not to ride the bus home that day; I was to take the bus that would go to my grandmother's house instead.

There was no further explanation.

I did as I was told.

When I got off the bus, Mrs. Deborah, my grandparents' next-door neighbor and close family friend, greeted me. Without disclosing what was going on, she took me to her house instead of to my grandparents'. Her behavior seemed guarded, as if she wasn't at liberty to talk about why I had been summoned to their house. Although the homes were separated by several acres, as we pulled into her driveway, I noticed a number of extra cars parked outside of my grandparents' house.

That was odd.

It wasn't my birthday—or theirs—so this couldn't be a surprise party. I knew my grandparents had big family get-togethers all the time, but nothing was scheduled for that weekend. The more I thought about the reasons behind the unusual situation, the more I sensed something might be wrong. I just couldn't figure out what it was. Had something happened to Grandma or Grandpa?

Did they have a fall?

Had one of them died?

They *were* older, so that was an option.

Mrs. Deborah tried to distract me with chitchat while stalling for time. The longer I had to wait, however, the more persistent I became in my search for answers. *When can I go to my grandmother's house? What is going on over there? Who are all of those people gathered at their house?*

About all Mrs. Deborah told me was that I had to wait until we received a phone call—and not to worry. Again, that didn't make any sense. Why the mystery? I was fourteen at the time and had a more refined "baloney meter" that resonated whenever adults weren't being forthright with me. After what felt like an eternity, the call finally came. I hustled across the yard between the two houses.

As I crossed the small ditch separating the homes, virtually out of the blue, a heavy feeling weighed down on my chest as if someone were standing on my rib cage. I was overwhelmed with the foreboding sensation that something bad had happened to my daddy. Something really bad. Between the short hike and the uneasy premonition gnawing at my stomach, my heart started to race.

As I pushed open the side sliding-glass door, a distinct hush fell on the room. All eyes were immediately fixed on me—which felt strange, as if I were some kind of endangered species being studied. Why was I suddenly the center of attention? I was just a kid. Since I hadn't done anything wrong, I knew I couldn't be in trouble. When I said, "Hi, everyone," with a wave of my hand, they responded with a somber "Hi" that seemed to fit the restrained mood.

Scanning the room for a clue as to what was happening, I noticed my pastor sitting on the sofa with a number of my extended family members. For some reason the sight of him heightened my fears. This gathering wasn't for a wedding, it wasn't a Bible study, and it wasn't for a meal. That left very few options as to why he was present. Besides, upon closer inspection I noticed several people clutching wads of crumpled tissue.

Not good.

I was directed down the hall to the last bedroom on the left. I knew it was Aunt Dot's bedroom, which, at first, made me wonder if she had fallen ill. For a fleeting moment I was relieved to discover Aunt Dot was fine. After I settled on the edge of the bed, I was informed that Daddy had passed away earlier that morning. The words knocked the wind out of me, striking me with the force of a jolt of electricity.

More words of explanation came . . . something about a blood clot lodged in his heart took his life . . . he was now at peace with Jesus . . . Daddy was reunited with Momma . . . but I was too numb to care. Never in a thousand years would I have expected to hear that news. Daddy was just forty-six years old. He was way too young to die. I turned on my heels and ran out of the house screaming "*Noooooo!*" at the top of my lungs.

Shaking uncontrollably as if standing on the epicenter of an earthquake, I collapsed. Still shrieking out my disbelief, I didn't care what anybody might have thought about the scene I was making. My heart was shattered into a million fragile pieces. The grief was beyond comprehension. I had no strength to cope with the finality of his death.

First Momma. Now Daddy.

Gone.

When Momma was gunned down, I didn't get to say good-bye to her. And now, without warning, Daddy died when I was at school.

Once again I didn't get the chance to say a final good-bye. It just didn't seem fair. I would have given *anything* to have been at his side, to have hugged and kissed him one last time.

I think his death hurt me at such a core level because after losing Momma, Daddy had made me a promise: He pledged he would never leave Daniel or me. Like a prizefighter before stepping into the ring, Daddy had a rock-solid focus in his eyes as he spoke. That look assured me that he meant every word of his commitment. His words provided the security I needed to face the world. Now the words ran through my mind as a reminder that the promise he had made had been broken.

At just fourteen, I was an orphan.

What was I going to do without Daddy? Who would teach me how to drive? Who would screen my dates? Who would walk me down the aisle on my wedding day? I can't say I had all of these thoughts immediately upon hearing the tragic news. And yet somehow, some part of me knew my world would never, ever be the same without Daddy.

A few minutes after I went back inside the house, Danny arrived. I was with him in the back bedroom when he was told that Daddy had died. He fell across the bed, sobbing his little heart out. Watching him fall apart intensified my pain. I was hurting for both of us now. How could two young hearts bear so much grief?

At nine, Danny had been getting into sports. Daddy had been so proud of his progress. But now my brother wouldn't have his father cheering him on. Who would take Danny hunting and fishing? Who would mentor him into becoming a young man? Who would teach him how to love, respect, and court the hand of a woman? In a way, Danny needed Daddy even more than I did. Daddy was supposed to be Danny's compass on the road to manhood. Without him, that road would be a long and difficult journey.

I wanted him back.

+ + +

Daddy's funeral was held on October 11, 1984, at the Belmany Mortuary in Mobile. Three ministers gathered together to officiate the celebration of Daddy's homecoming—Ernest Miller, Daddy's lifelong friend who knew him from the early days when Daddy got saved; Kenneth Draughon, Daddy's pastor at the time; and Mitchell Smith, Daddy's assistant pastor from Sellerstown.

People traveled from across the country to honor the man they admired. In a way, I wasn't surprised. Daddy had led hundreds of people to the Lord. He had planted churches in several states. He had been driven to pursue the lost and feed his flock. He had preached faithfully under fire and had been willing to lay down his life, if necessary, to care for his congregation. No wonder when it was time to sing "Heaven's Sounding Sweeter All the Time," the packed service erupted in praise.

I listened to the music while looking at Daddy's casket. I remembered something he once told me: "Rebecca, if anything ever happens to me, don't go to my grave. I'm not there." I knew he couldn't wait to shed his earthly shell and get a new body, one that was free from pain. He didn't want my brother and me to mourn over an empty grave.

During the family's private viewing, I noticed that Daddy's hair wasn't quite right. It didn't make sense to me why someone didn't comb his hair to the side. I wanted him to look his best, so I took my brush out of my purse to fix his hair as he lay in the casket. Tucking the brush back into my purse, I reached in to touch his hand the way I had with Momma just seven years earlier. I had to hold the hand that had held mine so many times before.

I tried to imagine the joy Daddy would receive in heaven after all he had sacrificed to bring his heavenly Father glory. I know his face had to have been beaming as bright as the sun when Momma walked up to him to say, "I've been waiting for you!" My parents were both gone, but they were together. They were safe forever in the presence of Jesus. Proverbs 10:25 says, "When the storms of life come, the wicked are whirled away, but the godly have a lasting foundation" (NLT). That was the good news.

However, I was old enough to really understand my personal loss. I knew what it felt like to live without Momma in my life for the last seven years. Admittedly, after Daddy's funeral I didn't experience the same sense of peace I had felt when Momma died. In fact, I had quite the opposite reaction.

When Momma died, I knew it was because a man shot her.

When Daddy died, I felt as if God took him from me.

I blamed God. Why couldn't He just heal my daddy?

Although I confess that my first reaction was to blame God, I'm grateful I was in church three times a week—Sunday morning and evening and Wednesday night in my youth group. I believe staying in fellowship with other believers, hearing about God's goodness, coupled with my personal journaling and Bible study, kept my anger at God from taking up a permanent home in my heart. And when the early signs of anger began to surface, Aunt Dot, my youth pastor, and his wife helped pray me through it.

I can see why I struggled with depression at times as a teenager. I was a prime candidate for medication, although I didn't take any. My depression was rooted in a combination of issues. There was the trauma I experienced at the hands of Mr. Watts during my childhood. There was the string of new schools, new friends, and the uncertainties that came with the transition whenever we relocated. But losing *both* of my parents was so emotionally over-the-top, the weight of my feelings knocked me to the floor.

I could tell Daniel was doing his best to cope too. He and I shared an unspoken sadness: the missing, the hurt, the loss, and, yes, the questioning why we had been asked to endure so much injustice and pain. I could see the haze of trauma lingering in his eyes even if he didn't say a word. I tried to be there for Daniel when I was home, and yet I was torn between supporting him and trying to stay busy with friends and activities, hoping that in some way, somehow, I might outrun the nagging feelings of grief that nipped at my heels.

For me, the first two years after Daddy died—when I was fourteen to sixteen—were the hardest. I literally sat in the corner of my room, staring at nothing for hours. I wondered how my life had come to such a place of emptiness. I couldn't imagine ever experiencing the "green pastures" promised in Psalm 23. I wanted to move forward with my life but felt as if I had been stuck on the pause button. I didn't want to accept the fact that there were things in my life I couldn't change—forget about trying to deal with the nitty-gritty of living in the present.

And the future? That was too overwhelming to envision. I needed the steady hand of my father to keep my free spirit tethered to earth. His spiritual leadership was essential to my understanding of who God is. I needed Momma's guidance to walk me through the changes that were happening to my body and my emotions. I had neither. Instead, I felt wrung out and hopelessly broken.

I even tried hanging out with friends from school who weren't Christians. I figured maybe they could provide some escape from the questions and pain that constantly taunted me. But the more time I spent with them, the more confused I became. I quickly noticed that these friends didn't exhibit any sense of inner peace. And regarding the choices they made, they trusted in their own ways rather than seeking God's wisdom. Grandpa Welch used to say, "Some children are trained—others just grow up!" I knew I had been trained in the ways of God; trying to live any other way would not bring me peace.

Yet I remained fractured.

Here's the best way I can describe those years. Imagine taking seven different one thousand–piece puzzles. Then, imagine doing the unthinkable—mixing them all together in one giant pile. Then, after you've created the mess, you look at the pictures on the various boxes and realize there are tons of pieces of nondescript sky and fields of grass. Your job is to re-create the seven puzzles. That's when it dawns on you it might take a lifetime to figure out which pieces fit into which puzzle.

Is it any wonder I was depressed?

Thankfully, Daniel and I had Aunt Dot. At age forty-six, single, living with and caring for her parents, Aunt Dot chose to love us with everything she had as if we were her own children. She made sure we had our homework finished, our lunches packed, and our breakfast eaten before getting us off to school on time—while getting ready for her own full-time job. That was no easy task.

For years Aunt Dot was bivocational, working as a paralegal while doing ministry as a missionary in India and Africa. She tripled her workload the moment she made the decision to become a single parent for her brother's children. I later learned that in her twenties, Aunt Dot felt that God had spoken to her in her heart not to marry. She wrestled with that for years. She wanted children. Her mothering instincts drove her to seek a mate, settle down, and raise children. Why, then, did God ask such a difficult thing of her? After Daddy died, God's leading made perfect sense.

She would have children, just not biologically.

Not only did Aunt Dot provide comfort and the security that blossoms from the rich soil of a loving home, she counseled me through this fragile time. She helped me realize that I could only take each day as it came. She encouraged me not to dwell on all that had happened nor fret over what the future might be like without my parents. She said the best thing I could do was to ask Jesus to reach down and pick me up. I had to be totally dependent on Him, to be okay without knowing all the answers to the questions echoing inside of me.

In time, I came to see that only God could take my impossible situation and make sense of it. As I leaned into Him, He looked at my upside-down world and said, "Becky, do you think that's hard or complicated for Me to sort out?" Before I could give all my justified reasons for wondering, fretting, and failing to exercise the faith that, indeed, the task wasn't impossible for Him, He snapped His fingers, and everything fell into place.

No, I didn't get my parents back. But I was able to rest in the knowledge that He knew where, and how, all the pieces of my life should fit together. I knew He said in the Bible that He's a father to the fatherless and to the brokenhearted. I was both, so we had a perfect fit. There was one more insight I came to embrace.

I needed God more than I needed to blame God.

One of Daddy's final wishes was for his sister, my aunt Dot, to adopt us if he were to die. In the summer of 1986, two years after his death, the adoption was complete. I was sixteen, and Danny was eleven. Aunt Dot did an incredible job filling in for my parents. She made sure we were able to participate in school activities and sports, and since we were living with her at my grandparents' house, we saw our uncles, aunts, and cousins often. Her desire was to provide for us a sense of family unity while protecting us from any more harm, which is why she made a point of knowing who my friends were, what we were doing, where we were going, and who was calling for me at the house. She knew we had experienced a lifetime of hurt already. The last thing she wanted was for another crisis to rock our world. And, as God would have it, for the better part of a year things were calm.

That's when the phone rang.

There was nothing ominous or unusual about the ring.

I was in the family room watching television, too preoccupied with my show to break away from the action. I continued to watch as Aunt Dot answered the call and, for a few minutes, talked to the caller in muted tones. She asked the man to hold and, with her hand covering the receiver, called me to her side. She appeared guarded, as if contemplating the wisdom of handing me the phone.

"Becky . . ."

"Yes, Aunt Dot?"

"There's someone who wants to speak with you."

"Okay—" I reached for the phone. She hesitated. She didn't immediately hand it to me. I wondered what was driving her reluctance. She seemed to be studying me, searching my face for the answer to an unspoken question. As I learned later, she was weighing the decision whether to crack open a doorway to the past. She understood she couldn't shelter me forever. There would be a time to confront the events that took place on Sellerstown Road.

Evidently, she decided that time had come.

"Honey, it's Mr. Watts. He'd like to speak with you."

My heart exploded against my chest.

"Mr. Watts? From Sellerstown?" I felt my face flush.

"Yes . . . but Becky," she said, her voice dripping with caution, "you don't have to take the call if you don't want to, okay?"

I took the call. I placed the phone to the side of my head as my heart pounded out warning signals that pulsated around the edge of my ears.

"Hello?"

"Hi, Becky. This is Mr. Watts."

His voice was painfully familiar to me ten years after we'd left Sellerstown. The husky, gravelly tone triggered a rush of mental images of the man . . . pacing the street in front of our house, under a full moon, in his pajamas and brown fedora hat . . . shaking his fist at our car as we drove home . . . and cutting up in church, trying to distract Daddy from pew number seven.

"Hi, Mr. Watts."

It was about all I could think to say at the moment. The truth was, I hadn't spent any time rehearsing what I'd say to him if, by chance, I ever spoke with him again. I had no prior plans to read Mr. Watts the riot act for what he'd done to me and my family, and that didn't change with him on the other end of the line.

"Becky, I know talking with me might be difficult for you. I don't mean to make you feel uncomfortable—"

"Don't worry, Mr. Watts. I'm fine."

"Well, then, what I have to say won't take but a minute." He paused. At first I thought the line went dead. Then I got the impression that someone—Mr. Watts?—was fighting back tears on the other end of the connection. He continued. "Becky, I'm out of prison . . . but I'm not the man you used to know. Believe me when I tell you I'm different now."

I listened. In the back of my mind something didn't make sense about the fact that Mr. Watts was out of jail so soon. We knew two of his four 5-year sentences were to be served concurrently, but that still meant he should be in jail for fifteen years. We'd later learn that Judge Britt had cut Mr. Watts's sentence to four years and then granted him parole after serving just one year.

"I . . . I was wrong for what I did to you and your family," he said, his voice catching on several of the words as he spoke. "Your parents didn't deserve any of the things I put them through. I'm sorry about what I did."

I wasn't sure where this conversation was headed, but my impression was that this couldn't be the same man who had harassed us for so long. The Mr. Watts I had known *never* apologized to anyone for any reason. But here he was clearly fighting back the tears, offering me an apology. There was more.

"Becky, when I was in prison, I got right with God," he said, and then he broke down and sobbed.

The floodgate of repentance had opened, and Mr. Watts no longer attempted to choke back the years of regret. "I need to know that you'll forgive me for all I've done to you and your family. I can't live the rest of my life without knowing you've forgiven me. Can you?"

Mr. Watts never sounded more human.

I'm sure what I said next surprised him. I told him my brother and I *did* forgive him. I told him, in fact, we had forgiven him long before he had asked for forgiveness. I explained that my parents not only taught us these words of Jesus, but they modeled them for us as well. Jesus said, "But I tell you who hear me: Love your enemies, do good to those who hate you, bless those who curse you, pray for those who mistreat you" (Luke 6:27-28, NIV). Mr. Watts had given me plenty of years to live out those words in my life.

And while I didn't go into many more details with him, my parents had taught me quite a number of things about forgiveness. If I found myself questioning why they didn't fight back after one of Mr. Watts's attacks, Daddy would say, "Becky, the Bible says we are to 'bless those who persecute you; bless and do not curse'" (Romans 12:14, NIV). To be sure, the seeds they planted in my heart took root and allowed me the freedom to forgive Mr. Watts rather than to become a prisoner of anger and resentment.

Daddy knew that Mr. Watts had been tormenting us because he, in spite of his power, money, and political connections, was a tormented man. And as I spoke with Mr. Watts that afternoon, I sensed that while he had been physically released from prison, he wouldn't be completely free until he had called me. As difficult as this might be to believe, it made me happy to see Mr. Watts set free from the guilt that he had unnecessarily carried for so long.

As I finished speaking, I could hear Mr. Watts struggling to regain his composure, fighting the tears as he expressed gratefulness for our forgiveness. While I don't remember all that he said during that first phone call, it was clear that Mr. Watts experienced the heavy burden of guilt lifting from his heart.

Before we said our good-byes, Mr. Watts told me he wanted to make some sort of restitution. He had set up trust funds for Daniel and for me to receive when we graduated from college. He made it official by putting this in his will. I was stunned and grateful. I accepted his kindness.

Through the next several years, we kept in touch with letters. His written words often echoed the heart of a repentant man. The hardness in his speech that frightened me as a child had melted away into a graciousness and an understanding of second chances. He truly came to the realization that we are all sinners, saved by grace. The grace exhibited by my parents was now something he knew firsthand.

Speaking of the old Mr. Watts, the last time he mailed my parents a letter, it was an unsigned threat promising we'd leave Sellerstown "crawling or walking . . . dead or alive." About a year after my first phone conversation with the new Mr. Watts, I received the following letter. His words reflected the love and care of a changed man. The contrast between these two pieces of correspondence was as polar opposite as the North is from the South.

His cold, anonymous letter had been typed to obscure any trace of the sender; this message exuded the warmth and crafting of a personally handwritten note. He had been trying for some time without success to come see me. Barring that, he wrote,

*August 29, 1988*

*To: Miss Becky Nichols, Daniel, Dorothy, and*
*Mr. and Mrs. Nichols,*

*Greetings to all of you,*
*Looks like it does not work out for me to go see you all. I have talked to several [drivers], none seems to want to go with me but I have not given up hopes. I do want to see you all. As you know, I am 82 years last February 16, not quite as spry as I was once. But the good Lord is helping me. I am enclosing a check for $100. Hope this will help a little. My best wishes and prayers goes with it. And if we never meet here on earth I do hope and pray we will all meet in Heaven when this life is over. May I have your prayers with mine. May God bless you all.*

*Becky, I am treating you as good or better than any one else except my own family. I would like to see you have a new car when you graduate from college. That [is] what I have done for my 5 children who graduated. Will certainly be glad to help.*

*Daniel, I plan to do for you the same as for Becky. Be good children. Don't smoke, drink, or do dope. It can ruin you. Please take this with love and gratitude. Give my love and best wishes to all and please pray for me.*

*Your sincere friend,*

*H. J. Watts*

*P.S. My dear wife expired one year ago today. I miss her so much. Living by myself [is] so sad and lonesome. Again, remember me Becky and Daniel. I have given your names to my lawyer. You will be in my write up. We are still working on my Trust and Will. Let me hear from you when you get to college.*

*Best wishes, H. J. W.*

As difficult as it may be to believe, I accepted his apology. I don't remember hearing from Mr. Watts again after I received this letter. However, I did learn that he died from cancer in 1991.

I have no doubt that God used the sacrificial love exhibited by my parents to bring Mr. Watts to a saving faith. Although none of us saw that back when the bullets were flying through my window and the bombs were exploding outside in the yard, I can see that now. And you know what? If that's what it took to bring a lost sheep into the fold, then I'm thankful our Shepherd knew that the hardships we would endure would be used for His purposes. Genesis 50:20 says, "You intended to harm me, but God intended it for good to accomplish what is now being done, the saving of many lives" (NIV).

Yes, life is hard, but God is good.

CHAPTER 15

# No Apologies in Heaven

"I forgive you."

Those just might be the three most difficult words in the world to say to someone who has wronged you—especially if you mean what you're saying. Come to think of it, it's even more difficult to forgive the offender *before* he or she has asked for forgiveness—and virtually impossible to extend forgiveness to a person who, by all appearances, may never apologize for his or her actions.

A friend of mine had a near meltdown when I told her about my first phone conversation with Mr. Watts. I had been reaching out to her for some time. One day while we were dining at a favorite lunch spot, I thought it might be a good idea to tell her the whole account. She knew I was a Christian and was peripherally aware of my early childhood trauma. While I had talked with her about God's love and His gift of forgiveness over the years, I hadn't gone into the details of my early life.

From the time I began telling her about the anonymous threatening letters from Mr. Watts, through the sniper shots and bombings he orchestrated, and then to the day when my parents were gunned down, she listened on the proverbial edge of her seat. When I told her Mr. Watts called to say he was sorry—a twist in the story she never saw coming—I could tell she was starting to get feisty.

But when I got to the part where I told Mr. Watts that my brother and I had forgiven him even before he had asked for our forgiveness, my friend became indignant. To say she was visibly angry would be an understatement. Livid might be a more appropriate word. Having attracted stares from the adjacent tables, I actually had to calm her down. I explained that I had no strength within myself to forgive Mr. Watts. Rather, it was the love and power of Jesus that enabled me to extend love to the man who was responsible for the persecution of my family.

Her reaction isn't uncommon.

In fact, the one question I'm most often asked after sharing my story is, "Becky, how in the world could you *possibly* forgive Mr. Watts for all the horrible things he did to you and your family?" I'm not surprised that people wrestle with that reality. Humanly speaking, it's natural to think that anyone in my shoes should have the right to seek revenge. Just listen to how we talk when we're wronged on a much smaller scale than, say, someone bombing your house. We say things like . . .

"It's payback time!"

"So when are you going to get even with her?"

"Watch me turn the tables on him for messing with me."

"You're gonna get what's coming to you, pal!"

People have this notion that I ought to get my "pound of flesh," or that I have a right to harbor a deep resentment against the man who vowed to run my parents out of town, who terrorized my childhood, and who got little more than a hand slap on the wrist for his crimes. That's a tempting response. Maybe it's your response too.

If so, I don't fault you for that reaction.

This side of heaven, it's easy to be preoccupied with settling the score . . . of fighting back . . . of hurting those who have hurt us . . . or, at the very least, withholding forgiveness out of spitefulness to those who have wronged us. I've never claimed to be an expert on the subject, but I do know this: If I allow myself to go down the pathway of rage and retaliation, several things happen, and none of them are good. Here are my top four:

My sins will not be forgiven by God if I refuse to forgive those who have sinned against me.

I miss an opportunity to show God's love to an unforgiving world.

I'm the one who remains in jail when I withhold God's grace by failing to forgive.

If I have trouble forgiving, it might be because I'm actually angry at God, not at the person who wronged me.

Let's unpack those briefly, one at a time.

## Forgiving As He Forgave Me

Why is forgiving others such a big deal to God? As you might imagine, I've had several decades to explore this question. The pain I've suffered at the hands of Mr. Watts and Harris Williams, the man who shot my parents, has driven me to dig deep into understanding the heart of Jesus. My personal study can be boiled down to this statement:

Forgiveness is the language of heaven.

What do I mean by that?

Jesus wants us to be fluent in speaking forgiveness to one another. He wants forgiveness to be on the tip of our tongue, rather than something we begrudgingly offer after weeks, months, or even years of rubbing the offense in the face of the culprit before doling out a reluctant "I forgive you."

Here's why you and I should practice the language of heaven with the persistence we'd bring to the study of any foreign language. As I've thought about it, God's forgiveness is mankind's greatest need. Against the backdrop of eternity, the thing you and I need most is ***not*** food, air, water, shelter, love, money, family, friendship, or a lifetime companion. While those are wonderful things to have, our single greatest need is to be forgiven by God for our sins. Why?

Because the debt we've incurred by offending a holy God with our sins is unfathomable. We have no means to repay what we owe Him. A platinum American Express card with an unlimited credit balance wouldn't cover the down payment. Unless our outstanding debts are paid off—or forgiven and wiped clean—we cannot enter into His presence. And without God's forgiveness (since He's the only one who has the means to forgive us of our debts), we remain outcasts, eternally separated from His love, His joy, His peace, and His fellowship.

But because Jesus died on the cross for you and me, He paid the debt we owe. His sacrifice purchased our freedom from the bondage of sin. Because we have been forgiven so much, we have an obligation to forgive others. When I look at it from God's perspective, I begin to understand why forgiving my husband for the petty things that might upset me, or forgiving my kids when they interrupt me for the thousandth time when I'm on the phone, or forgiving the neighbor who telegraphs his hatred every time I drive by is required of me.

You and I have an obligation to forgive because we've been so richly forgiven. In that respect, forgiveness is the language of heaven. That's the message in Jesus' parable of the unforgiving servant found in Matthew 18:21-35 and following. Read it sometime, and as you do, don't overlook the powerful warning at the end: "That's what my heavenly Father will do to you if you refuse to forgive your brothers and sisters from your heart" (NLT).

After teaching His disciples how to pray what has become known as the Lord's Prayer, Jesus says, "If you forgive those who sin against you, your heavenly Father will forgive you. But if you refuse to forgive others, *your Father will not forgive your sins*" (Matthew 6:14-15, NLT, emphasis added). There's not much wiggle room in that verse, is there?

Jesus doesn't qualify His statement with a list of disclaimers. Notice what He *doesn't* say: "But if you refuse to forgive others *except* if it's your spouse who has cheated on you . . . or a business partner who swindled you out of a fortune . . . or a crazy man living across the street trying to blow up your family. . . ." Nope. Jesus offers no such exceptions.

There are no loopholes.

Plainly and simply put, my sins will not be forgiven if I fail to forgive. That's the first good reason to forgive.

But . . . when is enough enough?

Peter, a follower of Jesus, once tried to pin down Jesus on this "requirement" of forgiving someone who wronged him. Peter asked, "Lord, how often will my brother sin against me, and I forgive him? As many as seven times?" I'm a lot like Peter. I like specifics. You tell me I've got to forgive others, then I'd like to know what a reasonable number is. Surely there's a limit, right? Seven sounds reasonable; it's much more generous than the "three strikes and you're out" rule.

Watch how Jesus answers Peter: "I do not say to you, up to seven times, but up to seventy times seven" (Matthew 18:22, NASB). I'm tempted to do the math. I've got my pen and notepad out with a series of little marks grouped in units of five so I can easily keep track of my progress. Let's see, over the last three decades I've forgiven Mr. Watts 475 times . . . 480 . . . 485 . . .

I'm pretty sure that's not what Jesus had in mind.

I think Jesus was saying that you and I should forgive so many times that it *becomes second nature to us*. If forgiveness is the language of heaven, then forgiveness should be *a way of life* for me. Notice, I didn't say it should be easy. It's not. I won't sugarcoat it for you. In my case, I'm tempted to protest and say, "But, Lord, I'm on number 489. Will I *still* have to forgive Harris in my heart after forgiving him 490 times?"

Frankly, I've missed His heart if that's my thinking.

It's not about counting; it's about grace.

God will never say it's okay *not* to forgive.

Personally, I want forgiveness to become my heavenly habit, not an obligation. There's a big difference. The first approach reflects a lifestyle that flows from God's Kingdom and changes my way of operating in all my earthly relationships. The other approach is all about duty; it's about as heartfelt as paying income taxes.

## For the Love of God

Second, I have an opportunity to display God's love whenever I offer forgiveness in the face of hatred, personal betrayal, and persecution. When I forgive, that act of divinely inspired grace allows me to become a light in a dark world, pointing the way to Jesus. Make no mistake about it. People are observing you and me to see how we, as Christians, deal with the hard knocks of life. When they see that we've been wronged, offended, wounded, ripped off, shortchanged, or "done a wrong turn," our response can either attract those who are watching us to the Savior or give them yet another excuse not to follow Him.

Jesus said, "In the same way, let your light shine before men, that they may see your good deeds and praise your Father in heaven" (Matthew 5:16, NIV). I've got to admit, while I desire to be a light for Christ, while I can think of nothing more important than to be a living tribute to His grace, this can be a challenge when you've been hurt as deeply as I have been wounded. I'll be the first to admit that it's easy for the bitterness from the past to surface and weasel its ugly taproot into my heart.

To be perfectly blunt, when you finish reading this book, when you place it on the shelf or pass it along to a friend, that's it—you're done. You get to move on from my story to other worthy books if you choose to do so. Our lives will have intersected for a moment in time, and for that I'm grateful. But long after you've put down the book, I'll still be carrying the story in my heart every waking hour—and it still sometimes pops up at the most unexpected moments.

Like the time when I, at age thirty-five, was sharing a meal with friends at a restaurant. We had just watched a movie with a lot of violence. As the conversation turned to other violent and scary films, I found myself alone, transported into my own world without anyone knowing I had mentally checked out.

I pretended to be engaged in the exchange but in my mind I was suddenly a five-year-old all over again . . . in my bed . . . eyes wide open . . . scared . . . listening to the footsteps outside my window. The unnerving sound of a home intrusion spiked my heart; someone uninvited was on our property. I could hear the grass yield under each step.

Was there more than one assailant in our yard? Were they outside my window? Were they going to come in our house this time or continue to hide in the blackness of night until the moment when they'd launch their attack? Should I scream? If I did, they'd know where I was. I had been taught to remain quiet, to keep the lights off, to stay away from the windows—and to get down if I heard gunshots. But this time would it be another round of bullets flying through my window or the blast of a bomb?

Before something bad could happen, I willed myself to join the present moment and reenter the conversation with my friends. Even though we were sitting close around the table, they had no idea I had been alone in my own frightful world of memories. Sure, I tried to appear interested in the banter over film violence, but somehow I couldn't escape the questions I had had as a five-year-old: Am I safe now? Will I ever be safe? When the sun comes up, will this nightmare finally be over?

Even though the events took place thirty years prior to the movie night out with friends, an old wound was cut open. The trauma required more than a few days for me to get over. I went to my Bible, as I have done so many desperate times before, to find healing and peace once again. I had to remind myself that God promised to be with me every second of every day. He said, "Fear not, for I am with you; be not dismayed, for I am your God. I will strengthen you, yes, I will help you, I will uphold you with My righteous right hand" (Isaiah 41:10, NKJV).

Even when I'm alone with my thoughts.

I didn't ask for this abrasion on my soul to be a part of my life; it just is. Now, day after day, I have the choice to forgive the two men who took so much from me, or I can choose to wallow in a toxic brew of bitterness. True, I forgave Harris Williams a long time ago. But that doesn't mean I still don't have to forgive him again and again . . . on my mother's birthday when she's not there for us to celebrate her . . . every Easter because that was the season when gunshots cut down my parents and shattered my world, and the list goes on and on.

Don't get me wrong.

I'm not suggesting I'm the only person who has experienced deep and abiding hurt. Far from it. In this fallen world, all of us have had—or will soon experience—wrongdoing at the hands of others. Some of those actions are petty, bush-league stuff; other actions cause major league–size wounds. Maybe you were molested as a child, or were raped, or live with a verbally abusive spouse, or are haunted by the mean-spirited pronouncements of a friend who betrayed you. You and I cannot walk away from what's been done to us.

At the same time, as crazy as it sounds, we're *commanded* to speak the language of heaven, to forgive as we have been forgiven—generously, fully, and freely. That means we forgive with no strings attached; that may require us to forgive repeatedly. When we do, we shock the world with God's power at work within us. When they shake their heads in wonderment, when they struggle to understand how anyone could forgive like that, we have the opportunity to point them to the Cross, the ultimate act of forgiveness.

## Get Out of Jail

The third lesson I've come to discover in my journey of forgiveness is that I'm the one who remains in jail if I withhold God's grace by failing to forgive when wronged. As I've presented my testimony at various women's conferences, someone invariably approaches me with her "strategy." She views withholding forgiveness as a means of leveraging control over the offending party, like meting out some sort of punishment.

Guess what?

Aside from the fact that such a strategy is not an option for the believer, it often backfires. The offending person might not even have a clue that he or she has hurt you. Not all offenses are intentional, right? So, while you're harboring bitterness toward that person, when you fail to release him or her through forgiveness, you end up punishing yourself in the end. As someone once said, "Bitterness is like drinking poison and waiting for the other person to die."

Author Lewis Smedes, whose book *The Art of Forgiving* is one of the best on the subject, put it this way: "When you forgive a person who wronged you, you set a prisoner free, and then you discover that the prisoner you set free is you." I love that perspective. In a way, when I forgave Mr. Watts, *I* was the one who benefited in the long run. If, however, I had allowed the root of bitterness and unforgiveness to take hold in my life, I'd be the one in jail—not him.

Why? Think about what happens when we don't forgive. For me, rather than forgive and move on, I become preoccupied. I overanalyze the offense and, in turn, find that my thoughts are dominated by how I was hurt. That, in turn, creates a huge distraction in my daily routine. I remember once being so engrossed with unforgiveness that I had forgotten to make dinner. As the dinner hour came and went unnoticed by me, my kids said, "Hey, Mom, are we still having dinner?" I was completely shut down because I hadn't taken the steps to forgive the person who had hurt me earlier that day.

The writer of the book of Hebrews says, "See to it that no one misses the grace of God and that no bitter root grows up to cause trouble and defile many" (12:15, NIV). Being quick to forgive, then, prevents bitterness from keeping my heart captive to the wrong that's been done to me; what's more, it breaks the bondage of bitterness from being passed to the next generation.

I don't want my children to be harboring anger at Mr. Watts or Harris Williams because they've watched me be destroyed by their actions. To be sure, if I had given in to the trap of having a pity party for myself over the fact that Mr. Watts got out of jail early, my kids would have watched me serving his time in my own self-pity-induced prison. I'd much rather that they see their mother being free in Christ and learn, as I'm continuing to learn, about the power of forgiveness to set us free.

At times, when I was younger and feeling self-pity about my situation, Aunt Dot would help me put my life in perspective. She'd say,

"There are a lot of people who have been through worse things than you have, Becky. What's more, they didn't necessarily have a supportive family or God to help them through it." I hadn't thought of that.

She reminded me, "There are children who have never heard their parents say, 'I love you.' Your parents loved you and Daniel so much and said so regularly. More importantly, God loves you, and you know He'll never leave you. He's right by your side until you're reunited with your parents in heaven." The thought that other kids had gone through worse things than we had awakened compassion in me and got my focus off myself and my pity party. It also opened the doorway to forgiveness.

My aunt Dot went a step further by giving me a practical way of knowing whether I've truly forgiven someone from my heart. She said that, if I were to see the offender walking down the street, I should be able to wish him or her well. Forgiveness is a choice, she said, not a feeling. Aunt Dot wasn't suggesting that I have to have a relationship with such people again or invite them into my life or be their friend.

Some people still have serious issues.

Others have toxic personalities.

For some with unresolved problems, the damaging things in their lives could spill over and hurt me. But that shouldn't prevent me from wishing them God's best . . . from a distance if necessary.

## No Apology in Heaven

The journey of forgiveness takes an interesting turn in the road with the fourth observation: If I have trouble forgiving, it might be because I'm actually angry at God, not primarily at the person who wronged me. Our inability to forgive others often has to do with our unwillingness to make peace with God over what has happened. Whether or not we've stopped long enough to see that this dynamic is at work, subconsciously it's possible we're mad at God for not preventing our pain in the first place.

You know, it's God's fault that such and such has happened.

For example, God could have stopped a spouse from committing adultery—or from being a lazy bum who's unwilling to provide for the family. God didn't intervene, and now we're mad at Him because our marriage has fallen apart or because the bank has foreclosed on our home.

Perhaps we think God could have stopped a business partner from embezzling the profits or kept a prodigal from leaving home after all of our prayers on her behalf. He didn't. We're so filled with anger and disappointment that God didn't show up at the last minute and answer our prayers, there's no way we'd ever forgive the business partner or wayward child.

What's more, it's tempting to think that God owes *us* an apology for the betrayal, suffering, insults, hard knocks, or wounds we experience here on earth. When we get to heaven, we're gonna have it out with Him; we'll march right up and say, "Why, God, didn't You heal my mate of cancer?" . . . "Why, God, did You allow my sweet daughter to marry that creep of a guy?" . . . "Why, God, did You blah blah blah?"

I've got news for you.

There isn't an apology coming.

In my case, the devil was in pew number seven, and God knew about him all along. He knew what kind of fellow Mr. Watts was, as well as the severe damage that his actions were having on my daddy's nervous system. In spite of this knowledge, God didn't prevent Mr. Watts from carrying out his five-year campaign of terror against us. Had God stopped Mr. Watts in his tracks, Daddy wouldn't have suffered with paranoia. Perhaps he'd still be alive.

If I'm honest, I must admit that my real issue could be with God, not necessarily with Mr. Watts. I might be tempted to withhold forgiveness because I'm actually mad at God. Thankfully, with the help and teaching of my parents, I learned to keep things in perspective. They helped me see that God is still God even when things don't make sense. God hasn't made a mistake yet, so He can be trusted even when my circumstances suggest otherwise.

He is the Potter; I am the clay.

God is still good even when life is hard.

As I mentioned in the last chapter, my need for God trumped my need to be mad at Him. I'll admit I lost track of the number of times I pounded my fists on the gates of heaven, demanding an explanation from God as to why He permitted what He had allowed. Somewhere in the midst of that ongoing wrestling match, just after my sixteenth birthday, I found the Scripture that says that God is a Father to the fatherless (see Psalm 68:5). I hung on to those words with everything I had.

I came to see that I had to make a choice: I could contend with God, exhausting myself every day in the vain pursuit of securing an apology from Him. Or setting aside that fruitless quest, I could immerse myself in the Scriptures where the Maker of my soul was quick to meet me and give me His peace.

What's more, God reminded me that He has the long view in mind. I only see through a glass dimly. As 1 Corinthians 13 puts it, "Now I know in part; then I shall know fully, even as I am fully known" (v. 12, NIV). To paraphrase evangelist and American reformer Hannah Whitall Smith, a great many things in God's divine providences do not look like goodness. But faith sits down before mysteries such as these and says, "The Lord is good; therefore, all that He does must be good no matter how it looks."

Again, in my case, the long view that God had in mind was the use of our suffering to bring Mr. Watts into a place where he accepted Jesus into his heart. I'd love to believe that one day the same will be true for Harris Williams. Which brings me back to something I mentioned earlier—forgiveness isn't necessarily a once-for-all action on our part.

Even if we've made our peace with God and have set aside that crazy notion that one day He'll apologize to us in heaven for exercising His sovereign will on earth, forgiving someone might require repeated doses of grace.

Such was the case with Harris.

## Say It Isn't So

Things aren't always as they seem.

When Harris Williams was sentenced to life in prison, I thought that meant exactly that. He had taken my mother's life and robbed Daddy of his wife and livelihood. The court said Harris would have to serve those years behind bars for his crime. But in April 2005, out of curiosity, my husband, Kenny, looked up Harris's status on the Internet. Much to his amazement and to my shock, Harris had been released from prison in 1999 and given five measly years of parole.

Ironically, in 1999 we lived in North Carolina, working just two-and-a-half hours from where Harris was living. Did anyone contact me or my family to inform us that Harris was up for parole? No. Did anyone ask us if we wanted to be at the parole hearing? No. Did anyone tell us that he was released after serving twenty years and that he would return to the same town he had lived in before he was imprisoned? *No!*

The news tore open my old wounds.

Where was the justice?

If given a million years, I would never have thought that a man could take someone's life—and shoot with the intent to kill another person—and then, after a short stint in jail, be walking around as a free man. So many questions ran through my mind when Kenny told me this news. The feelings I had laid to rest regarding the loss of my mother reemerged.

I knew I had a decision to make.

I had to choose to forgive Harris all over again.

The first time I worked through the forgiveness of Harris, I was an innocent child; I had been following the teachings and the example of my parents. Now, however, I would have to forgive Harris on my own, as an adult. It would be harder for me this time. I kept dwelling on how unfair it was that Harris had his freedom back while I was still without my parents.

It bugged me that Harris had served less time than my mother had been gone. He got his life back, while mine would never be the same. I found myself wondering what he was doing with his freedom. Had prison reformed him? Would he return to his drinking and hardened behavior? Or would he make something of his second chance?

I wish I had a second chance with Momma.

I had to let go of my anguish over and over again. I called a friend and shared with her the endless mental gymnastics I was having upon hearing the news that Harris was out. She said, "Becky, you have two choices. You can let these negative thoughts continue running through your mind like a locomotive, robbing you of the God-given peace that you have, or you can stop these thoughts right now dead in their tracks by forgiving him again."

Did Harris deserve my forgiveness?

That wasn't for me to decide.

I'm not his judge. God is.

Besides, Jesus commanded me to forgive him. Did that strike me as being unfair? Of course it did. And yet, as I pressed myself into the Scriptures for answers, I was drawn to the story of the criminals who were crucified beside Jesus on the two adjacent crosses. It dawned on me that if I were to ask the families who had been wronged by those convicts if they thought the felons should receive the full penalty of death for their crimes, they'd say, "Absolutely."

But Luke, the only Gospel writer to give this version of the incident, describes a conversation between one of the criminals and Jesus. During their exchange, the criminal freely confesses that he deserves his death. He makes no excuse. He doesn't shift blame. He accepts his punishment. That's when an interesting thing happens.

This condemned man, after asserting the fact that Jesus has done nothing wrong, says, "Jesus, remember me when you come into your kingdom."

Jesus replies, "I tell you the truth, today you will be with me in paradise" (Luke 23:42-43, NIV).

As I reread that familiar passage, I didn't understand how Jesus would forgive a criminal who had broken the law and hurt people and then allow him to receive the same eternal salvation as someone who had led a godly life. I still don't know the answer to that mystery, but I do know that God, in His wisdom, knows why He extends the gift of grace to any of us. That's His business. My part is trusting God and praying for His will to be done in my life.

After the initial shock of hearing that Harris had been released from prison, I spent some time listening to my daddy's testimony, which he had recorded on a cassette tape before his death. When he got to the part about Harris and the shooting, Daddy's tone changed; there was an unmistakable compassion ringing clear in his voice as he said, "I forgive the man who shot me and my wife. I know alcohol makes people do things that they would not normally do. My hope for him is that he would be saved."

His words touched my heart in a deep and profound way, both then and even now as I write these words. My daddy and hero displayed the forgiveness he had modeled so many times before. His words reminded me that I have to walk in forgiveness and that my prayer for Harris should be the same as that of my daddy's, namely, that Harris would be saved. That Harris, like the criminal on the cross, would know the saving power of Jesus; that nothing he has ever done would be unforgivable to His Creator.

That Jesus loves him and died for him.

Once I prayed that prayer for Harris, the burden and accusation lifted.

I felt free again.

## The Heart of the Matter

If I were to boil down what I've learned about forgiveness, I'd say it's ultimately a matter of the condition of my heart. Momma demonstrated that reality with her life. Her goal, her driving purpose every day, was to become more like Jesus, to conform her heart to His heart. He forgave, so she forgave. He loved without placing conditions on His love; she loved others with the same fervor.

He extended grace; she did the same.

Because Momma was teachable and tender toward the things of the Lord, her heart was highly receptive to the things that the Lord wanted to plant there: love, joy, grace, peace, kindness, and forgiveness, among other things. Momma was willing to do anything God asked her to do. And because she kept the garden of her heart free from the weeds of anger and bitterness, those weeds were powerless to choke out her love of people. In turn, she found it easier to forgive those who persecuted her . . . even if it cost Momma her life.

Perhaps the clearest enduring example that Momma's greatest desire was to align her heart with that of the Lord is represented in a poem she penned in 1966, twelve years before her death. You can almost read between the lines the words of Jesus in John 15:13 (NIV), which says, "Greater love has no one than this, that he lay down his life for his friends." She wrote,

*Has the meditation of my heart been acceptable to my Lord, or have the words of my mouth caused some soul to go astray?*
*Have I shed enough tears to wash my Savior's feet, or is my hair long enough to dry them with?*
*Have I pointed Him to the world with Judas's finger, and lost my love for Him because of gold?*
*Have I forsaken all to follow Him the last mile, or do I prefer the mob that scorned Him?*
*Could I have watched His blood trickle down the stones without a guilty conscience, or stood in silence from fear of man?*
*Did I hold the nail they pierced Him with, or did the thorns pain Him with my sins?*
*Do I, as Peter, deny that I ever knew Him by not confessing Him to my friends?*
*Do I love my brothers and sisters enough that I would lay down my own life for them, or do I love Him enough to introduce my Savior to a lost world?*
*Oh Lord, may I be aware daily of Thy sufferings for me, for I am not worthy of Calvary.*

I think Momma would agree that I'm the keeper of the door to my heart. To love and forgive others as I've been loved and forgiven by Jesus, I have to guard what I allow to take root in my heart. If I open my heart to self-pity, anger, grudges, and unforgiveness, I give the enemy of my soul an invitation into a very expensive home—a home purchased by the blood of Jesus. But as I become fluent in the language of heaven, as I open the door of my heart to Jesus and in His strength forgive others, that's when I'm set free.

# Afterword

After I share the details of my story and how I survived those unbelievable years, I'm often asked, "So how's your brother, Daniel? Where is he now? And how did he cope with everything?" I'm happy to report that Daniel made it through those storms as I did. He's been a strength to me when the waves are high and winds are blowing.

I credit much of our "post-traumatic success" to Aunt Dot. When she promised Daddy that if anything happened to him, she'd take care of his children, she became both Momma and Daddy to us. She made a decision to do everything in her power to give us the life that our parents would have wanted us to have and enjoy. I am forever grateful for her love and investment in our lives.

For example, in middle school when Daniel showed an interest in music, Aunt Dot didn't hesitate to help him get a saxophone. He polished his skills and ultimately played in the band from those early years well into college. He's so musically inclined he plays the guitar by ear and can read music—just as Momma did. I know Momma would be pleased that her love for music and talent were passed down to her son.

One of Aunt Dot's goals was to help us get our college degrees. Having pieced together a patchwork of grants, scholarships, and personal savings, we did. I graduated from Missouri State University with a bachelor of science degree in interior design; Daniel graduated from the University of Alabama with a mechanical engineering degree. I know Daddy would have been proud of Daniel for working so diligently to obtain that degree.

I should point out that Daniel is a spitting image of Daddy. He's six foot three and handsome just like my daddy. He loves the Word of God and cares about people and living out his purpose here on the earth. Even though Daddy is gone now, we have a big part of him here in Daniel. I'm so proud to call him my brother.

What's more, my brother has felt the tug of ministry on his heart. Loving and serving God has taken him to Scotland and Mexico on mission trips as well as on several homeless-outreach missions. Daniel followed the call of serving others just as my parents did. It has been a blessing to me to have such a friend in my brother and to watch him walk out a life of integrity and service.

The world would have lost a lot had Daniel died the night Mr. Watts blew out two windows in his bedroom, sending glass and wood into his crib. God obviously had—and continues to have—big plans for my brother.

After I got married and Daniel graduated from college, Aunt Dot was left with an empty nest. Through the years she has kept herself busy going on mission trips to India and holding women's conferences along the Gulf Coast. She continues to work part-time in the legal profession. Aunt Dot still lives in the Nichols family home in Mobile where she finished raising me and Daniel. She loves the fact that Daniel bought a house only a few miles from her. Although I'm living in the Nashville area, we all get together on holidays and other times during the year, visiting and building memories together in our old homeplace. Aunt Dot says that one of her greatest joys in life now is being "Grandma" to Kolby and Katelin.

Permit me a final thought.

One of my favorite verses is Job 42:10, which says, "After Job had prayed for his friends, the LORD made him prosperous again and gave him twice as much as he had before" (NIV). Like Job, I've experienced suffering. And yet, like Job, I believe that God has given me blessings beyond my imagination. For me, my "twice as much" is my family.

Take, for instance, my incredible husband, Kenny. When we first started dating, I felt the need to warn him that, because of my past, I was probably going to be a "high maintenance" person. I put Kenny through a small tidal wave of emotional testing just to see if he was in the relationship for the long haul.

In a way I was surprised when Kenny passed my exam, proving to be even more than I could ever have hoped or asked for. He was not scared off by my brutal honesty and continues to stand beside me when my past, like a thunderstorm, rains on the present moment. On my wedding day, Daddy's absence was felt. Thankfully, I had Daniel, who did a first-class job filling Daddy's role of giving me away.

Then there are my two heaven-sent angels, Kolby and Katelin, who complete me as a mom and are a daily reminder of God's goodness and restoration. I pray that when they grow up, they will carry with them the insights into the Lord that Kenny and I have imparted to them and that those life lessons will sustain them until their race is finished. My life is beautiful because of the love they so freely give me.

# ACKNOWLEDGMENTS

In a moment of panic, realizing I needed to somehow try to thank all the wonderful people in my life who stood with me through thick and thin, I grabbed book after book off the shelves in my office. With books piled high, I read at least a dozen different acknowledgments written by both the famous and the everyday writer. My hope was to find just the right words to express my gratitude.

Thank you seems insufficient to describe how grateful I am to have had such an army of prayer warriors and advisers who have steadied me through the front lines of so many battles. These strong people held my arms when I grew weary during those times. I'm thankful to the ones who have so carefully dressed my heart wounds and prescribed the medicine (the Word) to direct me on to my purpose and the next victory.

Because of you, my journey has been filled with love, grace, and lots and lots of patience. My heart is filled to the brim with a sense of indebtedness and joy as I thank the following people:

Kenny, the one my soul loves, I know God gave you strength for both of us. Thank you for slaying all the dragons of fear as I wrestled with the past while writing and living in the present; for all the years you've listened to my story as I repeated it countless times to those who wanted to hear it; for helping me live beyond the pain; and for reminding me that it's not just about surviving but about living a victorious life with the help of Jesus and those around me.

I greatly appreciate all the days you filled in the gaps and kept our family world normal when I had to work on the book. Your understanding meant everything to me on the days you came home from a long day at work only to discover that dinner was nowhere in sight. I'm thankful that you are a great cook—I know the kids are grateful too. You amaze me with your endless talent and God-given abilities. I'm so blessed to be loved by you.

Kolby and Katelin, thank you for making Mom smile on the days when I wanted to cry and for giving me hugs and laughter when I thought about all the things I've lost. You are my "so much more"—my exceedingly, abundantly, blessing-upon-blessing gifts from God. You fill my life with joy and hope. I look with anticipation to the future and all that God is going to do in your lives so that you can bless others and bring glory to Him. You know what I love about you both? Everything!

Daniel, my dearest brother, I am thankful that you have such a forgiving heart and that you don't hold grudges. That's important, being that you're my little (big) brother. You are one of the most kind and most caring people I know. The character of God is clearly seen in you and in the way you love your family and friends. You bless my life with your friendship and love. Thanks, too, for your input on the book.

Aunt Dot, your life of grace and godliness has been a wonderful gift to me. You have been the lighthouse in the storms of my life. Thank you for shining the light of love on my heart and always directing me back to the Word. You have carried well the parental responsibilities of raising Daniel and me to love God with a genuine and sincere faith. I am so grateful for you and for the love you show so selflessly. Thank you for being my memory when I was too young to recall some of these events. I am so blessed to call you Mom and friend.

The following family members were part of the glue that held the pieces of my life together with their love. Without them, Daniel and I would have been unloved and placed in an orphanage. They truly are what life is all about.

To the Nichols family (Dad's side): Grandpa and Grandma Nichols, Daniel and I will be forever grateful that you took us in and gave us a loving and safe home and that, after raising seven kids of your own, you cared for us during your later years and had the courage to love and discipline us like our own parents would have. Thank you. One day we'll be together again.

Likewise, Aunt Daisy, Joe (your memory lives in our hearts), Jim, and John Wade; Aunt Martha and Uncle John, Billy Sasser, and family; Lynn and Rick and Kristi; and Uncle Richard and Aunt Judy, Grant, Shannon and family, you all mean the world to me.

To the Welch family (Momma's side): Grandpa and Grandma Welch, the time we shared was too short, but your love lives on in our hearts. The memories we have with you are love, laughter, and wonderful family holidays. Even the tears tied us together as a loving family. And Uncle Ed (we miss you) and Aunt Shirley, Eddie and Beth and family; Aunt Sue (we'll see you on the other side) and Justin Price and family, you all rounded out my world in ways that only a devoted family could.

Thanks to the extended Alonzo family (my in-laws), Norman and Nancy Alonzo: Norm, in your sweet and funny way, you asked me if I thanked you in my acknowledgments. The truth is, I can't thank you and Nan enough for welcoming me into your family and loving me like your own daughter. When the Bible says that God restores what the locusts have eaten, I was blessed with y'all. Your support and encouragement mean more to me than I can express in this small thank-you. Likewise, Norman Jr. and Lori and Becca; Roland and Pam Savin and family, you have been a treasured gift to me.

To my family in the Lord: Your belief that this story needed to be shared with the world kept me going on days when I wanted to throw a brick at the computer screen and run out the door. Thank you for praying and standing with me.

Jeff and Courtney Ball and family, Mark and Melinda Flint, Curtis and Rhonda Gray, Steve and Cindy Hollander, Shino and Kelli Prater, Derek and Linda Schujahn, Peter and Nicki Penrose, the Barker Family, and my little sis, Wren Wimmer: I can't write this without tears welling up in my eyes. You have been our "through thick and thin" friends. Your friendship has made this journey we're on together full of love and laughter and always God centered. Thank you for letting me and my family be a part of yours and for sharing holidays and fun times together. And the thank-yous could go on and on.

Thanks to my Bible study group for your constant prayers, love, and support: Maretta Rohrer, Kellie Seboa, Alice Bray, Sharon Campbell, Kathi Katina, Jane Hayes, Cristi Robinson, Missy Worton, Lenair Sparks, and Robin Mowbray—thank you for your encouragement and writing accountability.

Breeon Phillips, who heard my story and sent the synopsis to a friend and got the publishing ball rolling, thanks for being the flame that started the fire.

Bob DeMoss, I have written so many thank-yous to you in my mind while we have colabored over this book. You are an amazing writer and collaborator. I'm thankful that God allowed your abilities to grace this work. Thank you for the countless hours of constructing this story from tiny pieces of information and then turning it into a masterpiece. Only God knows all the sacrifices you and Leticia made to make this dream a reality. For all the time we asked ourselves if this book would ever be finished, I am deeply grateful for your persistence to push through to the last written word. Because of your commitment and effort, this story of forgiveness and redemption is forever recorded, and I am eternally thankful to you and your family.

Missy Worton, thank you for introducing me to Bob DeMoss. Your heart for this story blesses me beyond words.

Greg Johnson and WordServe Literary Group, thank you for taking a chance on me by flying to Nashville just to hear me tell my story and, in turn, believing it was "book worthy." Thank you for your support and prayers throughout this project. Your patience and assurance that this book would be written brought peace to my soul on days when I could not see the end in sight. Thank you.

Tyndale House Publishers, I am thankful that my life has been touched by such people of integrity and sincerity. You have blessed me with your notes of encouragement and thoughtful gifts. I have a new respect for the publishing world. I had no idea of all that is involved in forming a story into a readable project. I simply took reaching over to grab a book and reading it for granted.

My thanks to the Tyndale book team, especially Jan Long Harris for taking time to listen and agree this story had to be told; Sharon Leavitt for being so real and making it easy on me as a first-time writer; Mark Taylor and his commitment to continue his father's legacy through Tyndale, which publishes my favorite translation of the Bible, the New Living Translation; and Doug Knox and the rest of my new friends at Tyndale—please accept a lifetime of thank-yous for making my dream come true.

My thanks to Sam Chappell and Andy Miller, who offered their advice on the legalities of writing this book.

A special thanks for sharing your memories, love, and faith go to E. J. and Pat Sellers, Missy Sellers Gore and Terri Cox, Carolyn Sellers, Sue Buffkin, and James and Eleanor Tyree. For the time and memories of Eddie and Johnnie Sellers. Thanks to the members of Free Welcome Church who stood with us in the line of fire and for loving us like part of your own family. I, as well as my family, thank you for your undying devotion and service to the church and Kingdom of God.

To Detective George Dudley, who came to our home countless times to protect and investigate and for sharing your own account of what happened, thank you.

To Captain David Mobles of the sheriff's department of Whiteville, for your willingness to help locate any information concerning our story.

I am so thankful to know that there are people in the world who will lend a helping hand in a time of need, even if they've just met you. That is the case with Niki Dennis, clerk of the Superior Court in Bladen County, North Carolina. For your time, compassion, and persistence to help us locate information on a thirty-year-old case. I am thankful for your assistance and to know a kind person like you.

Clara Cartrette, because of your coverage of our story in the newspaper, you provided us with a tremendous foundation of accurate information upon which we could build the details of this book. Your passion to get this story out for the public to read during the years of terror brought an awareness to the community and now to anyone who reads this book. Thank you for your tireless effort.

How can I thank ATF Agent Charles D. Mercer? Wherever you are, I thank you from the bottom of my heart for being relentless in seeing justice served for the bombings my family experienced while living in Whiteville. All those years of investigating paid off.

My thanks to the pastors who have ministered countless times to me and my family through prayers, counsel, and just being there when we needed them: Rice and Jody Broocks, Ron and Lynette Lewis, John and Maretta Rohrer, Jim and Kathy Laffoon, Rafe and

Liz Young, Charles and Barbara Green, Dave and Ina Newell, Sam and Jody Hawkins, and Rick and Karen Long. Also thanks to our Bethel church family here in Nashville and Grace Fellowship of Slidell, Louisiana, led by Pastors Curtis and Rhonda Gray.

To my mom and dad, your willingness to pick up your cross and follow Jesus at any cost demonstrated your unquestionable obedience to God's Word and love for others. Your desire to reach a lost world and bring hope to the brokenhearted continues to be a powerful testimony of God's unending love. Even though our time together on this earth was short, your love will last a lifetime in my heart. I'm thankful that we don't have to say good-bye, only "see ya later," until we are reunited for eternity.

Most of all, I am grateful to Jesus. I am forever thankful for Your unfailing love and mercies that are new every morning, for making Yourself more real to me each moment we spend together. I love You more than life itself. I am so grateful that Your Word is a lamp to guide my feet and a light for my path. That everywhere I go, You go with me. Surely goodness and mercy shall follow me all the days of my life, and I will dwell in the house of the Lord forever.

My Savior, my Friend, and my soon-coming King: Praise be to You forever and ever.

# NOTES ON CHAPTER OPENER PHOTOS

p. 1 Rebecca Alonzo

p. 5 Robert and Ramona (Welch) Nichols on their wedding day

p. 23 Robert and Ramona Nichols, while doing evangelistic work in Brinkley, Arkansas, in March 1967

p. 39 Free Welcome Holiness Church in Sellerstown, North Carolina

p. 57 Rebecca Nichols standing in front of the parsonage

p. 75 Robert and Rebecca Nichols during the family's 1973 vacation to Cherokee

p. 93 Robert Nichols along with H. J. Watts (behind him and to his left) and two unidentified men

p. 113 Five-year-old Rebecca Nichols on one of her many "wedding days"

p. 129 Free Welcome Holiness Church

p. 147 The last photo of Robert and Ramona Nichols with their children, taken in fall 1977 after Robert performed a wedding

p. 207 H. J. Watts in 1981, just after he had changed his plea from not guilty to nolo contendre in his trial for bombing and conspiracy

p. 225 Rebecca Nichols with her aunt Dot in 1987

p. 243 Kenny, Rebecca, Kolby, and Katelin Alonzo

p. 261 Daniel Nichols

# ENDNOTES

### CHAPTER 3: SHOTGUN JUSTICE IN SELLERSTOWN

31 *Willie Sellers comes to mind*: E. J. Sellers, interview with author, October 10, 2007.

### CHAPTER 4: THE DEVIL'S IN PEW NUMBER SEVEN

46 *Old-timers claimed that, as a youth*: E. J. Sellers, interview with author, October 10, 2007.

47 *Mr. Watts was quick to swallow the small fish in town*: Mr. Watts is described as "a county kingpin," which speaks to his reputation and character. Debbie Norton, "Watts's Guilty Plea Climaxed Surprising Case," *Star News*, February 20, 1981.

47 *The farmers took the bait*: Clara Cartrette, "Watts Pictured As 'Rich, Powerful Man' Who Plotted," *The News Reporter*, n.d.

47 *One of Watts's favorite lackeys*: Debbie Norton, "Watts's Guilty Plea Climaxed Surprising Case," *Star News*, February 20, 1981. Clara Cartrette, "Witness Says Watts Asked Him to Kill Nichols," *The News Reporter*, February 19, 1981. Roger Williams testified in court that "he acted as a paid 'strong arm' for Watts . . . to help collect unpaid debts."

48 *"That's the way to go, buddy"*: Clara Cartrette, "Witness Says Watts Asked Him to Kill Nichols," *The News Reporter*, February 19, 1981.

49 *"Mr. Watts, I get my advice"*: Clara Cartrette, "Nichols Testifies to Bombings at Sellerstown," *The News Reporter*, February 5, 1981.

50 *"Mr. Nichols, it doesn't look"*: Ramona Nichols's journal.

51 *"You had better not tell my wife"*: Robert Nichols's journal. He also testified to these statements in court, as reported in Clara Cartrette, "Nichols Testifies to Bombings at Sellerstown," *The News Reporter*, February 5, 1981.

54 *crawling or walking*: Clara Cartrette, "Nichols Testifies to Bombings," *The News Reporter*, February 5, 1981.

### CHAPTER 5: UNDER SIEGE

62 *The antics of Mr. Watts in pew number seven*: Clara Cartrette, "Tyree Tells of Disruptions," *The News Reporter*, February 9, 1981; Debbie Norton,

"Witness Tells of Hearing Key Suspect in Case," *Wilmington Morning Star*, February 6, 1981.

67 *And, while Detective Dudley had a hunch*: George Dudley, phone interview with author, January 22, 2009. This explosion, as well as the others directed at the Free Welcome parsonage or church, are itemized in Clara Cartrette, "Many Charges against Three County Residents," *The News Reporter*, January 29, 1981.

68 *During the Sunday morning service*: Robert Nichols's journal.

**CHAPTER 6: NOW I LAY ME DOWN TO SLEEP**

78 *Mr. Watts, arms folded high across his chest*: Robert Nichols's personal journal. Details of the bombing itself were reported in "Field Near Parsonage Dynamited," *The News Reporter*, December 5, 1974; "Minister's Family Is Harassed," *Fayetteville Observer*, December 6, 1974.

79 *"Last week's dynamite hit out behind the house"*: Larry Cheek, "The Embattled Pastor," *Fayetteville Times*, December 9, 1974.

82 *The handwritten note told Mr. Watts "to keep your mouth"*: Debbie Norton, "Writing Expert Testifies Suspect Printed Notes," *Star News*, February 10, 1981.

82 *From the detective's point of view*: "George Dudley, phone interview with author, February 9, 2009.

84 *"Tribute to Sellerstown"*: The article written by Ramona Nichols appeared in the *News Reporter* on December 16, 1974. Used with permission.

86 "*We used to look for the siege*": Wray Thompson, "More Harassment at Sellerstown Parsonage," *The News Reporter*, December 16, 1974.

**CHAPTER 7: THE TOUGHEST GUY IN TOWN**

94 *Aunt Pat's older daughter, Terri, had a ringside seat*: Terri Cox, interviewed in person by author on October 20, 2007, in Sellerstown.

101 *As we'd soon discover, on Saturday, June 28, 1975*: Clara Cartrette, "Witness Says Watts Near Sellerstown Bomb Scene," *The News Reporter*, February 9, 1981.

107 *The strategy of this, the third bombing*: Wray Thompson, "Explosion Damages Church Home Again," *The News Reporter*, July 3, 1975.

108 *"Don't go out there"*: Carolyn Sellers, interview with author, October 20, 2007.

109 *Eleanor asked, "Where's Danny?"*: Pat Sellers recounted details of this exchange in an interview with the author, October 19, 2007, in Sellerstown.

112 *"I'm no quitter"*: Wray Thompson, "Explosion Damages Church Home Again," *The News Reporter*, July 3, 1975.

112 *"So many of God's soldiers"*: Ray Wyche, "Tenacious Pastor Bucks Violence," *The Carolina Scene*, July 24, 1975.

## CHAPTER 8: HOLDING ON TO HOPE

113 *Daddy was toying with the unthinkable*: Robert Nichols's journal testimony.

114 *"They felt like they could get to my husband"*: Doug Cumming, "Attacks on Minister, Church Probed," *The News and Observer*, July 11, 1975.

115 *Everyone in the community knew*: Ibid., David Eskridge, "Preacher Knows Bombers," *Wilmington Morning Star*, September 24, 1975.

116 *With the exception of his sea green eyes*: Clara Cartrette, e-mail message to author, March 2, 2009.

117 *Sharing an office with George Dudley*: Clara Cartrette, "Witness Says Watts Near Sellerstown Bomb Scene," *The News Reporter*, February 9, 1981. Cartrette reported that an ATF agent testified that when interviewed by ATF agent Charles Mercer on November 10, 1976, Charles Wayne Tedder said he "understood Agent Mercer was offering a $10,000 reward for information that Watts was bombing the parsonage."

117 *"We battle fear from time to time"*: Ray Wyche, "Tenacious Pastor Bucks Violence," *The Carolina Scene*, July 24, 1975.

118 *He had done so much to chase my family away*: Clara Cartrette, "Tabor City Man Says Watts Would Remove Nichols," *The News Reporter*, February 5, 1981.

120 *"We were clicking on the same clock"*: James Tyree, interview with author in person on October 20, 2007.

120 *"Brother James, God can do the same thing for you"*: Ibid.

126 *"You can see how closely they are watching us"*: David Eskridge, "Preacher Knows Bombers," *Wilmington Morning Star*, September 24, 1975.

## CHAPTER 9: HEARING VOICES

131 *"The search warrant is merely a tool"*: Wray Thompson, "Feds Search Premises in Sellerstown Probe," *The News Reporter*, October 2, 1975.

132 *For instance, because the drama in Sellerstown*: Ibid.

132 *"On October 16, 1975, the governor publicly offered"*: "State Offers $2,500 Reward," *News Reporter*, October 16, 1975.

132 The details of this fifth attack appear in a newspaper article contained in a scrapbook owned by the Nichols family. It is titled "5th Explosion" and dated November 10, 1975; however, the name of the reporter and newspaper are missing. This incident is also mentioned in Cartrette, "Many Charges against Three County Residents," *The News Reporter*, January 29, 1981.

133 *A federal grand jury was assembled*: Wray Thompson, "US Subpoenas Eight for Bombing Inquiry," *The News Reporter*, n.d.

135 *"I've never been a violent person"*: Dot Nichols, interview with author on November 24, 2008, in Franklin, Tennessee.

135 *"It will take at least three weeks to come around"*: "Rev. Nichols a Patient in University Center," November 25, 1975. (Note: Author's newspaper clipping does not indicate the reporter's or newspaper's name.)

136 *The generous church family voted to purchase Daddy a new 1976 Buick*: Robert Nichols's journal has a handwritten note: "Church helped buy car, 1976 Buick, made Mr. Watts mad."

137 *"You're a thorn in a friend of mine's side"*: Clara Cartrette, "Williams Says Watts Would Frame Tedder," *The News Reporter*, February 19, 1981.

138 *"I've just got to get out"*: Ibid.

138 *"You're a good ole boy"*: Cartrette, "Witness Says Watts Asked Him to Kill Nichols," *The News Reporter*, February 19, 1981.

140 *"One more valley, one more hill"*: "One More Valley," words and music by Dottie Rambo and Jimmie Davis, copyright © 1966.

141 *That evening, Mr. Watts returned to his old tricks*: Clara Cartrette, "Many Charges Against Three County Residents," *The News Reporter*, January 29, 1981.

142 *"If you make it look like an accident"*: Clara Cartrette, "Williams Says Watts Would Frame Tedder," *The News Reporter*, February 19, 1981.

143 *"We're all sort of shaken"*: "Blast Rocks Parsonage in Columbus," *Morning Star*, October 14, 1976.

143 *"I walked outside to see"*: Clara Cartrette, "Blast Rocks Church, Suspect Questioned," *The News Reporter*, 1976. (Note: Author's newspaper clipping does not provide the specific date for this article.)

144 *"This thing's got to come to a close"*: Ibid.

144 *What Mr. Watts failed to report*: Clara Cartrette, "Witness Says Watts Asked Him to Kill Nichols," *The News Reporter*, February 19, 1981.

**CHAPTER 10: BLACK THURSDAY**

147 *The visitor came*: The story of the Ku Klux Klan member's visit was told to the author by Dot Nichols in an interview with the author on November 24, 2008, in Franklin, Tennessee. She learned of it from a conversation with Robert Nichols.

149–150 *Wanted these officers to know he was "well off"*: Clara Cartrette, "Witness Says Watts Near Sellerstown Bomb Scene," *The News Reporter*, February 9, 1981.

153 *"Please get out of there"*: As told to the author by Dot Nichols in an interview on November 24, 2008, in Franklin, Tennesee. She first heard about the exchange through a conversation with Grandma Welch.

153 *She was well aware of his criminal record*: Star Regional Staff, "Columbus Minister Injured, Wife Slain," *Wilmington Morning Star*, March 24, 1978.

155 *"You know, Ramona, I'm not sure how safe"*: As told to the author by Pat Sellers in person at her house in Sellerstown, North Carolina, on October 19, 2007.

157 *"How are you doing, Harris?"*: The following conversation and movements are from a transcript of the trial *State of North Carolina vs. Harris Kelton Williams*, as well as Rebecca's memories of the event.

**CHAPTER 11: UNANSWERED PRAYERS**

172 *At 6:09 p.m., as I would later learn*: Clara Cartrette, "Bizarre Shooting Described," Clara Cartrette, *The News Reporter*, August 14, 1978.

173 *"How badly are you hurt?"*: The following conversations and movements are from a transcript of the trial *State of North Carolina vs. Harris Kelton Williams*.

179 *The phone rang*: Dot Nichols told the story of James Tyree's call to Robert's parents' home during an interview with the author November 24, 2008, in Franklin, Tennessee.

182 *"We're putting you . . . and her . . . in God's hands"*: Ibid.

186 *"Hands were raised in glory"*: Clara Cartrette, "'We're Here in Victory' Call of Memorial Service," *The News Reporter*, March 27, 1978.

186 *"It would appear that we're here in defeat"*: Ibid.

186 *"Ramona was a servant of the church"*: Ibid.

**CHAPTER 12: EIGHT MEN AND FOUR WOMEN**

197 *"Now, Rebecca, you see that thing"*: Excerpts taken from the court transcript of the *State of North Carolina vs. Harris Kelton Williams*. Dialogue has been edited slightly for readability.

203 *"I would like to see justice"*: Clara Cartrette, "Nichols Did Not Seek Vengeance," *The News Reporter*, August 14, 1978.

203 *"It's so hard to look at him"*: Ibid.

204 *Assistant District Attorney Mike Easley was the first*: Details from the closing arguments reported by Clara Cartrette, "Williams Is Given Life Imprisonment," *The News Reporter*, August 14, 1978.

**CHAPTER 13: PUTTING THE DEVIL ON TRIAL**

217 *According to the newspaper account*: Clara Cartrette, "Jury Selection Begins in Sellerstown Bombing Case," *The News Reporter*, January 26, 1981.

217 *This move prevented the prosecutor*: Clara Cartrette, "Watts Pictured As 'Rich, Powerful Man' Who Plotted," *The News Reporter*, n.d.

218 *"I have to take tranquilizers"*: Bill Gaither, "3 Columbus Residents Indicted in Bombings," *Fayetteville Times*, n.d.

218 *"If you're not very careful"*: Clara Cartrette, "Spivey Says Attorneys Harassed, Scared Him," *The News Reporter*, n.d.

218 *"A rich and powerful man in Columbus County"*: Clara Cartrette, "Watts Pictured As 'Rich, Powerful Man' Who Plotted."

219 *One of the most damaging . . . was a government witness who claimed*: Debbie Norton, "Watts Pleads Guilty in Bombing," *Wilmington Morning Star*, February 20, 1981.

219 *"The picture painted of him"*: Clara Cartrette, "Watts Given Four 5-Year Terms; Fined $25,000," *The News Reporter*, February 23, 1981.

220 *the judge, who had represented him in years past*: Debbie Norton, "Watts's Guilty Plea Climaxed Surprising Case," *The Wilmington Star*, February 20, 1981.

221 *"When the Reverend Robert F. Nichols came to Sellerstown"*: Clara Cartrette, "Watts Given Four 5-Year Terms."

221 *After commending Agent Charles Mercer for a "thorough and relentless investigation"*: Cartrette, "Watts Given Four 5-Year Terms," describes the judge's actions and comments during sentencing.

**CHAP**

252 ... , "Five Things ... ober 5, 1997, ... ed August 28,

255 ... *fort*, chapter 7.